Drum Circle Spirit

Facilitating Human Potential through Rhythm

by Arthur Hull

Edited by Angela Marie

White Cliffs Media
Reno, NV

White Cliffs Media, Inc   Phone: (775)-831-4899
P.O. Box 6083   Fax: 1-760-875-6202
Incline Village, NV 89450   Email: wcm@wcmedia.com
                                 Web: http://www.wcmedia.com

Printed on acid-free paper in the United States of America

Library of Congress Cataloging-in-Publication Data

Hull, Arthur, 1947–
    Drum circle spirit : facilitating human potential through rhythm / Arthur Hull.
        p.   cm.   —   (Performance in world music series ; no. 12)
    Includes bibliographical references and index.
    ISBN 0-941677-84-2 (alk. pbk. w/CD)
        1. Community music—Instruction and study. 2. Musical meter and rhythm—
Instruction and study. 3. Percussion instruments—Instruction and study.
4. Group facilitation. I. Title . II. Series
    MT85.H9
    786.8'071 — dc21
                                                98-14751
                                                  CIP
                                                    MN

Rhythm Temple

by Arthur Hull

The MALLET—built of skin, bone, and pulsating blood
powered by primal emotion, personal history, and the
never ending search for the one,
FALLS with its own weight, inertia, and the
spirit being channeled through it,
BOUNCING off the animal skin stretched
across the top hole of the wooden temple.
The SKIN receives the mallet,
sending it back with equal force,
DANCING with the energy,
living again as
one note in the larger song.
That NOTE vibrates
inside the belly of the temple,
SHAKING the wooden walls,
making its presence felt as well as heard,
as it forces itself, by its own compression,
out through the small hole at the bottom of the TEMPLE
and into the universe
with the same power, spirit, and vitality of the mallet
TOUCHING bodies, bones, hearts & souls of those
WORSHIPPERS nearby.
BOOM!

Table of Contents

Foreword

Arthur Hull has taken a giant step in contributing to our understanding of what is real, not only about drum circles, but also about the evocative power of the drum, and how to use it as a necessary tool of communication empowerment, bringing people together, sharing very positive vibrations amongst all participants regardless of their color, creed, religion, and gender.

This is the first comprehensive literature that deals with the subject of Drum Circle Spirit, the role of the facilitator, and the major tool itself, the drum. In this book Arthur has endeavored to show us how important the drum is, as a tool to be employed by the facilitator—who no matter how enthusiastic, charismatic, or happy-go-lucky he or she may be, must understand the language of the drum. This does not simply mean knowing many rhythms nor having the ability to display many rhythmic patterns spontaneously. The ability to lead a drum circle depends on the personality of the facilitator.

How important is the role of a facilitator? Who is he or she? What qualifications and knowledge of the tools are at his or her disposal? If the drum is regarded as the main tool of the facili-

Babatunde Olatunji and Arthur Hull

tator, the knowledge of the language of the drum must be acquired and understood by the facilitator, who employs that knowledge to unify everyone in the circle. Facilitators do not have to be master drummers. Not everybody can or should be a facilitator even though the skills can be learned, yet the energy and enthusiasm may be lacking. Accumulation of knowledge about a subject matter is one thing, how to impart that knowledge is another matter entirely.

A facilitator is like a conductor of a symphony orchestra who may not know how to play all the instruments in his orchestra, yet through his training as a conductor must develop the skill as well as the knowledge to guide the players through the rendition of a musical piece effectively and harmoniously from the beginning to the end. Other qualities of a facilitator of a drum circle are the ability to motivate and direct the performance of the group so that each participant, by the end of the gathering, can feel accomplished as a member of the community.

Yes, the community is the benefactor of the drum circle, gaining a unity of purpose from successful experiences.

I strongly recommend this book to all who are interested in personal healing, learning unique methods of facilitating, becoming familiar with new vocabularies introduced by Arthur, and in healing our planet.

Congratulations to Arthur Hull for making a major contribution to our knowledge of facilitating a drum circle.

—Babatunde Olatunji, New York City, March, 1998

Arthur Hull and Babatunde Olatunji

> "Yesterday is history. Tomorrow is a mystery. And today?
> Today is a gift. That's why we call it The Present."
> —Babatunde Olatunji

Dedication

I dedicate this book to my friend, brother, teacher, mentor, and inspiration, Babatunde Olatunji.

The mission to create peace and harmony amongst communities is much older and much greater than any one of us. It starts with creating peace within ourselves, and then within our communities. Babatunde Olatunji brings to us a way, through drum, dance, and song, to identify, strengthen, and celebrate elements that, when functioning in any population, create a community that is healthy, wealthy, and wise.

It is my view that a major part of Babatunde Olatunji's mission is to be a rhythmical evangelist. For the last 45 years, he has been birthing "rhythmaculture" into the biggest cultural mixing bowl on the planet, the USA. Baba uses traditional African music, dance, and drumming as models for us as we learn how to use rhythm to connect us to the Earth our Mother, to each other, and to our collective spirit as we build healthy communities.

"Rhythmaculture" is something that America lost somewhere along the way on its path to "progress, our most important product."

The grassroots surge of personal percussion now appearing in many forms in the U.S. is more than an overnight phenomenon. I've watched

> "All people from all walks of life, all colors, have various things that they can do together to create harmony, and it is the simplest thing to make music and sing together."
> —Babatunde Olatunji

many different parts of this drumming community grow for many years and almost any person on the North American continent who is drumming today can follow their teaching lineage back to Babatunde Olatunji. Of all the great drumming teachers that I have had the privilege to work with, I've learned as much about the why of it, as about the how of it from Babatunde Olatunji.

As Babatunde Olatunji once told me, "We are trying to balance the technological society that has taken us away from the reality of the Earth that supports us. It gave birth to us in the first place. We need to recognize that it will always be there. It's there for us to use, replenish, and leave for forthcoming generations, so we cannot afford to destroy it. We are learning to do that now. We are also finding the simple things that people can do together. All people from all walks of life, all colors, have various things that they can do together to create harmony, and it is the simplest thing to make music and sing together."

I support Baba's mission of creating peace in the world through the celebration of life. I take this mission as my own. By reading and utilizing the information in this book, so do you.

Acknowledgments

The inspiration for this book came from one of my oldest teachers, drumming buddies, and friends, Rick Walker. His comment, "Arthur, you wrote the book on facilitation!" caused a bell to go off in my head, "Ding!" and with an Arthurian gleam in my eye, I responded, "Not yet." Thank you, Rick.

Something does not come from nothing. I would like to acknowledge that the universal principles and wisdom taught in this book have their foundation in rhythmacultures from around the world, including African, Asian, Arabic, Polynesian, Native American, and South American. With deep respect, I am thankful for the ancient cultural forms and traditions that the drumming masters from source cultures bring to us. They give us guidance, wisdom, and techniques to help us create our own, long-overdue rhythmaculture.

This book grew from the foundation given to me by my teachers who represent many different drumming cultures. I would like to acknowledge and thank many people who have brought this knowledge and wisdom to me through their teaching, mentoring, and friendship: Rick Walker, Abrihame Adzinia, Layne Redmond, Simbo, Michael Pluznick, Dumisani Maraire, Titos Sompa, Danjuma Adamu, Benét Luchion, Pedro De Jesus, Don Davidson, Kim Atkinson, Fred Simpson, Mabiba Baegne, Marcus Gordon, John Santos, Sedonia Cahill, Luis Raul Rivera, Wilfred Mark, Sammy Norte, Marian Oliker, Chalo Eduardo, Mbimba, Candido Obajimi, Abdoulaye Diakite, Allassane Kane, John Amira, Hamza El Din, Yaya Diallo, Suru Ekeh, Gordy Ryan, Onye Onyemaechi, Nurudefina Pili Abena and of course Babatunde Olatunji. They all contribute to this path on which I walk and to this mission that I serve.

Having information about drumming, rhythms, and rhythmacultures gave me the foundation for teaching village music at the University of California, Santa Cruz. I would like to thank and acknowledge a whole other group of people who helped me develop my personal philosophy, performance practices, body language skills, platform presentation skills, and group leadership skills: Nita Little, T. Mike Walker, Sensei Charlie Badenhop, Ernesto Munoz, Jackie Wilson, Ken Okulolo, Ian Browde, Samba Ngo, Joanne Bailey, John Malloy, Wilma Marcus, Gabrielle Roth, John Grinder, Judy Delozier, Charlie Shepard, Charllotte Bretto Milliner, M.A. Bjarkman, Dick Markus, and Baba Hari Dass.

I would like to thank all my students for the parts they play in my growth, and their contributions to this book. The better the student is, the better the teacher becomes. I would especially like to acknowledge Don Davidson and Cameron Tummel who, as my students, have taken this knowledge out into the community and have brought their experiences back to Village Music Circles™. They have become my teachers, associates, and friends.

I first began to learn how to teach beginning-beginner facilitators in facilitators' playshop programs. I would like to acknowledge Michael Wall for his help and suggestions during the Hawaii programs as he taught me how to teach, making the knowledge transmittable, so I could write this book.

Thank you, Mickey Zeckley, for letting me use the *Lark In The Morning* music camp, nestled deep in a northern California redwood forest, for three years as a writing retreat.

I would like to acknowledge *Drum*™ magazine, *Reach into the Pulse*™ newsletter, and *Percussion Source*™ magazine for allowing me to reprint parts of earlier interviews and articles. Thank you to Interworld Music for permission to reproduce the poem *Rhythm Temple* from my book/video *Guide to Endrummingment*™.

This book has been manifested using skills from within our local hand-drumming community. Its construction has been dependent on interactions with friends with whom I have had a relationship for many years. I would like to acknowledge Bill Muench for computer technical support and advice, Cliff Warner for the interior book design, layout, and his overall perspective, and Kim Dowling for transcribing many hours of teaching tapes. Peter Cerny's original artwork represents the spirit of my words in visual form. Thank you, Peter. Also, a special thank you to my music therapist friend, Jean Anne Nevling, for helping me develop the book outline. T. Mike Walker and Rick Walker provided insightful fine editing, for which I am grateful.

I would like to thank my word sculptor, Angela Marie, for the years we spent together in front of a computer, molding Arthurian gibberish into a readable and useable format, and also acknowledge and thank her for excellent editing and perspective.

To all the people who gave up a day to be a part of the Drum Spirit CD, I thank you. Also a big thanks to Daniel Thomas, who recorded, edited, mixed, and mastered our playing into the final product.

I am indebted to Remo D. Belli of REMO™ Drum Company for his friendship, mentoring, his continuing support of rhythmical evangelism, and his courage to follow the convictions of his vision.

To all the community networkers and rhythmical evangelists who are tireless grassroots workers creating a strong foundation for building a healthy community through drumming, dance, and song, thank you.

Finally, I would like to acknowledge my family's support during this process. From the inception to the final editing of *Drum Circle Spirit*, my children have grown into teenhood, my wife has grown more patient with my elf self and I have grown into a writer.

Thank you for being a reader.

Introduction

Drum Circle Spirit teaches about facilitating community through rhythm-based events. Although I discuss the application of rhythm-based technology to specific populations, I use the open community rhythm circle as my model. A community rhythm circle is open to anyone and everyone who comes to participate. These circles need not be culturally specific, gender specific, or musically, technically specific.

Facilitating is about being able to help a group get together and make music as a percussion orchestra. I want to empower you to take the tools presented here into your community and help support the community's need to create beautiful music together.

It is not necessary to be a music or hand drum teacher to learn to facilitate. In fact, music and hand drum teachers sometimes need to unlearn some of what they know to facilitate properly. If you are a middle school or high school teacher, a kids-at-risk counselor, a personal growth or gender group facilitator, a music therapist, or a drum circle participant, then you have an opportunity to integrate information from this book into your musical community.

Welcome to your community!

There are many different populations who will benefit from circles you facilitate. These circles include women's groups, men's groups, trance dancers, school kids, kids-at-risk, well elderly, personal growth groups, music therapy classes, corporate team-building groups, and community drum circles. The tools that you assimilate by following the exercises presented are applicable to many groups. *Drum Circle Spirit* can help you build a foundation of tools and principles with which you can grow and develop your own facilitating style.

This book is about building a functional understanding of basic facilitation principles, as well as developing a solid foundation for creating your own style of community empowerment through the expression of rhythm on drums and percussion.

I have found at least one developing drum circle facilitator in every city where I have traveled over the last few years. Each person, in various stages of development and discovery, creates their own unique way to guide a group to its highest potential.

Until now there has been no book or course on how to facilitate rhythmically-based events,

> *I want to empower you to take the tools presented here into your community and help support the community's need to create beautiful music together.*

except the school of hard knocks, where the person goes through trial and error experiences of the sort that I've gone through during the last 30 years. This is the book I wish I could have had many years ago. My intention in writing this book is to help you so you do not have to reinvent the wheel, thus making your learning time shorter and getting you out into the world sooner to do rhythmical community service.

The personal expression of rhythm is a healing experience. Group rhythmical expression is a community healing experience. As a rhythmical evangelist, I know that helping a group or an individual find and express their lost rhythmical spirit can be profound. Every time a group of kids or a community sits down and creates rhythmical synergy together, the world is a better place. The world needs more facilitators. This book is my contribution to that goal.

> *Every time a group of kids or a community sits down and creates rhythmical synergy together, the world is a better place.*

If you gather together a study group for the purpose of using this book in a group learning process, then I will respond to any written questions that your group might have as your process develops. You can have your group designate a liaison person to work with me, through my office, to handle any group situation not readily covered by our correspondence. Contact me:

Arthur Hull, Village Music Circles, 108 Coalinga Way, Santa Cruz, California, 95060.

This book is inspired by all the questions and inquiries I've received over the years. It is based on the curriculum created for the Facilitator's Playshop series that I teach. I define "Arthurian" words in Chapter 7 and they appear throughout the book. These are words I bring into use to describe processes and ideas for which I could find no appropriate ways to express with existing language. Enjoy.

You may already know more than you think you know!

Turning a Bone Into a Tool

According to my mother I've been a drummer since her third trimester of pregnancy with me. When I was 12 and 13, in San Bernadino, California, I would sneak out my bedroom window on Friday nights with my tunable bongos and go down to the Hell's Angel biker/beatnik joint and play for beat poets and folk singers. Many a time I was shoved underneath the stage when the police came in.

I made my first drum in wood shop in junior high school. It looked a lot like the *Ashiko*-style drum that is one of my signature series designs built and sold by REMO drum company. Back then those *Ashiko*-style drums were called Desi Arnez BaBa-Lu drums. I was self-taught, doing what is now called spirit drumming, and did not start my formal training and drumming apprenticeships until my early twenties.

My first experience of drummers coming together in a group and playing together was in the late sixties, at a Rainbow Gathering.

A Rainbow Gathering is held in early July each year, usually in some national park near a wilderness area.

The Rainbow family drummers and camp builders would get to the Rainbow gathering a few days early to help set up the campsite that would turn itself into a small city for a week. Then we would dig the drum pit with a fire pit in the middle so that we could sit on the edge of the pit with our drums and play together.

With drummers constantly coming and going, the drumming literally lasted for three or four days without a break. However, the rhythms were not well maintained and didn't last very long. Other than the raw input of our spirits translated into the dance our hands did on drums, we were ignorant of drumming technology then and didn't understand what made a drum circle work. Someone would start a rhythm and we would all pick up on it and play around, experiment, and stumble along, sometimes getting connected and going to that magic place where time stops. Then somebody would play on top of the rhythm and solo. That would excite someone else and they would also play on top and solo. We would have three to six soloists, with some people playing the rhythm groove and other people holding down the bottom. Eventually the rhythm would be top heavy, with more people soloing than people supporting the groove, and the rhythm would collapse, and come to a stumbling close. We would all stop for a second, look at each other, and somebody would ask, "Were you there man? Were we all there at the same time?" looking for validation that we had all been to "that magic drumming place."

> *Someone would start a rhythm and we would all pick up on it and play around, experiment, and stumble along, sometimes getting connected and going to that magic place where time stops.*

The magic place, as we called it, is when you are lost in the rhythms and you are being played by your own drum, as well as by the drum circle that you're in. The frustration for me was that each time we would get into a solid rhythmical song as a group, somewhere along the way we would reach rhythm burnout (RB).

Rhythm burnout is usually created when a certain percentage of players are no longer paying attention to the group rhythm. This can happen when a person is too involved with their own rhythm part to listen to the song of others in the group. Another way RB can happen is when someone is playing on top of the group rhythm so loud that it affects others, and pulls them off rhythmically. The group then loses the pulse, the rhythm falters and falls apart. Typically, some people in the group who do not want the rhythm to fall apart as it does with RB play with their heads up and feed their energy to the rhythm. But if not enough of the rest of the group "play with their heads up," rhythm burnout happens. You can hear when a group is heading to that place of faltering, stumbling stoppage. Some people keep playing until they suddenly notice that they are the only ones playing and everyone else has stopped. Other people just play softer, then give up and wait for RB to complete itself so someone else can start another pattern.

The magic place, as we called it, is when you are lost in the rhythms and you are being played by your own drum, as well as by the drum circle that you're in.

At a Rainbow drumming circle, as one of these rhythm burnouts approached, I looked around and noticed that at least fifty percent of the other drummers' heads were also up, looking around. That told me that they were also noticing that we were heading to RB. The drummers with their heads up were the ones feeding the group rhythm with the intention of finding and redefining the foundation of the ever-changing ongoing rhythm song. They did not want to go to RB just because the rest of the drummers were losing their focus and not paying attention. As the group was playing itself closer to RB more heads were popping up, but not enough to prevent final RB resulting in a rhythmical train wreck.

I realized that a lot of the players in the circle had the same goal as I did. We wanted to re-focus the rhythm and make it live again before it fell apart and died. But they didn't know how to achieve it. I had the same goal, had an idea about how to achieve it, and decided to implement it into the ongoing rhythm to see if it would work.

Before the rhythm totally fell apart, I solidly threw another rhythm into the circle, over the top of the faltering rhythm. All the drummers with their heads up jumped right into the new groove. All the other drummers, who were heading toward RB, pulled their heads up out of their drums, looked around, and joined us as we headed off into another rhythmical adventure. The transition from one rhythm to the next happened without the traditional fumbling rhythm-burnout ending. It was an exciting moment for me, and I realized that I had recognized something that other people in the group had also noticed. The difference was that I had done something about it.

At the end of the piece that I had initiated, it was obvious that we were heading for another RB. The same heads were up and they were looking at me as if I were going to start another rhythm. Instead I gestured over to one of the other drummers who was looking at me, as if to say, "Will you take us through this transition?" That drummer got the message, looked around to see that all the other drummers who had their heads up were now watching him, and then he started another rhythm. We made another transition out of a faltering rhythm to another rhythmical place. More people paid attention so that the rhythm that we initiated had drive, solidity, and lasted longer before the group went into another RB.

I realized that now some of us in the circle were listening for the indications of rhythm burnout starting to manifest itself. We were listening not just for rhythm burnout, but also for a style and intention of playing within the group that signaled that it was time to go somewhere else rhythmically. To go to that other place, the group mutually changed the dynamic, volume, speed, or rhythm. Some of us discovered that it wasn't necessary to wait for RB to make a transition. We realized that we could read the group prior to reaching RB, and could re-focus its attention to take it to a higher rhythmical place. It was during this time before rhythm burnout that we were beginning to acknowledge, as a group, that we wanted some sort of change to happen. Instead of a rhythm burnout point, I recognized this as a transition point. Some of us drummers had given each other permission to play with that point in the group when it was obvious that we were going into RB.

This new style did not sit well with some of the members of the circle who were traditional anarchist drummers. In an anarchist drum circle there are no leaders and no rules. I was new to any kind of drum circle, and I didn't know the rules of this one. One of the drummers walked up to me after that session in the circle and told me that he believed that what I had done was improper for the culture that we were in and that the circle didn't need a leader. I realized I had initiated something that was out of context with the rules of the game in this drumming community. I apologized to the person, but the cat was out of the bag, so to speak. Throughout the remainder of that Rainbow drum circle gathering, different drummers led us through the transition point to save us from the dreaded RB. By the closing of the event, on the last day of drumming, the group was heading for a big crash, burn, and die rhythm burnout. I looked around to see if anyone in the group might lead us out of the rhythmical mess into which we were obviously heading. I looked across the circle to see the person who warned me about not leading the group a few days earlier. He looked at me with a smile and gleam in his eye, and then initiated the first true rumble signal I'd ever heard. Everyone in the circle followed his lead. We went crazy, creating a big rumbling crescendo, and then we all stopped together by following his hands as they came down onto his drum signaling the last note. He came over to me afterwards and said, "Well, if we're going to end it, we might as well end it right."

When I first discovered the transition point, I felt like the ape must have felt who had picked up a bone and for the first time discovered that it could be used as a tool.

I realized during that Rainbow Gathering that just before rhythm burnout occurs, a nebulous, usable energy exists inside a drum circle. I now call that the "transition point." When I first discovered the transition point, I felt like the ape must have felt who had picked up a bone and for the first time discovered that it could be used as a tool.

Rhythmaculture, Circles, and Drum Circle Etiquette

The Birth of Rhythmaculture in America

You won't find the word rhythmaculture in your dictionary. It is an Arthurian word that describes a culture that has integrated ritual, dance, song, and music into almost every aspect of its existence, its expression of itself, and its celebration of life. In a rhythmaculture, rhythm and music serve specific purposes. There are songs and dances for courtship, weddings, births, funerals, planting, harvesting, and spiritual expression. Song, dance, and ritual permeate nearly all rhythmacultures' community gatherings.

Historically, rhythmacultures have used drums or percussion as tools of expression. These people have evolved their cultures out of an intimate relationship with the earth and animals. A lot of their rhythms, songs, and dances have been modeled from the movements of the animals, the songs of the birds, and the community's dance for survival, such as the movements of planting, harvesting, and hunting. Asians, Pacific Islanders, Native Americans, and Africans are all people who come from rhythmacultures.

> *Drumming, dancing, singing, and the art of ritual have been used by rhythmacultures all over the world as ways of celebrating community and energizing the spirits of those communities.*

By studying these rhythmaculture traditions, I find the roots of humanity—full of ancient and timeless wisdom as well as universal principles and truths.

The people of European descent started losing parts of their rhythmaculture around the historical period called the Inquisition. Back then, social conditioning was affected in such a way that anything that was considered primal or pagan was frowned upon. Certain white Anglo-Saxon religious orders instigated persecution of the Druids, Witches, Gypsy and Jewish cultures that still continues today.

European colonizers tried to suppress drumming among the African people they had taken from Africa and brought to the Caribbean as slaves. They thought that the slaves were talking to each other and their ancestral spirits through the drums. This was true. The colonists also were afraid that drumming among the slaves might unite them into a rebellious spirit. This was also true. The first slave revolt in the Caribbean was in Haiti. The children of Africa successfully kicked the colonists off the island and created the first third world country in the Caribbean. The rhythm and dance that fueled that particular revolution was called *Petró*.

Many colonists tried to ban drums, but the spirit of rhythmaculture cannot be stopped. Through the suppression of the drums by the colonists, many other rhythmical art forms were birthed, such as the Cuban *Yambu* rhythms and dances played on wooden boxes, the steel pan bands of Trinidad, and tap dancing in the southern United States.

> *We North Americans are now starting to rebuild and redevelop our relationship with the drum as a tool for unity and expression.*

Haiti is an example of a new rhythmaculture being formed. Three different rhythmacultures from Africa were thrown together with the French and original native cultures on the island. Haiti was the mixing bowl, and these five cultures were the ingredients. The result, after two hundred years of cooking and evolving is a rhythmaculture that is distinctly Haitian—where dance, music, and drumming permeate many aspects of its social interaction. The Afro-Cuban rhythmaculture is also a good example of this type of two-hundred-year mixing bowl evolution.

America is the largest mixing bowl in the world. Immigrants from all parts of the globe have come to this land. The first generation immigrants were able to maintain some of their traditions and rhythmaculture from the old country. As each succeeding generation has become more Americanized, some if not all of that tradition has been lost. As our cities have gotten larger, our lives and communities have become more fragmented and disconnected. We Americans have become so isolated that we are seeking different ways of recreating safe, supportive, and healthy communities.

> *By recreating rhythmaculture we are reaching inside ourselves for the essence that fuels the evolution/revolution of our society back toward community values.*

Drumming, dancing, singing, and the art of ritual have been used by rhythmacultures all over the world as ways of celebrating community and energizing the spirits of those communities.

The birthing of rhythmaculture in North America is in its beginning stages. We are modeling master drummers and dancers who have come here from all over the globe. They give us knowledge, tools, and the blueprints we need to create what, in two hundred years, will be a rhythmaculture that will be distinctly American. It will be more than a mixture of African and European cultures. It will include Asian, Arabic, Polynesian, Mexican, and Native American contributions as well.

We North Americans are now starting to rebuild and redevelop our relationship with the drum as a tool for unity and expression. Drumming and dancing are appearing in churches as a tool for worship, in music therapy as a tool for healing, in corporations as a tool for team building, in conferences as a tool for synergizing, in schools as a tool for learning, in men's groups and women's groups as a tool for gender empowerment and goddess worship, and in communities as a tool for entrainment, entertainment, and community building.

A person who is drumming in a men's group could also be doing shaman drumming on his own or with a group. While occasionally playing in a community drum circle he could also be studying with an ethnically-specific drum teacher and playing for a dance class that relates to those rhythms. The drum is being used as a glue for all these populations throughout the United States today.

Over the years, I've been working with these different groups. They have been growing and overlapping into a strong and diverse population, dedicated to creating community and unifying itself through rhythmaculture. By recreating rhythmaculture we are reaching inside ourselves for the essence that fuels the evolution/revolution of our society back towards community values.

Evolving Terminology

Some words that represent African-style instruments have "devolved" as they have been assimilated into American culture. The African word *doundoun* refers to the largest of three double-headed bass drums used in some West African rhythm ensembles. In Europe the same type of drum is called a *dun dun*. The word *djun-djun* that I use in this book is an Americanization of *doundoun*.

Similarly, when I refer to an ashiko drum in America I'm talking about a "mutt" drum created in America that incorporates features of different African drums. These features include the cone shape of both *ngoma* drums of central Africa and ashiko-style drums of Nigeria, and the rope-head tuning system, called the "Mali weave" in the U.S., used on west African *djembe* drums. The resultant American drum only vaguely resembles its African ancestor.

Timeless Rhythm

This story unfolds just as I completed an evening community drum circle in Phoenix, Arizona. It was at a park on the outskirts of the city appropriately named "Pa Pa Go Park." For anyone unfamiliar with Babatunde Olatunji's verbal notation for the sounds on the drum, "pa" represents slaps and "go" represents tones, so the name of the park, when played on the drum, would be "Slap Slap Tone Park." In actuality the park was named after the southwest Native Americans who lived in this area for hundreds of years. The drum circle was held on an island in a small manmade lake.

Diana and I sat high up inside one of the holes of a meteorite, under a moonless southwest desert night sky full of brilliant stars.

After the official closing of the drum circle, many of the families were on their way home. Meanwhile, ten to fifteen die-hard drummers stayed on the island and played into the evening.

My wife Diana and I, in no hurry to leave, decided to take a twilight walk. After crossing over the bridge from the island into the park, we passed a group of Native American families who were setting up a barbecue across the lake from the island where the drummers were jamming out. Between their barbecue and the lake sat a large pow-wow drum with seven chairs around it, and a container of long-handled beaters sat next to it.

Scattered throughout the park were massive four-story-high boulders sticking out of the ground. They had large holes in them that made them look like meteorites that fell from the sky. By the time Diana and I had hiked up to the top of one of the meteor boulders overlooking the park, each drum group, located only a few yards across the lake from each other, was drumming full blast. Diana and I sat high up inside one of the holes of a meteorite, under a moonless southwest desert night sky full of brilliant stars. We could hear the different rhythms of the two distinct groups of drummers drifting up to us from the lake.

One group consisted of mixed genders, cultures, and timbral groups with each person expressing their individual rhythmical part, contributing it to the "in-the-moment" song that would be gone when they were finished playing.

The other drumming group consisted of brothers, fathers, sons, and uncles, all from the same culture, playing the same drum and rhythm, while singing the same prayer songs that have been passed on from generation to generation. These songs and rhythms will live on to the next generation, long after they are finished for the evening.

By chance, the rhythms of the two cultures would melt together for a few beats then clash into each other again across the lake. Each time the rhythms of the two groups would meet and melt into one expression the hairs on the back of my head would stand up and I would get goose bumps. It felt to me that for those few brief moments these two extremely different, almost opposing, representations of rhythmical expression were sharing the same rhythmical space and collaborating to create something that went beyond what each one of them represented separately.

> For me, time had stopped. The rhythm song that we could hear emanating from the shores of the lake could have been played a thousand years ago, or a thousand years from now on some other planet.

Slowly, and likely unconsciously for the players, the rhythms of the Native American pow-wow group and those of the island drum circle entwined into one song.

I am unsure exactly how long the song lasted. For me, time had stopped. From where Diana and I sat in the meteorite, the rhythm song that we could hear emanating from the shores of the lake could have been played a thousand years ago, or a thousand years from now on some other planet.

With my roots that grew from the free expression of my drumming spirit as a hippie drummer, coupled with my respect for culturally-specific drum circles that comes from 16 years of teaching "Village Music™" at a university, the opportunity to stand between and enjoy the melding of these two worlds was a powerful moment. When the song was done my face was wet with tears and I was at peace.

Circles

A Circle is a Series of Points Equidistant from a Central Point

A circle is one of the most natural forms found in our physical universe. It has no beginning and no end. For longer than we have written history, people have gathered together in circles in ritual fashion to celebrate and to pray in community.

A community drumming circle is a modern day version of an old-time community social. People come together to sing, dance, play music, and socialize. Instead of going to a concert to be entertained, we go to a community drumming circle to actively participate in entertainment by and for the whole community. A rhythm circle is just another style of community drum circle. Rhythm circles include a wider range of possibilities instead of emphasizing drums.

Everyone standing or sitting in a circle can see and hear everyone else equally and has an equal position. The circle is easily expandable and contractible in relationship to population changes. It is the optimum formation for a gathering of people who are all participating, as listeners and players, in a musical event where the participants are both the audience and the entertainment. In a circle, when an individual is playing their part in the musical ensemble, it is a gift to the center of the circle, where all the individual parts join into a musical group vision that manifests via sound. The quality of the music is based more upon the group's relationship with itself than the group's rhythmical or musical abilities.

Community drum circle at It's Beach in Santa Cruz, California

Rhythm is a basic universal language that everyone understands. It is a natural aspect of the human experience. It permeates our lives as a functional aspect in every action we make, from getting something from the fridge, eating, driving a car, having a conversation, or making love. One of the easiest ways of expressing your rhythmical sensibility, regardless of your rhythmical expertise, is on drums and percussion instruments.

A drum circle is a fully-participating group, sharing a rhythmical and musical experience. This experience results in harmony, camaraderie, and a feeling of wellness amongst the participating population.

Regardless of the group's level of rhythmical expertise, a good drum circle facilitator with the proper skills and focus can help guide, direct, and orchestrate a group to its highest musical potential. It's a powerful moment when people who might think they are rhythmically impaired are empowered to express their life's rhythmical experience on a drum or percussion instrument. They come to an understanding that they don't have to be a musician to make music.

When a group of like-minded people come together in a circle and merge their rhythmical experience into one musical expression, they create a community drum or rhythm circle. When they gather together and drum they are physically entrained by the dance they are doing with their hands on their drums and percussion. The result of that dance is the music the group creates. The quality of that music is a representation of the quality of their relationship with each other.

Participating in a drum/percussion circle of any kind is a healing experience for the heart, mind, and body. A drum circle creates a kinesthetic, subsonic vibration that gives a rhythmical massage to everyone near it. This massage affects each person differently, but positively influences the harmonious alignment of our physical cells, emotional states, and our spirits. It goes to the place where the person most needs that vibrational massage. Drum circles create physical vibrations that relax the body. They also massage the heart and the emotions. I've watched inner city gang members channel their anger and frustration through their drums to a place of peace. I've facilitated drum circles at numerous funerals where the rhythms flowed with the tears.

> *Participating in a drum/percussion circle of any kind is a healing experience for the heart, mind, and body.*

Drum vibrations massage the head and the brain and calm the mind. I've watched drumming bring a group of autistic children out of that mysterious other world into this reality—to drum and play. A drum circle creates physical exercise, and the entertainment of the whole group—as everyone gives a little of themselves, leaning forward into the circle, trusting, into one song. That one song creates a harmony that vibrates your physical state of being, your emotional state of being, and your mental state of being. People walk out of the drum circle totally excited and relaxed at the same time. The experience of being in a drum circle is very similar to that of being in church, where the entire congregation is participating in creating an environment conducive to generating a deep cathartic spiritual experience. To me, a well-facilitated drum circle is Rhythm Church.

Rhythm is a universal language, allowing dialogue among us at the most basic creative level. Drumming together cuts through racial, cultural, and gender differences to the core of who we are as human animals. That's why I say, "The drum is a tool for unity."

Universal Language

As this story unfolds the program planners of a particular U.S. shipping line were having a Pacific Rim managers' meeting in Bangkok, Thailand. They were concerned about the meeting and asked me to take instruments to Bangkok for fifty people to do some rhythmical synergizing. They hoped that I could relieve the cultural tension that they had experienced in a similar meeting that had been held the year before. They were certain that recent cultural history was preventing the managers from being fully open and friendly with each other.

Their managers represented particular regions of the east and southeast Pacific Rim. Each manager came from and represented a particular region: a specific country, culture, and religion. Because of the history of the last fifty to a hundred years the Japanese distrust the South Koreans who distrust the Chinese who distrust the Taiwanese who distrust the Cambodians who distrust the Pakistanis who distrust the Indonesians, and on and on and…

What I found when I arrived at the meeting was exactly what the program planners feared. Everyone was being polite to each other, but not much was getting accomplished in the meeting. The people were using English as their second language in the meeting, but of the fifty participants, at least seven cultures were represented. I decided to speak only when needed and facilitate just enough to create rhythmical dialogue among the group. I did this so that it was as much their responsibility as it was mine to create a musical piece together. By running the program this way I created more of a need for the participants to collaborate in the creative expression being produced.

Since they were using rhythmical expression instead of verbal language to create their music, they were using the most universal communication we humans have. The musical dialogue started flowing and some excellent creative percussion pieces were produced by the group. Laughter and the quality of the music being played were excellent indicators of the synergy they had found. A good time was had by all!

Since they were using rhythmical expression instead of verbal language to create their music, they were using the most universal communication we humans have.

After my part of the program we all went to a fancy dinner on a flatboat on the Chao Phraya River that flows through Bangkok. At the end of the dinner all the participants started sharing their traditional drinking and toasting customs in what seemed to be a conspiracy to get their hosts drunk. The next morning everything was bright and cheery and the meeting proceeded as planned with a high degree of energy and exchange. The program developers complimented me on my synergizing and team building work and gave me credit for the good energy. I am unsure whether it was my doing, or some combination of events including the drum circle and all of us sharing toasting customs on the boat together.

Types of Drum Circles in the U.S.

Anarchist Drum Circles

Many of us were thunder drummers back in the '60s. We were pulled into the power, mystery, and altered state of consciousness offered to us by the drum, which is right in front of us at a touch. In an anarchist drum circle, we were sailing the rhythm seas without a rudder in a blissful state of ignorance. We didn't know that we did not know anything nor did we care. Unless we lived in a large metropolis, thunder drumming circles were the only choice we had at the time, and there was nobody around who knew any better to help us or judge us. With lots of testosterone, little technique, and not much knowledge, we thought that calluses were tools we needed to develop to play a drum. Now of course we know that our body develops calluses to protect us from our own ignorance of drumming techniques.

> In an anarchist drum circle, we were sailing the rhythm seas without a rudder in a blissful state of ignorance.

This type of drum circle became popular as a traditional part of the Rainbow gatherings. Every July at the Rainbow Gathering, thousands of people get together at a national forest somewhere in the U.S. They stay there for a week, living in peace and harmony with each other and the earth and keeping the forest not only as clean, but cleaner than they found it. Some of the drum circles at these Rainbow Gatherings have hundreds of people participating—the drumming doesn't stop for days.

The unwritten rule in this kind of circle is that everyone is free to speak their rhythmical spirit, and nobody takes charge, leads, or teaches the group. It's an anarchist situation. It's about agreement. Once that rhythmical agreement among the players happens, rhythmical alchemy is created. It's in that rhythmical alchemy that the potential

Anarchist thunder drummer circle in Seattle, Washington

for musical magic exists—where the group, in their "in-the-moment" musical collaboration, creates one harmonic voice. In anarchist drumming circles that magic moment usually will only last a short amount of time before some player gets excited and starts jamming on top of the music with their drum. We call it soloing. A solo in a rhythm circle is a wonderful thing to hear, as the soloist weaves his or her instrument in, around and on top of the group groove like a bird flying through the trees in a forest. But as more people get excited and start soloing instead of dialoging with each other, they start bumping into each other rhythmically. The magic leaves. The group rhythm gets mushy. The drum circle loses its agreement, and the rhythm fumbles into chaos, falls apart and stops. Then someone starts another rhythm for the rest of the group to join in, and the cycle starts over again.

I would never get in the middle of this type of circle and say, "Hi, I've got some information that will help us maintain this wonderful groove a lot longer so we can bathe ourselves in it." I would get thrown out of the circle. In this anarchist drumming circle environment, saying, "Let's all agree to play to one pulse as a rhythmical reference point," would be interpreted as trying to make a rule where the rule is "No rules allowed." An anarchist drum circle can be facilitated, but only in a subtle and most basic way.

Benét Luchion is one of the best anarchist drumming circle facilitators I've seen. Benét facilitates using his understanding that the group is looking for agreement. He walks into the circle with the biggest double-headed drum he can find, such as a *djun-djun* or a big bass drum, and with a big mallet plays nothing but a simple pulse on the drum. He finds that common denominator groove that the players are looking for and rein-

Benét Luchion

forces it, until even the players who aren't listening to each other can't avoid it. He is, as we drummers say, "holding down the bottom." The bottom is the rhythmical foundation that's a reference point for all the players in the circle. Benét is one of the better players in almost any anarchist drumming circle he enters, but instead of getting on top of the rhythmical groove and soloing with a loud, high-pitched *djembe* drum, he's hitting the quarter note, the pulse. This locks the rhythm together with a bass drum. He's playing the most simple part, the most important basic element needed to create agreement among the players.

Culturally-Specific Drum Circles

Culturally-specific drum circles sit on the other end of the drum circle spectrum. They involve a deep respect for cultural source while studying in an oral tradition handed down from teacher to student from generation to generation. In some traditions there are drumming families with a lineage that goes deep into their cultural history. The ethnic arts community in the U.S. is about the study of the drum, dance, songs, and music of a particular culture that is still alive and vibrant today. There are master drummers and what I call "people of source" who are in the U.S. from many different countries. They are teaching us about the basics of the expression of their cultures through the music and the traditions that go along with their rhythms and dances.

In a culturally-specific drum circle you will find a chorus of tuned drums, with each drum playing a prescribed part. When all the parts are played together they create a specific musical drum song that may be hundreds of years old—recognizable and reproducible.

Today, in colleges, universities, and metropolitan areas throughout the United States, wherever you find a culturally-specific drum circle you will also find a dance teacher and dance class that is specific to that ethnic culture. Some of the culturally-specific drum circles that can be found in the United States today are the Afro-Cuban folkloric study groups and drum circles. Very popular today are *djembe* and *djun-djun* drumming of West Africa. You can find strong Congolese drum and dance communities across the United States, as well as stick drumming from the Ewe culture of Ghana. Along with culturally-specific drumming that comes from the Caribbean area, you will find Haitian drumming. Calypso drumming of the Trinidad/Tobago Islands is also popular in the United States.

Community Drum Circles

Anarchist drummers see a culturally-specific drum circle like a wild horse sees a corral; a culturally-specific drummer sees an anarchist drummer as ignorant and disrespectful of indigenous drumming traditions.

I stand in the middle, between the two. I respect the free flowing, "knowing without knowing" drummer's spirit that comes from the inside out, as an anarchist drummer lets his or her freeform drumming spirit fly. At the same time, I respect and appreciate the guidance, wisdom, and techniques that ancient cultural forms and traditions of source cultures provide to us.

The community drum circle is an open space for people to come together and share the love of drumming, dancing, and singing. It is a celebration of life and community.

The community drum circle offers some of the best of both of these seemingly opposite drumming worlds. It's a place where everybody is welcome regardless of their level of musical expertise and drumming knowledge. In a community drum circle we are encouraged to express our individual rhythmical spirit, and at the same time adhere to some of the basic universal principles found in culturally-specific drum circles.

The community drum circle is an open space for people to come together and share the love of drumming, dancing, and singing. It is a celebration of life and community. The population of a community gathering reflects the wide diversity of interested drummers, from the thunder drummer to the culturally-specific drumming student. The reasons for coming to a community drum gathering reflect that diversity. Folks may say any of the following: "I'm just curious," "We are here to have fun and entertain each other," "I'm here to be a part of Rhythm Church and have rhythmical communion with this group," "I'm here to achieve an altered state of consciousness through rhythm," "I'm here to relieve stress by banging on a drum," or "I'm here to celebrate life." Many of these points of view are often reflected in a single rhythm circle.

When we drum together as a community, it changes our relationships.

Thunder Drummer Roots

The thunder drummer song is as ancient as the first music circles in Africa. These circles eventually evolved into the specific African rhythmaculture that drummers are studying today. A thunder drummer's song is the sound of the primordial search for rhythmical agreement among the players, and at the same time it is the full expression of the rhythmical spirit within each of us. It is simply "the search for the one."

There is an ongoing thunder drumming circle at the picnic benches on the bluff above the beach where I teach in Santa Cruz, California. The beginning-beginner drummers soon find out that their tackhead bongos or tambourines won't fit into the culturally-specific West African *djembe/djun-djun* circle nearby, and that they are not allowed to play with the Afro/Cuban circle up the beach until they know the 2/3 *clavé*. Other than a facilitated community drum circle, at this entry level an "anything goes" drum circle is the most accessible place they have to drum with others.

Occasionally, I'll stop by the picnic benches with a *djun-djun* on my way to my classes. I'll sit for a while listening to the search out of chaos, find the leverage point in the beat, and begin to gently play a pulse into the rhythm. Consciously or unconsciously, we all come to rhythmical agreement, locking the rhythm into a groove and taking off. (Thank you, Benét!) I then hand the *djun-djun* over to someone waiting to play who has no drum, and go down to the beach to teach my classes. Later that day they will come down to my teaching circle with my *djun-djun* and a "thanks."

> A thunder drummer's song is the sound of the primordial search for rhythmical agreement ...and the full expression of the rhythmical spirit within each of us.

I've watched the population of this thunder circle evolve and change as the ultimate internal question comes up in their individual beginning drummers' hearts. "Is this all there is?" The answer (in time) for all but the most die-hard thunder drummers is "No." That's when I find them waiting for me at the beginning beginners' class at the beach.

One such student said to me, "Arthur, you've spoiled the thunder drum circle for me. You've taught me how to listen and now all I hear in that circle is the noise." My answer is, "Don't abandon the thunder. Now that you know how to listen, listen through their noise for the group spirit. Then feed that spirit back to them with your rhythm. In doing so, you'll help guide the groove to a fuller expression of the circle's musical spirit."

Do the white arrows make the black arrows? Or do the black arrows make the white arrows? YES!

Specific Population Drum Circles

The spirit of the drum is being discovered as a tool for unity in many populations. The spirit of the drum has brought me to kindergartens, middle schools, high schools, personal growth venues, corporations, kids-at-risk, the mentally challenged, blind and deaf kids' programs, well elderly, music therapist events, colleges and universities. The list continues with religious organizations such as the Protestants, Episcopalians, and Quakers, shaman and trance drumming communities, Veteran's groups, and men's and women's empowerment groups. Group rhythm allows us to bypass any perceived differences we might have. Our rhythm brings us to a place of common purpose where we share our personal expression.

> *Rhythm is a universal language, allowing dialogue among us at the most basic creative level. Drumming together cuts through racial, cultural, and gender differences to the core of who we are as human animals.*

More and more people involved in the facilitation of the types of populations listed above are discovering the use of rhythm-based events to help synergize their communities' purpose and goals. Only fifty percent of the people attending my facilitation playshops are there to learn how to facilitate community drum circles in general. The others are there to learn how to facilitate their specific community.

The Plaza Circles

There is a large open courtyard plaza, downtown, on the campus of the University of California, Berkeley. It has been used as a meeting place for drummers for as long as the plaza has been in existence. In the sixties there was a culturally-specific Afro-Cuban group that met in one of the corners of the plaza. By the late seventies there were anarchist thunder drumming circles meeting on the weekends on the corner in the plaza kitty-cornered to the Afro-Cuban group. By the eighties there was a third group of drummers meeting on the weekends playing West-African rhythms with *djembes* and *djun-djuns*. By the nineties there was only one corner left, and you can still go to what is now called

> *Group rhythm allows us to bypass any perceived differences we might have. Our rhythm brings us to a place of common purpose where we share our personal expression.*

Stephen Biko Plaza at UC Berkeley and usually find at least three, and sometimes as many as five, groups of drummers playing. The drumming in these circles represents a range of types of drum circles that can be found throughout the U.S. That range includes anarchist drum circles and culturally-specific circles such as Afro-Cuban, West African drumming with *djembe* and *djun-djuns*, Haitian and Ghanaian stick drumming, Sabhar drumming from West Africa, and Niabingi drumming from Jamaica.

Drum Circle Etiquette

At no drum circle that I know of will you find a sign posted outside the event listing a bunch of rules you must follow to participate. But in every drum circle, no matter what type of gathering or for what purpose, the event is built upon numerous agreements created by the participants, sometimes over a long-time relationship. These unwritten agreements constitute what I call "drum circle etiquette." The etiquette is different for various populations, but even in an anarchist drum circle where anything goes there is a basic agreement that the people are there to share their rhythmical spirit and create the power of unity through music.

If you are walking into a particular drum circle for the first time, the best way to enter is with a service-oriented attitude. Be very observant of the actions and reactions of different drummers operating in the circle. Play in a supportive manner with the idea that you don't know the unwritten rules of this particular circle yet.

Some of the more universal rules of etiquette that you will find in most drum circles are listed below.

- **Sit in the circle so you can see everybody, and so that you are not blocking anyone's view.**
- **Ask permission before playing someone else's drum.**
- **Wear no rings, watches or bracelets while playing hand drums.** This protects the head of the drums from the metal.
- **Leave rhythmical space for other people in the circle to express themselves.** Listen as much as you play. In other words, don't take five-minute solos.
- **Don't smoke.** Respect the need everyone has for their air in this close space.

Kids' drum circle in Hong Kong

Some additional suggestions may be helpful for someone who is entering a rhythm circle for the first time. The first thing to do is to LISTEN to what's going on in the circle as you sit down, instead of jumping in and starting to play.

> *There is a basic agreement that the people are there to share their rhythmical spirit and create the power of unity through music.*

A second thing to do as you begin to play is to support the fundamental groove that you hear in the song being created by the participants. Get into the group rhythm before you solo.

A third thing to do as you're playing is to keep the consciousness of using your notes to make space for other people's creativity rather than using your notes to fill up space. Using these three Arthurian suggestions will help you merge into the circle's playing experience in an unobtrusive way, so that you can quickly be fully participating and have a sense of really being a part of the experience.

Using our notes to make space for other people's creativity

Facilitators

What Is a Facilitator?

The word facilitate means to make easier. As a facilitator you are a rhythmatist, a leader, a teacher, a team builder, an orchestra conductor, an inspiration, and an evangelist for the Church of Rhythm.

- You are facilitating the group beyond their preconceived capacity, to being a functional community drum circle.
- You are teaching them by their own experience about the elements that make a drum circle work.
- You are conducting the different pitches and timbral groups of the circle into a musical orchestration.
- You are guiding their growing excitement and synergy to a place of shared spirit.
- You are inspiring the group to its highest rhythmical potential.

Skills for Facilitating

There are three basic skills needed to successfully facilitate a drum circle: group leadership, platform presentation, and body language. Along with a description of these skills are listed occupations that could generate the experiences needed to obtain them. Even if you haven't experienced the situations or occupations listed below, you too can learn to facilitate. I will present, later in this chapter, different ways to create the experiences needed to acquire these skills.

Group Leadership Skills

A facilitator needs to be able to move and direct groups of people in a smooth and logistically economic way to achieve a goal. You do this with what I call leadership skills. Occupations where people learn and use these skills include musical instructors, hand drumming teachers, musical therapists, personal growth facilitators, new games instructors, school teachers, dance instructors, and sports coaches. You may also know of other livelihoods and experiences where you work with or facilitate groups of people using leadership skills.

Platform Presentation Skills

A facilitator needs to be able to speak in front of large groups of people using vocal dynamics to move and inspire them. You need to address the group with whom you are working with a voice that commands attention and respect. That voice should also have in its dynamic delivery the ability to move people's emotions, spirits, and attitudes. I call this "platform presentation skills." Occupations where people learn and use these skills include orators, poets, actors and actresses, announcers, masters of ceremonies, lecturers, preachers, singers, and comedians.

Body Language Skills

As a facilitator you need to be able to utilize body language skills as a major communication element in the performance of your work. You need to be able to communicate directions to your circle while it is fully involved in a musical piece. Your voice would not be heard, so you use your body to signal clearly understandable directions and commands. I call this "body language skills." Occupations where people learn and use these skills include clowns, mimes, actors and actresses, dancers, contact improvisationists, and martial arts teachers and performers.

> *Body language, like rhythm, is a basic universal language that everyone understands.*

Body language, like rhythm, is a basic universal language that everyone understands. I've facilitated hearing-impaired children in California and mentally-challenged children in Singapore into fully functioning, spirited circles. How? Our natural expression of rhythm glued us together. Through the use of sounds instead of words, and with only the rhythm of mime and body language, I have facilitated many successful drum and rhythm circles in non-English speaking populations around the world, from Jakarta, Malaysia to Moscow, Russia.

Body language communicates spirit.

The Russian Elf Story

I had been working extensively with two pioneers of Neuro Linguistic Programming (NLP), John Grinder and Judy Delozier. They had been using me as a *rhythmasizer* in their programs. It was the beginning of the period of Glasnost in what was then called Russia. Gorbachev was still president and Yeltsin was mayor of Moscow. John was invited to do an intensive NLP program in Moscow with doctors and educators. He brought me there along with eight of their top trainers. These trainers each had their own consulting or counseling businesses and taught NLP-related programs professionally.

I was there to create rhythm-based exercises that were metaphoric to the messages being delivered in the program. The program also involved state-consciousness and state-change work, which had a tendency to put the participants in a trance state. As a result, I was also there to use rhythm-based drumming events as a grounding force for the participants so they could stay in their bodies long enough to absorb more NLP. Some of the circuitry exercises that you will find in this book were developed in these programs.

The program was held at a state-run university, just outside Moscow, where a lot of the athletes and the artists are housed and trained for the theater, ballet, and the Olympics. I was told it is one of the few places you could get toilet paper, chocolate, and fruit from Cuba.

On the opening day of the program we were in a large auditorium with the 400 participants—doctors and educators from throughout Russia. The trainers were introducing themselves through the interpreter assigned to them for the program. John went first, introducing himself and giving his extensive credentials as well his specific goals for this program. That set the introduction pattern. Each trainer took a turn standing in front of the audience with their translator, introducing themselves, and sitting down. Each trainer gave their credentials, their university affiliation, the titles of the books they wrote, their NLP specialty, and finally, their goals for the program.

I was last to introduce myself. Following a long list of eminent professors and doctors, authors with high university credentials, I had little to say. I stood in front of the group at the edge of the stage with my translator and took my time just looking out at them before I spoke.

I then said, "My name is Arthur Hull and I'm from Santa Cruz, California, in the USA." The translator said, "Blah blah blah California blah USA." Then I said, "I teach village music at the University of California." The translator said, "Blah blah blah California." Finally I said "My purpose at this program is to be your elf trainer." The translator started translating "blah blah blah huhh?" He stopped in mid-sentence, turned to me with a quizzical look and said, "Alf? a-l-f?"

How was I to explain to the translator what an elf was in a way that he could explain to the audience?

How was I to explain to the translator what an elf was in a way that he could explain to the audience? I immediately turned to the audience and, using more body language than English, I let them know that an elf is a person with pointed ears by pulling on the tops of my ears to make them pointed. I made a pointed hat with both of my hands over my head to let them know more about my elfself and then I hopped lightly around the stage, slightly hunched over, looking at them with a little elfish grin on my face. At that point I walked back to the edge of the stage and lifted my shoulders in the universal questioning way. I looked out at the audience holding out my hands.

People from the audience started standing up and yelling at the translator. These people were from different regions of a country that covered over 24 different distinct cultures, from Siberia to Poland. Each culture had a name and a description of what an elf, or a fool, or a coyote is, and these people were standing up in the audience yelling at the translator and giving him their cultural version of what an elf is. When things calmed down the translator looked at me and said, "I think that they understand now." I then spoke to the audience through the translator again, saying, "My job is to help you build community through music." The translator said, "Blah blah blah" again. Then I said, "Music is a universal language," and the translator "Blah blah blahed." I then pointed to the translator as I said, "Because it's a universal language I hope to make his job obsolete."

> *The "body conversation" I had with the audience on the stage was the first step toward relieving the need for a translator.*

And so the translator told the people that, because we were going to learn to speak music, his job was going to *disappear.* The whole audience exploded in uproarious laughter, lasting a lot longer than I would have expected. I intended what I said to be funny, but I did not think it was *that* funny. I later found out that any Russian who spoke English and worked for the government at that time was usually a KGB agent, and the usual way for them to get fired was for them to "disappear."

The "body conversation" I had with the audience on the stage was the first step toward relieving the need for a translator. By the end of the program my translator's job had become obsolete, and he became part of the group as the universal music became our language and spoke for us. Luckily, he didn't *disappear.*

Body language transcends all language.

Celebrating Life at Lenin's Tomb

After a closing dinner celebration at the end of the Moscow NLP program some of us decided to go to Red Square. Carrying percussion instruments and a drum with us, we took the subway/bomb shelter, three stories down underground, into the city. The group sang, drummed, and played on the subway all the way to the heart of Moscow. Leaving the subway, we came out on a street that had huge solid yellow lines painted on the pavement. Arrows and merging lines from other streets indicated to me that we were walking toward the Kremlin, following the route of the military parades that dignitaries view in Red Square. The group continued to sing, drum, and make merry as we walked toward Lenin's Tomb near the center of the great plaza.

Because of Glasnost the people of Russia had been feeling their oats, coming to Red Square to protest about lack of food, gas, government, etc. The government had posted extra forces in the square to deal with the protesters. Now here came a noisy group playing instruments and singing. The celebration caught the attention of other people that were in the square. Slowly but surely, a celebration circle formed—people were clapping, singing, playing instruments, and laughing. Meanwhile, I could see behind our celebrating circle, gray military hats bobbing all around us. I realized that these guards, police force, and military personnel didn't know how to deal with a group of people who were celebrating life. They only knew how to deal with a group of people who were protesting.

Finally, after fifteen or twenty minutes, I saw the gray caps begin to converge from all around the circle. As they got closer, the music suddenly stopped, the circle dissolved, the people all fell silent and started meandering around. It seemed like some unwritten notice had been given by the military to the people, and the celebration disappeared. I was suddenly surrounded by three of my tall Russian friends and gently escorted out of Red Square.

> *Slowly but surely, a celebration circle formed—people were clapping, singing, playing instruments, and laughing.*

Our group reformed, moved off, and started celebrating again once we were on the subway going back to the university. One of my hosts commented to me that this was possibly the first celebration other than a military one in the Red Square in many years—the first spontaneous community rhythm circle in the Red Square in Moscow!

Is the energy you give out the energy you get back? YES!

Basic Facilitation Principles

When you apply basic facilitation principles, they will enhance your chances for successful group participation at any rhythmical event you facilitate. Successful participation happens when your players feel completely immersed in the process. They feel that their contribution is just as valid as anyone else's, that they are not being overly challenged in the process, and at the same time they are being given creative license to explore and take risks. They can push their musical listening and playing abilities while participating in an ongoing, in-the-moment, ever-changing, rhythmical and musical event.

Are your participants enjoying what's going on? Are they feeling fulfilled in their expression? Two barometers for success are whether you, as the facilitator, are having fun, and whether your circle of rhythmatists is having fun. The basic facilitation principles listed below will be explored thoroughly, point by point, in the chapters to come.

- **Know your purpose**—be the facilitator. Have a good understanding of your role in the event. See the event as a complete experience created in cooperation between you and the circle, with a beginning, a middle, and an end.

- **Have a clearly defined goal** for the event and clearly define that goal to the participants (as appropriate) at the opening of the circle.

- **Understand the use of the physical circle as an equalizer** for mutual communication using sight, hearing, and participation.

- **Understand the idea of orchestrational position** and use it as a communication power point to focus attention and direct the group.

- **Understand the importance of body language** for orchestration.

- **Understand the use of windows of communication** (quiet spaces between the rhythms) for giving verbal directions for setting up the next rhythmical piece and for delivering community-building metaphors to the participants.

- **Educate the group to be self-facilitating** by helping participants identify fundamental elements needed for a successful rhythm circle.

- **Read and assess the participants in the circle as one body** to determine the level of rhythmical expertise, listening ability, and ability to participate as a group. This gives you, as the facilitator, the ability to make decisions about challenging the group to its highest potential while avoiding crisis mode for the participants.

- **Understand transition points** in the process of a circle, and how to use them to further improve the quality of the music being produced.

- **Understand and implement the principal of small successes.**

- **Open and close the circle in ritual fashion.**

Philosophy and Attitudes of Facilitators

For community drum circles, an attitude of service to the community is the foundation from which to operate. You want to communicate an attitude that welcomes anyone who comes to your circle to participate at any level they want, even if it's standing outside the circle and tapping their feet. Welcome any instrument they bring, including drums, other percussion toys such as bells and *clavé*, and homemade toys such as a can of rocks, as well as their voices and clapping hands.

> *For community drum circles, an attitude of service to the community is the foundation from which to operate.*

The ultimate objective of a community drum circle facilitator is to make yourself obsolete by guiding the circle to a place where they won't need to be facilitated to play well together. I call it leading the people to lead themselves. As the facilitator, you do this by communicating directly, sometimes specifically, sometimes guiding them with metaphors, to the basic principles that make a circle successful. When the group becomes able to self-facilitate the logistics of making music together, that frees you as the facilitator to guide the dynamics, energy, and direction of the event. My personal end goal in an event is to be a part of the circle, playing with it instead of leading it.

Create a drum circle with whom you can play.

By serving the community through rhythm you give a community a sense of who they are as a collaborative group. This guides you to one of your ultimate objectives as a facilitator: you guide the group to the place where it facilitates its own spirit into the circle. This spirit comes into play as you implement the Golden Rule of Facilitation: have fun creating fun.

If you have the right attitude toward your circle, then the tools and techniques you need as a facilitator will develop. When you enter the circle with your heart, coming from a place of selfless service, you have an opportunity to showcase other peoples' skills and spirit. If you are still developing your facilitating tools and techniques, but have the right attitude and intention, then magic can happen. If you use your tools with a selfish, egotistical attitude people may feel entertained, but the magic will elude you. Understand who you are and why you are in the middle of that circle. You, as a facilitator of a rhythmical event, have the unique opportunity to give the participants a gift—a part of themselves they may not have known they had.

> *The Golden Rule of Facilitation: have fun creating fun.*

As a facilitator you want to remember your innocence, curiosity and amazement as a beginning beginner so that you'll have empathy with the children and adults who are coming to a community drum circle for the first time. That beginning-beginner feeling

Facilitator's Playshop in Hawaii

is something that you want to keep for the rest of your drumming days. Catch that feeling, listen to what it is, identify it, and then hang on to it. As you become a hotshot, superduper drummer, get your chops down, and learn a book full of rhythms from seventeen different cultures, there is still somewhere in your drummer's consciousness a beginning-beginner feeling curiosity, wonder, and amazement. As soon as you begin to think you know it all, you stop learning. There is so much to learn that you would have to live a few life times to start to understand it all. What you know now is showing you just how much there is to learn. The more you learn, the more you will realize how little you know.

You Need Not Be a Drum Teacher to Facilitate

Sometimes people who have studied with me in my facilitators' program have sent me video tapes of them facilitating a rhythm-based program and asked me to critique their work. One such person, with minimal technical drumming skills, did his first open community circle and sent me the video tape for my feedback. He facilitated his first event more gracefully than have most hand drum teachers in their early circles. The reason was twofold: he focused on serving his community and he facilitated a collaborative effort by the group to entertain each other. He was not burdened by superfluous technical knowledge or trying to teach particular drumming skills and rhythms.

A Cautionary Note for Hand Drum Teachers

Let your teaching skills support your facilitating skills, and know the difference between teaching and facilitating. Be careful that you guide the people in your circles to learn for themselves the basic skills of listening and of expressing their spirit.

A teacher is there to teach, and that is empowering. But there is a relationship between a teacher and a student that is hierarchical, "I know something you don't know. Here it is." It needs to be that way, because the students need to be in a learning mode, and the teacher needs to be in a teaching mode to give them that kind of information.

By contrast, in empowerment facilitation you want to guide the people to be able to learn for themselves how to make beautiful music, without overly-challenging them to learn technical skills or culturally-specific drum parts. They needn't

> As soon as you begin to think you know it all, you stop learning.

learn drum parts to be able to express themselves on the drum. If you lead a community drum circle like you teach your drumming class, then you will turn that circle into a class. Then the people in the circle will become students, learning to depend on you as a teacher while you, in the process, lose the sense of community where people come together for creative expression.

My best advice to hand drum teachers is to use your teaching talents to support your facilitating goals. Let your teaching tools support the facilitator in you. You will then find yourself facilitating the process of people learning how to listen to each other while sharing their spirit, instead of how to play parts and depend on you. Instead of creating a group dependent on you for guidance, you can lead the group to lead itself.

The Exchange Of Circuitry

Of the 50 participants at my first Facilitator's Playshop in Hawaii, eight were nationally-recognized drummers and performers who have their own albums, have written drumming-related books, have produced drumming instruction videos, and do endorsements for drum companies such as REMO, Latin Percussion, and Toka. On the other end of the spectrum were about eight beginning-beginner drummers who were just developing their rhythmical skills. As teachers of kids-at-risk, as music therapists, and as personal growth facilitators, these folks have well-developed facilitation skills.

> The players were amazed at how well someone who is a novice rhythmatist can facilitate an excellent rhythm circle.

The group of people on each end of this spectrum brought to the week something that the other group wanted. They exchanged individual information for a week. The players were amazed at how well someone who is a novice rhythmatist can facilitate an excellent rhythm circle. Much of what the expert players learned was how not to look and act like a teacher while facilitating.

Beware of Passing Out
Culturally-Specific Rhythms

Beware of passing out culturally-specific rhythms in a community drum circle. Teaching a culturally-specific rhythm in a community drum circle with mom, dad, grandma, and the kids, if you are not careful, can defeat the purpose of the event. Passing out parts in a circle can be fine as long as the participants have the technical ability to interpret them. However, if a culturally-specific rhythm part is not played correctly then it is wrong.

Passing out a culturally-specific rhythm in a community drum circle could do any of the following:
- turn a drum circle event into a drum class;
- disempower and frustrate some participants, turning them off to drumming, by putting them in "student crisis mode" instead of turning them on to their own drumming spirit;
- create a barely-recognizable version of a traditional rhythm that would not represent the source culture, and in some cases could be considered disrespectful.

I ask you to be respectful of the ancient traditional rhythms from other cultures. Please be aware of your methods of accomplishing your goals, and be careful in your presentation that you do not misrepresent these cultures if you do choose to use culturally-specific rhythms in your event.

I have seen culturally-specific rhythms used in community rhythm environments. A presenter's attitude toward their participants, and how they present their information, results in either success or failure. West African *djembe* rhythms and rhythms taught by Babatunde Olatunji are the most used culturally-specific rhythms in community events. Sometimes they are presented in a highly specific manner where all the related parts are given to the participants holding the appropriate drum or percussion. Sometimes just the heart part of a particular rhythm is presented to the whole group. The presenter usually does this in one of two ways. Either they name the rhythm, its cultural source, and then show the part, or else they use the rhythm as a format for a community groove, changing the pattern enough to avoid having it be culturally-specific, thus giving the circle lots of freedom to invest their personal rhythmical spirit into it. I have used both methods of presentation depending on the population.

The word of mouth community drum circles held four times a year at It's Beach in Santa Cruz are partially a graduation celebration for my students and those of Don Davidson, who also teaches Village Music classes downtown and at the university. Many people who come to these circles are students and drum enthusiasts. I think this is an appropriate venue for sharing the culturally-specific rhythms that these people have been studying. When I do this,

I ask you to be respectful to the ancient traditional rhythms from other cultures.

I empower those who are joining us just for the day to play whatever part they feel is appropriate for them. Babatunde Olatunji does the same with the closing celebrations for his workshops that are open to the public.

The community rhythm circle held every New Year's Eve at First Night Santa Cruz in the middle of downtown Santa Cruz is heavily advertised and heavily attended by a large (three- to five-hundred person) cross-section of the population. I discuss universal grooves that are not culturally specific later in this book. They are accessible to a range of experience levels and I use them at First Night to facilitate a positive community-building experience gracefully. I would not choose to use culturally-specific rhythms with such a mixed population in an open community drum circle.

Bumbershoot Circles

Bumbershoot is the largest arts and music festival on the west coast of the U.S., held annually in Seattle, Washington at the Seattle Center (where the Space Needle is located). The four-day event is held on the last official summer weekend and is named after the large umbrella used during the west coast winter rains. At each Bumbershoot I host twenty community drum circles, with three hundred drums provided by REMO Drum company. I do this in a drum corral, situated in the middle of the festival grounds, and the circles are open to anybody that cares to join us. My job as drum elder is to facilitate three of the circles daily myself, and to play master of ceremonies for other circles that are voluntarily facilitated by the drum teachers and facilitators from a very healthy Seattle drumming community (thanks to John Avinger-Jacques and the Seattle World Percussion Society). All together, by the end of each festival, ten to fifteen facilitators have given over six thousand people a community drumming experience. We are on the mission.

Throughout the weekend many of the facilitators hang out around the drum corral and watch each other work. A few hang out with me the whole four days and only miss one or two circles. It has turned into an unofficial facilitators' show and tell conference, where we meet after each facilitated event and share comments, critiques, and other feedback.

My only request to anyone who wants to volunteer to facilitate a circle is that they be a rhythmical evangelist, making their presentation accessible to the whole walk-in festival population, including moms, dads, and kids.

Hosting this event gives me a wonderful opportunity to observe a complete cross section of what a particular community has to offer in its facilitators. Their experience ranges from beginning beginners to advanced facilitators, and their presentation formats range from almost anarchist thunder drummer circles to ethno-specific drum classes.

The result was a complicated multi-part rhythm where everyone in the circle was successfully participating.

In the most recent Bumbershoot festival, I was most concerned about a rhythm circle where the facilitator was trying to teach a five-pulse rhythm; that's one more pulse than most non-drumming Americans can comfortably feel and play. The facilitator was so involved in teaching his rhythm that he did not notice that his population, mostly families, had dwindled from two hundred people down to seventy-five folks.

He was not getting the obvious feedback that his circle was giving him. That feedback was that he was putting them under performance pressure by making them play something that was out of their technical reach, creating frustration. They were not having any fun. Instead they were in student crisis mode, so they were getting up and leaving to go somewhere in the festival that might be more fun. Duh? I pointed this fact out to him and watched him go through "facilitator's ego death," learn the lesson, and then change his program. He became more accessible and created a fun rhythmical event with the seventy-five people he had left. When his event was over he had attracted a full crowd back into the drum corral.

At this same festival, the rhythm circle that I enjoyed the most was the one that was expertly facilitated by Geoff Johns. He is one of the first drum teachers to present a series of audio cassette tapes that teach basic hand drumming styles. Those tapes, entitled "DRUM! How to Play the Rhythms of Africa and Latin America," are still available. See Resources in the back of this book.

Geoff showed the circle a number of simple parts, giving the people choices, encouraging them to pick the part they felt most comfortable playing. Then he layered the parts on top of each other one by one, pausing at each layer to let the circle hear the change in the song the new part created. The result was a complicated multi-part rhythm where everyone in the circle was successfully participating. The rhythm was so full and complete and universal that it sounded to me like it could have been the foundational structure for any one of four culturally-specific rhythms that I could identify from four distinct rhythmacultures. But it was just an in-the-moment composition expertly facilitated by Geoff Johns, and expertly executed by three hundred moms, dads, and kids having fun.

Geoff Johns

Facilitation Exercises and Drum Circle Games

The facilitation exercises and drum circle games scattered throughout this book are designed to help you develop the tools, techniques and skills you need to successfully facilitate a rhythm event with any population. The difference between the exercises and the games is that, in the drum circle games, everybody is responsible for the group process and the result. In the facilitation exercises, one designated individual is responsible for the group process and the result. The exercises are progressive: the earlier exercises will give you the skills to execute the later exercises.

Three population sources available to you with which to practice the facilitation techniques and drum circle games include kids, your local drum circle friends, and especially-created study groups.

Kids' Circles

I first tested out on kids almost everything I do with any population in a rhythm-based event. If the kids don't buy it, I don't try it on adults. Children are the greatest teachers. They are a pure form of direct feedback on your total presentation, from the quality of your execution of the event, to reflecting back to you your level of sincerity. You can't fool the kids. They will reflect back to you the spirit you present to them. Children see past any surface agenda you bring to them to the basic core of why you are really there. If you are there to share your rhythmical bliss, the children will respond appropriately. If you are there just to make money, the children will know that and will make you earn it.

While teaching at the University of California in Santa Cruz I developed a teaching associate program for my advanced students. One of the prerequisites for any person entering that program was that they had to be doing a rhythm-based event or class on a regular basis with a group of kids. The school system is starving for rhythm and music-based programs. With the limited resources available to them, no school or teacher that I know of has turned down the offer of someone volunteering to come into a class, for forty-five minutes once a week or once a month, to do a rhythm-based event.

You say you don't have the percussion instruments you need to take into a class of thirty to forty kids? The fun and easy answer to that question is to make your own percussion toys and "found sound" instruments. You can also do it as a project with the kids with whom you are working. You can refer to a chapter on how to make homemade percussion and use found sounds to create rhythmical fun in my video/book, *Guide to Endrummingment*, published by Interworld Music. See the Resource section in the back of this book.

Drum Circle Friends

Drum circle friends are groups of people who meet on a regular basis to drum and explore traditional rhythms or to express their personal rhythmical sensibilities. Your friends and players need not be studying this book or working with you developing facilitation skills. They can just be coming together to have fun and create music. This type of group is a ripe candidate for the drum circle games that you might bring to them from this book. Most drum circle friends are usually open to anything that someone might bring into the circle that would help them be better players. They might be open to applying some of your facilitating exercises to their process. Remember to make it fun!

Creating a Facilitation Study Group

Create a facilitation study group: a number of people who agree with each other to join together and help each other develop facilitation, listening, drumming, and teaching skills. You need to experiment with these concepts, ideas, and exercises in a small, nurturing environment that supports you in your growth. This way you can get feedback from a group of like-minded participants who understand your process and what you are trying to do.

Doing the facilitation exercises with a study group removes much of the public performance pressure. In your study group you can create situations that will give you the experiences you need to be able to facilitate a rhythm-based event. You also have the opportunity to receive feedback, advice, and critiques directly from the people with whom you are working.

> *Doing these exercises with a group of people who are playing together specifically to help each other develop facilitation skills is the most concentrated learning environment available.*

The most powerful learning tools I have in my Facilitation Playshops are the people themselves. Doing these exercises with a group of people who are playing together specifically to help each other develop facilitation skills is the most concentrated learning environment available.

For facilitators, experience is the best teacher. Some beginning-beginner facilitators have learned as much in our one week facilitation intensive as I did in the first four years of my drum circle experience. The material in this book is based on my thirty years of trial-and-error experiments in public drum circles. Most of the learning experiences came from mistakes. Inside every mistake is a lesson, and the only way that experience can become a failure is if the lesson isn't learned. My feedback for how well a new idea works comes by observing the quality of the music and the interactions of the group that get created as a result of the idea. Then I go somewhere, sit down by myself and figure out what worked and what didn't work.

As a participant in a study group, one of your roles is to help someone who has just finished an exercise with the group by critiquing their work. You might tell them several things:

- Specifically what you saw them do. It helps the whole group to understand and define the specific actions that were taken by the facilitator.
- What worked for you as a participant.
- What did not work for you as a participant.
- Ways you see that they could strengthen or fine tune their tools or techniques.

If you create for yourself a supportive group of people who are committed to playing together while doing these exercises, it will enhance your ability to facilitate and also make you a better-playing group and percussion ensemble. The process will also create sensitive players that are more responsive to each other.

My Commitment to You

The personal expression of rhythm is a healing experience. The expression of group rhythm is a community healing experience. As a rhythmical evangelist, I know what helping a group or an individual find and express their lost rhythmical spirit can do for them. Every time a group of kids or a community sits down and creates rhythmical synergy together, the world is a better place. The world needs more facilitators. This book is my contribution to that goal.

If you gather together a study group for the purpose of using this book in a group learning process, then I will respond to any written questions that your group might have as your process develops. Your group can also designate a liaison person to work with me, through my office, to handle any group situation not readily covered by our correspondence. The Introduction lists contact information.

Doing the Exercises

This book is a doing book. I've designed it to be an experience instead of just something you sit down and read. Your understanding will come from doing the exercises and from putting yourself in small circles and trying and experiencing different variations of these exercises.

As you do these exercises you will have successes and failures, and you will learn from both. Experience is the greatest teacher. The greatest learning is by doing, and in the doing you find out what works and what doesn't work. When you find out what works, you remember. When you find out what doesn't work, you remember as well. It is "a mistake" to label what doesn't work as a mistake. Finding out what doesn't work teaches you more about what can work. Labeling the failure of a process that you have tried "a mistake" makes that process a mistake and turns the result into a judgment rather than a teaching. Taking risks and learning from your failures makes failure into learning successes. A child does not know failure, only feedback. Avoid judging the feedback you get from doing these exercises—just learn from the exercises. Use your experience. Go make as many mistakes as possible to find out what works and what doesn't. The only real mistake you can make is not to try. It's up to you.

I've developed my facilitation skills over years of constantly taking risks, trying new variations on old themes, understanding foundations of what works, and stretching my limitations and the limitations of the people with whom I work. Take these exercises and concepts into a small community. Set up programs with the kids and work with the children in schools, for they are the greatest teachers. The children see through all agendas and only respond to spirit. If you come to them attached to a particular program and plan, they'll see that and respond accordingly. If you come with your exuberance and your bliss, prepared to share them as a gift, they will see that and respond accordingly. Children are the greatest truth tellers, the greatest reflectors. Take this to the children—they will be your greatest teachers.

> *Taking risks and learning from your failures makes failure into learning successes.*

Note to Hand Drum and Music Teachers

As a hand drum or music teacher, working with your students toward individual rhythmical expression gives you the chance to identify, develop, and fine-tune your facilitation skills. There are many fun games that are specific to small circles that you can create to develop the group song. Your student circles act as a built-in laboratory with which to experiment.

> *Create opportunities for each player to stretch their playing abilities.*

First, identify the different tools and circuitry you need as a drum circle facilitator. These skills are instead of or in addition to your hand drum teaching skills. Then, define your role clearly to your class by facilitating a drum circle segment at the beginning, at the end, or on both sides of your drumming classes. Let your class know that you are facilitating rather than teaching during that particular segment. Let them know that this is a time for learning how to improvise with each other rather than a time for learning a particular rhythm or technique.

In a smaller drum circle you can give more attention and focus to the individual players, as well as create opportunities for each player to stretch their playing abilities. They can each take risks in their rhythmical improvisation in a supportive environment. When players are improvising there are no mistakes. This is a vital difference between class time and improvisation time.

This Is Drum Jazz!

On the island of Taiwan, just off the Chinese mainland, there are schools designed to develop orchestrational percussionists. To become an orchestrational percussionist and go to Europe or America and play in a symphony is tantamount to being an athlete in college and moving onto the major leagues, like football or baseball.

I was working with fifty people from a particular school of percussion. I wanted to run a community drum circle format but the group requested technical information on culturally-specific rhythms. I did as they asked and put together a program of rhythms from different cultures that would satisfy this college-age group of aspiring orchestrational percussionists. Then I pulled an Arthurian sneak (that's coyote-style, for the uninitiated.) Toward the end of the hands-on class, I delivered a lecture on the universal principles that permeate world music. I passed out interactive drum and percussion parts that represent the use of universal rhythmical patterns found in almost any culture. These included pulse-oriented support bottom parts for the low-pitched drums, melody line parts for the medium-pitched drums, and more syncopated lead lines for the higher-pitched drums. I was careful to let the group be creative with the parts that I shared so that the parts would be accessible to whatever level of technical expertise each individual had available at that time. If a part was too hard then they could play any portion of the part that was accessible to them. If it wasn't technically challenging enough they could elaborate on the part that I gave them. Once the drum song was established I facilitated the group so that it slowly evolved into an in-the-moment drum jam. They were creating their own music.

When the piece was over, the participants started to question me about how I had orchestrated them from playing a song with specific parts to creating an interactive percussive improvisation. As I was describing the processes in technical orchestrational language, one of the students jumped up excitedly and yelled at me from the other side of the circle, "This is jazz!" and I said, "Yes, it's drum jazz."

> *One of the students jumped up excitedly and yelled at me from the other side of the circle, "This is jazz!"*

After the program, as I packed the instruments, I could hear a rhythm coming from outside the window. I looked out to the park across the street. The percussion students had started their own little drum jazz circle using the small percussion toys that they had brought with them to my program. They were also beating on the side of a trash can with some drum sticks and using some other found sounds that I could not identify. That was the first spontaneous, in-the-moment drum circle that I saw in Taipei. As more people walked up and joined the group in the park with whatever instruments they could find, I wondered if I might have disobeyed a major Star Trek prime directive, "Don't mess with their culture."

Circle Instrumentation

At the beginning of each of the facilitation exercises and drum circle games, you will see suggestions about what type of instruments to use with your circle to get the most out of that particular experience. The kids' circles, friends' circles, and facilitation study group described above will each work in the exercises.

Below I describe circles by what type of instrument they use. By using these circle types you can identify certain sound qualities when you are doing an exercise or game.

Drum Circle

When I use the term "drum circle" in the description for an exercise, I am referring to a situation where everyone is playing a hand drum. The three basic notes of a drum, combined with the different pitches of drums that you will find in an all-drum drum circle, create the melody lines and harmonies that make up the drum circle song.

Percussion Circle

An all-percussion circle refers to a circle where everyone is playing cow bells, wood blocks, shakers, etc. Playing percussion usually requires less technique than drums since many percussion toys are easier to play. Only one or two sounds are available on most percussion instruments, and the notes produced are usually of a shorter duration than those of drums. Thus there is more space in the music created by an all-percussion circle, so the

An all-drum drum circle

Shakers

Wood sounds

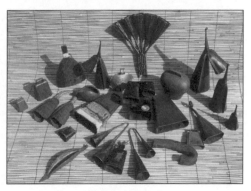
Bells and metal

all-percussion song is more clear and distinct than the all-drum song. To achieve a good timbral and pitch mix, in the in-the-moment percussion circle, try to have equal amounts of the following three basic timbral groups:

- **Wood sounds**, consisting of different kinds of wood blocks, *recko reckos* and *clavés*;
- **Shaker sounds**, including small shakers, *shékerés*, tambourines, *moraccas*, and cylinder shakers;
- **Bells and metal sounds**, cow bells of different sizes, African *gankoquies* and *atokés*, a couple of pieces of steel pipe hit together, a garden hoe without the handle.

If you don't have access to enough drums to do an all-drum circle, when that is specified you can use percussion toys instead. Although some of the games and exercises are more suited to an all-percussion ensemble than others, the all-percussion configuration will work most of the time.

Mixed Circle

A mixed-instrument circle includes an assortment of drums and percussion. It is the epitome of a community drum circle, representing the full range of timbral groups and pitches available in a rhythm orchestra. Simone LaDrumma, a Seattle area teacher and performer says, "Percussion is to drumming as spice is to cooking." Adding the percussion to an all-drum circle adds timbral texture to the ensemble. Each orchestrational idea described in Chapter 14, Orchestrational Ideas, is a facilitation exercise that can be done with a fully-mixed circle.

Simone LaDrumma

Vocal Circle

A vocal circle happens when everyone in the circle is doing the exercise by making percussion sounds with their voice. Our voice is the most expressive percussion tool that we have, and we carry it with us wherever we go.

If you have a chance to facilitate a rhythmical event in some sort of group gathering, but don't happen to have a load of percussion toys with you, you can use vocals instead of percussion in the exercises.

Mixed instrumentation

The Public Works Kitchen Band

This story unfolds at the first meeting ever of all eighty regional managers of the Canadian Public Works. This government organization met for a week-long leadership conference in the middle of Canada, in Winnipeg. I was brought in to be the rhythmasizer throughout the week, in addition to facilitating the opening and closing ceremonies. I arrived in Winnipeg at the hotel to find that all the drums and percussion for the program were sent to another hotel from the same chain, three provinces away, on the west coast in Vancouver, BC. Opening ceremonies were to be held that night, but all my instruments were hundreds of miles and two shipping days away.

I received carte blanche from the hotel manager to run through the hotel, with the concierge following behind me, gathering whatever "found sound" instruments would serve me for the evening ceremony.

Boy did I have fun! I found that the black plastic waste baskets from the guest bathrooms had a higher pitch than the white ones in the bedrooms. When turned upside down and struck on the bottom they made excellent hand drums. The food buckets made great bass drums when hit on the bottom with wooden serving spoons. I suddenly had all the drums I needed for the evening.

I found a trash can full of empty soda cans that hadn't been crushed for recycling yet. I had them washed, and put a hand full of the black grainy rocks from the hotel ash trays into each can. With the holes covered with duct tape they made great cylinder shakers. That led me to discover how good the metal ash holders sound when you hold them in one hand and hit them on the bottom with your other hand. So we used them as well.

I used the heavy-duty cafeteria-style coffee cups as my high pitch percussion bells, hitting them on the side with spoons. The plastic water pitchers hit on their bottoms with spoons served as my medium pitch percussion sounds. I found one-half inch diameter metal pipe and some thick wooden dowels in the hotel basement shop, and had them cut into six inch pieces that made two distinct sounds when struck together.

The food buckets made great bass drums when hit on the bottom with wooden serving spoons.

The kitchen staff got into the act and came up with two sets of stainless steel salad bowls that, when hit on the lip with wooden spoons, gave our growing percussion ensemble a full chorus of gongs. We liked the sound of the metal plate covers too.

The laundry staff heard about some crazy elf who was running around the hotel gathering up "found sounds." They showed up at the ballroom where all this equipment was being assembled and offered me a large fiberglass laundry cart with the wheels removed. When we turned it upside down the cart turned into a large bass hand drum, capable of accommodating four executives at once.

Needless to say, I ended up with more than enough found sounds to successfully facilitate our eighty-person opening drum circle ceremony. I also used this "stuff" for two more days, until my drum and percussion kit arrived from Vancouver. The group started calling themselves the Public Works Kitchen Band.

Using the "Kitchen Kit" did cause two problems. By starting up spontaneous Kitchen Band jams during the evening dinners, they would, in their enthusiasm, break the fine dinnerware, as well as disrupt the evening's poor keynote speaker. The second problem was that when the percussion kit with the "real" drums finally arrived, some of the participants wouldn't give up their favorite trash can.

Drums-R-Us

With the generous donation of three hundred drums from REMO drums, Village Music Circles does ten to twenty college and university programs a year.

Vanderbilt University, in Nashville, Tennessee had an orientation program for the incoming class of twelve hundred freshmen and transfer students who will form their graduating class of 2000.

Twelve hundred students was no problem, as we have facilitated circles with bigger populations. The challenge was the instrument logistics for that many people. We supplemented the three-hundred-drum REMO kit with three hundred percussion toys (bells, shakers, and wood blocks) from my executive program kit, but we were still six hundred instruments short.

As a solution we sent the university the chapter on homemade percussion and found sounds from my Interworld Music Video/Book *Guide to Endrummingment*. They reprinted it and put it in the students' orientation information packet in preparation for the event.

At the Vanderbilt orientation drum circle, hundreds of college kids showed up with homemade percussion toys and found sounds. There were four groups of kids from the residential dorms that collaborated together and came up with some very interesting instruments.

One group had each member of the dorm donate a pot or a pan, which they strung up on a clothesline. At the drum circle, the group had two guys hold up the pots and pans by pulling on both ends of the line at chest level. Then, the rest of the group hit their suspended instruments with wooden spoons.

Another group went to an auto wrecking yard and brought back hub caps, steel brakes, a car bumper, and other car parts as percussion instruments and strikers.

Another group went to an auto wrecking yard and brought back hub caps, steel brakes, a car bumper, and other car parts as percussion instruments.

A third group went to a carpet outlet and got a bunch of thick-walled cardboard cylinders that are used as the centers of rug rolls. They cut the cylinders to different lengths and then stretched and stapled the rubber from tire tubes over one end of the cylinders to make hand drums. Then they attached the cylinder drums to a stand made out of more cardboard tubing, so they could stand up in a line and play their homemade drums.

The most interesting group came in late, passing through our ongoing drum circle. They were wearing jackets and carrying no instruments that I could see. They worked their way through the massive circle as we were playing. As the group walked through the middle of the circle and passed by me, one of them winked at me as if to say, "We have something special for you." When they got to the other side of the circle, they lined up along the wall with their backs to the circle. They took off their jackets. They were all wearing white T-shirts. The group, in a line, all turned around at once, faced the circle, and played on their bellies with their hands. On the chest of each T-shirt was printed one big letter. The group stood in line and played their bellies in such a way that the rest of the circle could read the sentence that was formed by all their individual letters: "DRUMS-R-US."

Exercise: In-the-Moment Music

The basic musical format that we will use in the drum circle exercises is what I call "in-the-moment" music. "In-the-moment" music is what a community drum circle is doing most of the time during an event. It is the simplest form for bringing together a group of people to create rhythmical music. In-the-moment music happens when everyone in the circle plays with each other, creating their own personal rhythmic patterns so that they synergistically fit into the musical song created by the whole group.

Do this exercise with each of the four different instrument types I describe above: drum circles, percussion circles, mixed circles, and vocal circles. Designate one person to start the groove by playing a simple pulse with notes that are evenly spaced, as an anchor for the other players. Then ask the other players to listen to the pulse as a rhythmical foundation, and to create interactive patterns on their instruments, adjusting the music as they play to accommodate the other players. Once the rhythm and the melody line are well established, the pulse player no longer needs to just keep a pulse-oriented beat. They can also change their contribution to the musical song. Now that you have a group of drummers playing together you can apply any of the facilitation exercises that require an in-the-moment circle.

An in-the-moment music circle.

Drum Circle Game: Passing the Pulse

Use the all-percussion circle for this game. The passing the pulse exercise is an in-the-moment music exercise, but with added responsibility given to the pulse keeper's job description. Although this is a drum circle game, with no one in the middle of the circle, you as the pulse keeper need to use your facilitation techniques and sensitivity to complete the task.

- Start the song with the pulse.
- Let go of the pulse when the group song takes shape.
- Time the song from that point for three to four minutes.
- At the end of that time, call for and lead the closing group rumble.

A more detailed style of playing the game can unfold as defined below:

- Designate which instrument will be the pulse instrument, preferably using a cowbell or *clavé* that can be clearly heard when the other percussion instruments are being played.
- Start the circle with a pulse. Hold the evenly-spaced beat steady as the other players begin weaving their rhythmical patterns and timbral groups around your steady pulse foundation.
- Listen for the point when the song of the ensemble solidifies musically. One clue that will help you know when that is happening will be when the created parts begin to interact and dialogue with each other. The group becomes less dependent on your pulse and more dependent on the total group song. Another clue is when the whole group takes your pulse and runs with it, usually speeding up a little. That usually means it's time to let go of leading the group with your pulse, as they are now following the group pulse.
- When this happens, begin timing the group song.
- Three to four minutes after the group song takes shape, call verbally, and then lead a rumble to a close. You call, "Rumble," into the circle and the circle responds by stopping the rhythm song and going into musical cacophony. This cacophonous rumble is being led by you, and the circle is watching for your stop signal.

By physically telegraphing your last note in the rumble everyone in the circle can stop together on that last note. You telegraph the last note by raising your stick up in the air like an orchestra conductor and bringing it down deliberately onto your instrument. The group follows, ending the rumble.

The person on your left will be the next pulse keeper. The group exchanges instruments; everyone in the circle hands their instrument to the person on their left, saying, "Life is change." When you do this you give the pulse-keeping instrument, as well as the job description that goes with it, to the person on your left. You are passing the pulse.

Standing inside the calm center of a whirling hurricane.

Reading and Respecting the Circle

The circle is an ultimate source of information for you, the facilitator. That circle will tell you what it needs, where it wants to go, and how you can help it get there. Listen, and the information will come to you. Respect for the circle comes through your use of several techniques discussed in this chapter. I describe the three different ways of listening, and how to develop that most important facilitator's tool, your radar. Then I will teach you ways of building rapport between you and your circle and among the people in your circle.

Remember to Breathe

Before reading the group, place both your mind and your body in a receptive mode. To place yourself in that mode, consciously and constantly maintain deep breathing from the center of your being. If you find yourself overwhelmed by the information coming to you while you are reading the circle, you may notice that you have short and shallow breathing. Bringing your breath down into your body will ground you in preparation to facilitate.

Reading the Group as One Body

If you are always listening to your circle they will give you the feedback you need to create a learning experience for all of you.

A drum circle of any kind is a living, breathing entity that is interdependent on all the parts of itself. These parts are moving and dancing together on instruments with a force and a focused intention to create rhythmical synergy as one body.

All the information that you as facilitator need to help guide the drum circle to its goal exists inside the interaction in the circle. As a facilitator it's in front of you, behind you, and all around you at all times, and that information is ever-changing in-the-moment. The two most important aspects that will define the quality of your interaction with a drum circle are the following:

- **Your ability to read the group as one body.** Doing this allows you to access and utilize the information that is available to you at all times. When you see the group as one body, made of many different individual interactive parts, it helps generate the proper attitude, focus, and respect for the whole group's objective. This gives you access to a lot more information from the group in-the-moment.
- **Your ability to establish trust and rapport with the group.** This comes from having a complete understanding of your group's purpose and ultimate goal, and then using that understanding to actively advocate for that goal. In some events, part of your service as facilitator is to help define the group's goal as the rhythmical event unfolds.

An important aspect to balance, as facilitator, is the tradeoff between knowledge of facilitation tools and techniques, and an understanding of when and how to use them. Knowing when and how to use the tools is based on being able to read the group. When you read the group you see, hear, and feel where the group is, emotionally and technically, at any given moment. Remember that the moment changes with every beat.

The Three Reading Tools:
Peripheral Vision, Hearing, and Feeling

I trust your ability to develop your direct seeing, hearing, and feeling. You have been using those senses to get the information you need all your life. But in a drum circle, when you look at one thing, and focus on it, you may miss a hundred other things happening nearby. This section discusses ways to generate periphery-sensing tools that help you receive a tremendous amount of information at any one time. Instead of actively pursuing the information, you learn how to let the information come to you.

Peripheral vision, peripheral hearing, and peripheral feeling are three ways of receiving information from the group that will give you what you need to read the circle. The individual exercises for each reading tool that I discuss below will help you generate the ability to see, hear, and feel all the hundreds of things that are happening in a rhythm circle at any given moment.

Circuitry Exercises

There are many complicated actions that you take in your daily life of which you are only slightly aware. The simple act of eating is a good example. Just to get some food in your spoon and then get the food to and into your mouth takes a highly complicated set of commands, responses, and adjustments. All this action is happening almost automatically, usually while you are also reading a newspaper or talking to a friend at the same time. You have built, through a lot of practice over the years, the circuitry of eating. Your mind says to your body, "Eat," and your body and peripheral consciousness take over and get the job done. Although you may pause during the process for a moment to notice and enjoy a particular piece of food, most of your eating process is well-practiced body circuitry.

Every time you take action as a facilitator in a rhythm-based event you are developing your facilitation circuitry. Every exercise and drum circle game in this book will help you to that end. Until your facilitation circuitry is in place, every command, response, and adjustment that you will make in the process of running a rhythmical event will demand a large percentage of your focus and attention, just like when you were first learning to get that spoon to your mouth as a baby.

In a fully operational rhythm circle, it will seem that there are twenty things happening around you that you need to adjust in any given moment, and that you can only take care of seven or eight of them at any one time. This kind of situation can put you in what I call "facilitator's crisis mode." Facilitator's crisis mode is the feeling of being overwhelmed with too much information to handle, and too many decisions to make at any one time.

> *Every time you take action as a facilitator in a rhythm-based event you are developing your facilitation circuitry.*

Once you have developed your basic facilitation circuitry, you can use it to take care of all the technical aspects of running the event. This frees you to pay attention to and deal with the more subtle aspects of what is going on around you in your circle.

The facilitators' exercises and drum circle games in this book are designed to help you identify and deal with specific technical aspects existing at a rhythmical event. Meanwhile, the circuitry exercises in this chapter will help you generate the proper periphery sensing circuitry and listening tools to help you receive and deal with all that technical information.

You won't need any musical instrument to do most of these exercises, but you will need your facilitation study group, or a group of friends who would enjoy playing some personal growth type games. What they will need is their bodies and a willingness to be playful. Make sure that your group spends some time talking about their different experiences after each exercise.

Peripheral Vision

Peripheral vision is what my contact improvisation teacher and dance partner Nita Little calls "soft eyes." *Everything* that you can see in your field of vision without moving your head or your eyes is what I call "peripheral vision." You see the whole picture at once.

I contrast this idea with the concept of "hard eyes," what I call "looking out." We look out often in our daily lives, and are good at it. When we use hard eyes we project ourselves out through our eyes into our field of vision to look at something.

In the peripheral vision exercises you can compare the information you receive using "direct sight," or "looking out," with the information available to you when you use "peripheral vision," "or soft eyes."

Circuitry Exercise: Peripheral Vision

Prepare for the peripheral vision circuitry exercises by standing in a circle while holding hands with the people on each side of you. Ask each person in the circle to step back to expand the diameter of the circle as far as possible without letting go of their partners' hands. You know that your circle is perfect when you can see the two people on either side of you at the same time, out of the corners of your eyes, while staring straight ahead. When you can see both people at the same time, then you are using your peripheral vision.

Look across the circle at a particular person (I call this "looking out.") When you do this you are looking out of yourself with your eyes and accessing information across the circle. This is direct vision, or hard eyes.

Next, look at the whole group in such a way that you are not moving your eyes, and yet you can see the whole circle at once. I call this peripheral vision, or soft eyes.

With peripheral vision you let the information come into your eyes instead of going out of yourself to access that information. You can easily tell if you are using your peripheral vision simply by noticing that, not only do you see all the bodies in the circle at the same time, but you also see the spaces between the bodies.

Circuitry Exercise: Peripheral Vision Walking

This peripheral vision walking exercise helps you see the space between the bodies. Both Nita Little and Gabrielle Roth use exercises similar to this one in the beginning of some of their programs to establish how much moving space is available for each participant, as well as to activate the peripheral vision circuitry in the whole group.

By making the peripheral vision circle, you define the physical space in which your group will work. You will be walking inside the circumference of the circle you have just established.

Establish a circle, drop your hands, and begin walking, using "direct vision" to maneuver. Have the whole group begin walking around in random directions, inside the circumference of the circle, in a continuously smooth fashion.

Everything that you can see in your field of vision without moving your head or your eyes is what I call peripheral vision. You see the whole picture at once.

Begin moving faster, and have the whole group slowly increase their walking speed. Avoid collisions, but do not make sudden turns or stops. When the group has reached a speed that they mutually feel is unsafe, they will say so.

Next, re-establish the circle, instruct the group to use peripheral vision to maneuver, and have them drop hands and start the exercise again. Ask the group to pay attention to the holes opening and closing in front of them and to their sides, as bodies move around each other. Slowly increase speed, but do not go any faster than is safe. When it begins to feel unsafe, say so, slow down, and return to the perimeter of the established circle. Then, hold hands and relax as a completion to this exercise.

Discuss the differences between doing the peripheral vision walk with direct vision and with peripheral vision. While using direct vision, did you bump into somebody you didn't see because you were paying attention to somebody else? Did it seem that there was more room to maneuver in the same space while using peripheral vision?

The Birth of the Advanced Peripheral Vision Exercise

From a third floor corner office in the Soho district in downtown New York City, I look out the window, watching pedestrian traffic flow. It is a hot summer day at lunch hour. The streets are full of cars and the sidewalks are amazingly packed full of people going to and fro, weaving in and out of each other. The traffic light has a four-way pedestrian signal that stops all the cars crossing the intersection and lets all pedestrians walk in any direction, including across the middle of the intersection, to any one of the four corners of the intersection. They have thirty seconds to do it before the light goes green and the NY taxicabs try to run them over.

I watch this pedestrian flow phenomena happen several times. When the four-way pedestrian light goes green, some of the pedestrians are crossing from one corner to another directly across the street. But the majority of the pedestrians are walking kitty-cornered from one corner across the center of the intersection to the other corner. The problem is that when the pedestrian light turns green, there are four walls of people, like four walls of water flooding towards the same point in the center of that intersection. When they meet there should be a huge enormous crash and splash with bodies flying everywhere, because in New York nobody just walks across the street, they "get" across the street. But when the four rivers of bodies meet in the center of the circle they somehow miraculously dissolve into and through each other, and all of the parts of that particular group of bodies heading to the other side of the intersection get there in one piece, without crashing and bumping into each other.

Now in New York City there are some basic street rules that you adhere to, such as, you don't count your money in public, you don't take your keys out of your pocket when you are walking to your car until you are at the car, and you don't look straight in the face of anybody who is coming in your direction on the street unless you know them. "Hey, are you looking at me buddy?" So as I watch this phenomenon of masses of bodies flowing in opposite directions through each other, I realize that the people aren't really looking at each other. One body of people is walking toward another body of people as if neither of those bodies of people exist as a mass, or as something that would get in their way. So I sit and stare. If they're not looking at each other, how do they get by each other going in the opposite directions without crashing?

> When the four rivers of bodies meet in the center of the circle they somehow miraculously dissolve into and through each other.

At that point, I have a *blinding flash of the obvious*. I realize that what these people are doing in New York City at lunchtime, at a four-way pedestrian intersection, is an advanced version of the peripheral walk exercise. Instead of just walking in random directions, they have direct, solid focus and intention, as they are all walking through a point in the center of the street to get to the other side. It is precisely because they are *not* looking directly at each other that lets them merge and flow around each other. They are not looking at the people they are trying to avoid. They are looking for the holes between the people to maneuver through!

I run downstairs to the street, and spend the next hour crossing the intersection in every direction possible. Voila! the idea for the advanced peripheral walk exercise is born.

Circuitry Exercise: Advanced Peripheral Vision Walking

The sequence to this exercise is the same as the exercise above, except that everybody is walking through the center of the circle, then going out to the periphery in a figure-eight pattern, where the center of the 8 is the center of the circle. Each person then continues to walk back and forth through the center of the circle.

First, establish your circle. Then, drop hands and randomly start walking in figure-eights, using direct vision. Increase your walking speed until it begins to feel mutually unsafe. Then, slow down and return to the perimeter of the circle. When everybody has returned to the perimeter, hold hands and then drop them. Repeat the exercise, next time using peripheral vision.

How do all the people in the group get through the same spot at the same time, while coming from different directions? Contact cannot be avoided, but you need not always walk forward. You can roll around people, avoiding congestion, moving sideways or backwards while smoothly continuing along your path. What have you learned?

Peripheral Hearing

As the eyes, so the ears. Just like your eyes, your ears have the ability to hear peripherally. Of course the sounds that you are listening for are no more and no less important than the silence between them. Good luck.

Circuitry Exercise: Using Peripheral Hearing from the Edge

Your first peripheral *hearing* exercise is just like your first peripheral vision exercise. Begin by using your percussion circle to do this exercise, then use your drum circle, and finally, use your mixed-instrument circle. Everyone can do this exercise at the same time while playing in-the-moment music with their eyes closed. For this first exercise sit on the periphery of the circle.

To learn about your peripheral hearing, first listen to and identify particular sounds and rhythm parts being played across the circle, with your eyes closed. This is "direct listening."

Next, listen to the whole circle at the same time. This is "peripheral hearing." Not only are you hearing the notes of the whole circle, but you are hearing the space between the notes. It is the space between the notes that gives you a tremendous amount of information about your circle and the music it is producing.

Finally, go back and forth between direct hearing and peripheral hearing as you play. When the exercise is over, compare and discuss the difference between the two experiences with your study group.

Circuitry Exercise: Peripheral Hearing from the Center

Using the percussion circle, take turns sitting in the middle while the members of your circle are playing. First, listen to and identify each and every sound as they play. This is "hard hearing," going out with your ears and accessing the sounds.

Next, use your "soft hearing," letting the sounds come into your ears, without specifically identifying them. Let the space between the notes be no more and no less important than the notes themselves. Notice the differences between what you heard while sitting on the periphery of the circle in the last exercise, and what you are hearing now that you are in the center of your circle. Discuss the differences with your study group.

Circuitry Exercise: Listening for the Most Distant Sound

 Sit in your room, or in a park by yourself, and listen for the most distant sound that you can hear. Once you can hear it, listen beyond that sound for a more distant sound.

Keep listening beyond each sound for a further, quieter sound, until the most distant sound that you can hear is the one inside your head. Once you can identify that "inner sound," go to your drum circle and while drumming with your friends, listen again for that most distant sound until you find it among the noise.

Peripheral Feeling

Peripheral *feeling* has the same subtleties as peripheral seeing and hearing. Direct feeling is all the rush and excitement that you personally feel while you are in the middle of a circle of people fully engaged in a rhythmical percussion piece. "Peripheral feeling" is what you feel when you are feeling the emotions and needs of the people in your circle.

The dance that you do with your circle, as their facilitator, is very much like a dance that two people can do together in a contact improvisation exercise called the finger dance. Doing the finger dance exercise will help give you the experiences you will need to understand the metaphors I will use at the end of this chapter to talk about how to access and utilize the circuitry of peripheral feelings.

The Finger Dance

The finger dance is a contact improvisation dance designed to help two people get in touch with each other's energy and movement dynamics. It is a game where you touch somebody's finger with your finger and then you dance. Stand in front of each other, lightly touching index fingers, then close your eyes. You begin by leading that person with the finger touch, making random paths in the air, while that person's finger follows yours. Then you start listening to how that person is following you and you follow the person following you, until there is no leader. With your fingers touching, you are drawing, together, a path in the air between you. That path is continuously moving, changing directions and dynamics, and flowing in curves. This path is being mutually created by both dancers actively listening and following each other through the point of finger contact. We call this path the energy path. Have fun.

Circuitry Exercise: The Finger Dance

 The finger dance creates a path being drawn in the air at the point where the dance partners' two fingers touch. It is created together, in-the-moment, slowly and continuously, by both people leading and following at the same time.

Get a partner and designate one person as A and the other person as B. Stand loose and comfortable, feet planted on the ground but also ready to maneuver with your feet, so you can follow your partner. Check that the area around you is clear and safe from obstacles that you might trip over, as your eyes will be closed. If you both know that that you have mutually created a safe space in which to move then you can move your feet, with your eyes closed, while following the continuously curving path that you will create together during your dance.

Stand in front of each other, lightly touching index fingers, then close your eyes. A will lead B in a continuously flowing motion by drawing simple lazy circular designs in the air with a finger, staying in touch with the partner. Move in a smooth fashion so you stay connected to your partner. The objective is to keep the connection with your partner by avoiding making sharp turns, fast moves, or jerking movements. Don't be a jerk!

> *Good leaders listen to the people they lead.*

B will follow A, staying in finger touch, while their eyes are closed. A chooses a point in the dance and says, "transition." As slowly as possible, from the point where A says "transition," A begins to let B lead, and A begins to follow.

A relinquishes leadership of the dance, in a smooth fashion, to B, while continuing the dance. B now has complete control of the dance. At some point in the dance, B, who's leading A, says, "transition," and slowly begins to relinquish leadership of the continuous finger dance back to A.

Both A and B make the leading/following transitions as smoothly as possible and also take as much time as possible between A leading completely and B leading completely, without stopping the flow of the movement. This process will continue back and forth, with each transition point getting longer in time, until the finger dance becomes all transition. No one person is leading. It becomes a continuously-moving finger dance where A is following B who is following A.

> *When each person follows the other, an in-the-moment finger dance becomes a collaborative meditation and energy focus.*

Now together, with mutual consent, listen to the path that you are creating as partners, and find a mutual closing. Take a deep breath and open your eyes. Take time to talk about your experience.

Choose another partner, and do the finger dance. Notice the differences between the two dances.

The objective of the finger dance exercise is to get you to the place where neither you nor your partner is leading. You are both following each other. When that happens, the finger contact point becomes a window of communication—intimate, direct and deep. When that happens this in-the-moment finger dance becomes a collaborative meditation and focus. Together you and your partner draw a curlicue pattern in the air—the energy path. It is created when your energy and the other person's energy meet together where the fingers touch.

The Finger Dance as a Facilitation Metaphor

As a facilitator, an energy path is created between your energy and the group's energy. The event that you are facilitating is a collaborative energy path in constant motion. Like the finger dance, it has a beginning and a closing, with dynamic and directional changes created by the collaboration of all parties involved. The place where you all touch is the in-the-moment music that you and the rhythm circle are creating together. If you follow them while they follow you, together you go to a very magical musical place.

This is a metaphor for facilitating a group and learning about leading and following. The best way to lead a group is to be at that contact point and follow them following you, so there is a natural progression and the dance is smooth. The musical path you create together, even when you are leading, will be curvy rather than jerky. There is progressive movement in the music you create together.

Having and using the tools and techniques of a facilitator, when coupled with the understanding that much of your mission is to follow the people that you are leading, can create a powerful event. Good leaders listen to the people they lead.

The importance of the lessons learned doing the finger dance exercise goes beyond words. These elements of trust and rapport are essential. Trust is that delicate balance you establish by the intimate give-and-take relationship that happens in an ongoing drum circle.

The Contact Point

The point of contact is a window for the exchange of information between the two participants in the finger dance, as well as between you as a facilitator and the group with whom you are working. Both participants in the finger dance lean into and depend on that point of contact as a reference for where they are in any given moment. Similarly, a facilitator and a circle each lean into their contact point with the other and use that reference point during a community drum circle event. As the facilitator, the music that is created gives you your point of contact, and provides a window to exchange information between you and your circle.

It is through that contact point with the circle that all the information comes to you, the facilitator. It tells you what your next move in the dance is. The circle is dictating your actions as much as you are dictating theirs. They think you are leading them, but you are listening to them and following them following you. Together you and the circle take each other on a musical energy path full of dynamic volume, speed, and rhythm changes. Away you and the circle go, off into this other place where neither of you could have gone by yourselves. You each need to surrender to that point of contact. That surrender comes through a mutual interdependency and trust created by all the members of the circle, including the facilitator. With that realization, you as a facilitator can become a point *for* focus instead of a point *of* focus.

The Transition Point

The transition point between leading and following serves as a metaphor for what happens when, in a rhythm circle event, the group reaches a place in the rhythm where they start looking to each other and the facilitator with a question mark about what to do next. This is a place where the power of the circle, which the facilitator has given to the drummers to help them create their own music, is being passed back to the facilitator. The facilitator can then lead them to a closing, a speed up, or to the next piece. To see where a circle could go at any transition point, ask yourself the question "What is it I can do that will serve this group at this time?"

The Energy Path

The two fingers of the dancers in the finger dance exercise meet in constant flowing movement, drawing a continuous path with gentle curves. We call that path the energy path, and it is created by two participants collaborating together in movement. They are committing their energy to that point of contact, and the two energies together create the energy path.

The transition points that turn into a continuous mutual finger dance between the two partners in the finger dance serve as a metaphor for the type of relationship you, as the facilitator, want to have with your group. When you mutually create music with your rhythm circle, you are following the people who are following you. That place where you touch is where the music is made, and where that music goes represents the energy path that you mutually create.

Don't Be a Jerk

When a participant in the finger dance exercise makes jerky movements, both partners lose the contact point where the fingers touch, losing their reference and balance, becoming disconnected, and sometimes literally, physically falling over. If you are jerky in your facilitation you will disrupt your point of contact with your circle, creating an unbalanced experience for your participants. Sometimes when that happens, the rhythm can fall apart.

If you do make a sudden jerk with your community and lose that connection, you can learn from that and learn how to go from one direction to another in a smooth continuous fashion, without jerking your community around and losing your connection with them.

For instance, you want to avoid jerking the rhythm by leading a speed-up too quickly, or else you will leave a lot of your circle behind. You want to feel where the group is and play along with it. Then you can gently nudge up the speed, smoothly, to where the group can best maintain it.

Every Dance Is Different

The finger dance will be entirely different with different people, as the dance is determined by the combination of your energy with another person's energy.

No group you facilitate will be the same. Every group is different. Every circle experience will be different. The event is determined by the alchemy of your energy and that of your group.

Circuitry Exercise: Advanced Finger Dance

After you have completed five to ten finger dances you will have a sense of the flow of information between you and your dance partner. As you repeat this finger exercise, listen *through* as well as *to* the point of contact. That point of contact is your window through which to listen deep into the body of the other person. If you do this exercise enough you will be able to follow the muscle movements of your partner all the way down to the bones in the bottoms of their feet. Listen past your partner's center of balance, to their feet, where their basic movement emanates.

That place where you touch is where the music is made, and where that music goes represents the energy path that you mutually create.

It is a very powerful moment when you find the bottoms of your partner's feet for the first time in a dance. In that instant, with your eyes closed, and your only contact being a finger touch, you know exactly where your partner is, and where they are going. Without any fear of stepping on them or bumping into them you know exactly where to go to follow them following you.

The next step in deepening the finger dance is to recognize that your own balance and foundational movement comes from the bottoms of your feet. With that recognition comes the realization that the best place to listen for the bottoms of your partner's feet is from the bottoms of your own feet. And if they are listening deeply into you as well as following you following them, then you can never bump, or get lost, and you will take each other on some magical dances.

I've seen some dance partners, with their eyes closed while doing the finger exercise, do a very amazing dance. Both partners were very aware of where each other's body parts were. They never bumped into each other and they made many smooth transitions into different positions to follow the energy path being created by both of them.

"How can I best serve this circle at this moment?"

This finger dance is a metaphor for you as a facilitator. Listen to what the information you get represents about where your circle is, instead of only listening to the surface aspects of the drum circle sound. This directs you to a place where you can listen to the foundation of the music being created. This foundation represents where that drum circle came from and where it can go.

The best place to listen with the circuitry of peripheral feeling is from the "bottom of your feet" and the best way to initiate and maintain peripheral feeling is to constantly maintain a mantra in your head like this, "How can I best serve this circle at this moment?"

When Your Three Periphery Sensing Tools Are One

Your three periphery sensing tools are seeing, hearing, and feeling. When they are operating simultaneously in an ongoing circle, it is like standing inside the calm center of a whirling hurricane, where time has stopped, and you have all the time, information, and knowledge you need to do the right thing.

Imagine these periphery sensing tools as three rings, intersecting each other. That place in the middle, where all three intersect is the place of "knowing without knowing." That place is a scary place for the mind to be, because the mind thinks it knows everything and likes to control.

A lot of my best drumming comes from a place of mindless spirit, and if my mind would try to take over, I would surely drop a beat, like when I juggle balls with my body. If my mind tries to interfere, I drop a ball or two.

If I am listening to the rhythmical music of a circle with the bottoms of my feet, while at the same time asking the question, "How can I best serve this circle at this moment?" the answer usually comes from that place of knowing without knowing. Then my body and spirit react with the proper facilitation circuitry and body language, orchestrating the circle to their next level of rhythmical and musical potential before my mind even has a clue.

Life is such a dance.

Rock Hopping

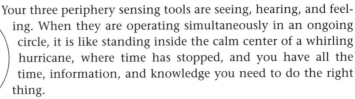

A few years ago, when I was at my physical best, I did a thing called rock hopping in the mountains on the Big Sur coastline of California. The streams flow down to the ocean at a 45° angle. In the summertime the streams were very small, exposing the very large rocks worn round and smooth by the constantly falling water. I would climb up the stream bed a quarter mile up from the ocean and half hop, half fall down from one rock to another, as if I were water flowing downstream. I never knew which rock I was going to land on next, except for the one on which I was landing. I was in total free fall, so that I couldn't stop at any one rock to decide which rock I should hop to next. If I tried to stop on any one rock, I would fall off of it. I had to trust that the rock I was falling toward was going to be solid enough for me to land and take off.

If it wasn't and it fell, or rolled with my weight, I had to fall with it to find the next place to go. I was basically in a partially-controlled, ongoing accident, where each decision in the moment could only lead me to the next decision in the next moment. After rock hopping down a streambed, my whole body felt exhilarated and my mind was totally quiet.

Sometimes while facilitating a rhythm circle you are rock hopping. You are looking for the foundation of the music in that ever-changing moment. Where can you put your foot to push off to the next direction? The music, like the water in the stream, is ever-changing, and ever-flowing toward its final goal.

The Radar

To facilitate a drum circle you need to create a 360-degree radar that's operating on an emotional, technical, and spiritual level, all at the same time, and at all times during your event. You want to be able to read the group as one body and at the same time pay attention to individual parts of that body that need help and support. You also want to be able to guide that body to its common denominator experience, and at the same time take it to its highest musical potential, beyond what it thought it could do.

The radar is an important internal tool that you can develop. You will know what kind of facilitation is required by using the information you are getting in that moment from your circle. The more developed your radar is, the more information you will receive. Developing a good radar starts with acknowledging the fact that you already have developed some radar circuitry in your activities as a drummer, musician, teacher, or counselor.

You can begin to further develop your radar by being aware of and honing the radar circuitry that you already have. A fully-developed radar has the ability to take information in at all levels. This includes being aware of the technical elements that are functioning in your drum circle at any given moment, as well as reading the musical and emotional dynamics of the circle.

Three-Point Radar

The most important technique for you as drum circle facilitator is to communicate to the circle as if it is one body made up of many parts. In the middle of the circle you will always have your back to someone. Remember to address your circle in the round.

You must start somewhere to generate the basic radar circuitry. You can use a three-point radar as a beginning technique. As you develop this three-point radar, sending information out as well as taking information in, you start developing more and more points on your radar, until every person in the circle is a point. The ultimate goal is to have no individual points in the circle, but instead just one body. In the fully functioning advanced model, you read, calibrate, address, and facilitate all the points in the circle at once, as one body.

Exercise: Three-Point Radar

Begin by picking three people who are equidistant from each other in the circle. Cut the circle like a pie, from the center where you are standing, into three parts. Identify three people in this triad and address them equally so that you are constantly turning and speaking to all the parts of the circle. Addressing and facilitating the circle in this way constantly reminds you that you are working in the round.

While facilitating an ongoing musical piece, use the three people you have chosen, and the general area around them, as focal points for the feedback that you need to tell you how the circle is doing and what needs to happen next, if anything. Make your instructional gestures to the drum circle once for each piece of the pie that you address.

Once you have established your three points, rotate the points by choosing another three people shifted to the right or left of the original people. Each time you need to signal the group, pick different people in the triangle. That way you are not signaling or addressing the same person over and over again. Address, make contact, and have a relationship with many different people in the circle, throughout the process.

The objective of this exercise is to evolve your triangle radar so that you have eyes in the back of your head. While you are addressing the whole circle at the same time, you can know which section of the circle you need to face and signal next, to communicate most effectively.

Slowly but surely, as your confidence and ability to use your radar strengthens, you will be better able to read and facilitate the group. Then you can add more points to your radar. Continue developing this radar until everyone in the circle is a point on your radar. After you have achieved that, you can dissolve all the points into one body by noticing you're not facilitating individual people in a circle, but one body of music made up of many cells.

Circuitry Exercise: Radar

Here is a game that you can play with your friends. Stand in the middle of a circle of friends and close your eyes. Ask them to face you, with their eyes open, hold out one arm and point their index finger at you. Then ask them to step toward you, a few steps at a time, and stop, at random intervals. People move one at a time. When you sense movement, turn and point at the moving person, while keeping your eyes closed. If there is someone where you are pointing, you stop their progression, until everyone else in the circle has taken another turn moving toward you. Your friends keep walking slowly toward you until somebody touches you. When you get touched, the exercise is over, and it is someone else's turn to be in the middle.

Rapport Skills

People don't care how much you know, until they know how much you care. The rapport between you and your drum circle reflects the level of mutual trust and emotional affinity between you. Another element that defines the quality of that rapport is the communication between you. Building rapport requires that you use your listening skills and your intuitive radar.

As a drumming teacher you would be using your radar to find things to fix. As a facilitator you use your radar to listen for the clarity of focus, energy, and direction that the group is manifesting. Although a lot of this information is detectable through the music that is being created, more information is coming in the form of the body language that you see in the group all around you, and the quality of responses you receive from your circle.

Building Rapport with Your Circle

Greet the people as they come into the circle during the beginning of your event. This is the first step in creating rapport with individuals. Doing this also creates relationship with the whole circle as its population begins to form and play together in the opening part of a community rhythm circle. I call this *Drum Call*. As greeter, you also start the process of reading the circle. Like a matador lets the bull run around the ring in order to learn its moves and temperament before going in the bullring to dance with it, *Drum Call* is an opportunity for you, as the facilitator, to read the group before fully engaging it.

As a facilitator, you will want to identify people who want to support the process of the circle. You might have even identified people ahead of time in a community with whom you have a relationship. This kind of person walks up to you and offers their services, perhaps to arrange chairs, play the *djun-djun*, etc. Alternatively, you may discover in the group an advanced player who is using her or his skills in obvious support of the group rather than to showcase their technical abilities.

> *People don't care how much you know until they know how much you care.*

Approaching and playing with that person, modeling what they are doing and supporting them in their support of the group will establish rapport with that person. Let them know that you will be giving them specific tasks within the circle later in the process. This opens up the possibility to use that person's skill and supportive attitude by moving them around to different timbral groups, having them play support parts, showcasing them, etc.

Establish rapport with the whole group: show them that you know where they are by being there and playing with them at their level of rhythmical expertise. Then let them know where they can go from that place by gently leading them to finesse their music and create a more articulate representation of the groove they are doing.

Creating rapport with the group creates a sense of trust between them and you as the facilitator. This trust lessens any performance pressure on you all, creating an environment that lets it be okay for individuals and the whole group to make mistakes and learn from them. Trust gives you all permission to laugh at your mistakes. This creates a bond between you that dissolves the perception of separateness and facilitates a sense of dialogue in sound and body language between you and the group, rather than a sense of monologue from the facilitator to the group.

As a facilitator, show with your body and tone of voice what your words are saying. If you put out in your physical attitude that you have some sort of authority over the circle, be it kids, adults, or a mixed group, then you won't have rapport with them, or access to their spirit. If you posture yourself above them, you are facilitating with an attitude, and so that is what you will get back from your circle. Instead, if you humbly assume the authority that they give you as a facilitator, then they respect you and are ready to be facilitated.

If you want them to have a transcendental experience, you have to have a transcendental presence. That presence cannot be faked. If you are living your bliss and sharing your love of rhythm with an open heart, the rapport door will be wide open.

Airport Rapport

As this story unfolds, I have just finished a team-building event with the Toyota company in southern California. At the beginning of the program, the executives saw me as a strange professor-type person from a Santa Cruz university, who was brought in from outside their corporate culture. After looking at my little hat and vest, and the pile of percussion toys in the middle of the room, some of them were afraid that I might make them do some new age, touchy-feely exercises. By the end of the event, we all had taken a collaborative musical journey. This journey created a synergistic interpersonal environment that made me a part of their world, and them a part of mine. We are in rapport.

After the event I go to the LA airport with some of these executives, who are now my cohorts and buddies. We are traveling on the same airline to San Jose. The airline that we are taking is the low-fare airline where there is no reserved seating. It is first come, first to get on the plane to pick out their seat. You wait in line to get a numbered, colored boarding card in order to get in another line so that you can board the plane.

We arrive the prescribed one hour prior to the flight to find a very long line. We get in the line to get our boarding pass for our plane. The line leads to one counter with one poor overworked person, who is taking care of all the people boarding two different planes through two different gates. The airport is very crowded and we think that we're at the end of the line to get on our flight. There are more people coming in and getting in line behind us. I relate with the person in front of me and find out that he is at the end of the line to get on the San Francisco flight that leaves just before ours. That means that I am first in line for San Jose, and that I could get the colored boarding card with the number one on it! Yippee!

Since there is only one ticket counter, we all stand in the same line. Chaos reigns at the ticket counter as the time for the San Francisco boarding draws near. The person at the ticket counter finally discovers that there are people for two different flights all in the same line. By this time I am relating with other people in line behind me, in addition to the Toyota executives. We are all joking about the predicament that the ticket counter person is in. Then she announces over the PA system that all persons that are in line to get onto the San Jose flight are to disperse, so that the people trying to get onto the San Francisco flight can move up the line to check in, and then get in the other line to board the plane.

> By the end of the event, we all had taken a collaborative musical journey. We are in rapport.

Nobody budges. I can see that their body language is defiant, but uncertain. Everybody has been standing in line for an hour or more, and most of the people behind me are going to San Jose. By dispersing, they will lose their place in line and have to scramble back into line after the San Francisco passengers get cleared through. The ticket counter person makes one more announcement, pleading for the people not getting on the San Francisco plane to disperse from the line. Still nobody budges.

I can see everybody in the line has the same goal, but they don't know how to achieve it. I have the same goal, know how to achieve it, and have the tools to facilitate them to that goal.

At that time, I turn around, and with my full facilitator's voice, I call back to the whole line,

"If there is anybody in this line that is supposed to board the San Francisco flight, please move forward." Nobody budges, but at least I have everyone's attention. So I then announce to the whole group, "If we want to keep our place in line, all of us who are here for the San Jose flight should take one step off to the right." Like a well-trained military marching unit we all take one step to the side, leaving only one person standing by himself where the line had been. The room breaks out in uproarious laughter, as the man left standing runs up to the counter to get his boarding pass, to get into the San Francisco boarding line, to board the plane, and find the last seat available, since he is the last in line.

This synergistic event makes everybody in line happy because nobody loses their place in the line that leads to the boarding line. It makes the ticket counter person happy because she finds the missing person on her computer's San Francisco roster, and it makes me happy because I get my first boarding pass with the number one on it. Yippee!

Even with my facilitation skills, it was necessary for me to establish rapport and a relationship with at least some of the people in that line, to achieve the results we all wanted.

Transition Point

The "transition point" is a very basic and important element that you as facilitator need to recognize inside the ongoing rhythmical relationships of the drum circle. The transition point in a rhythm circle's musical piece is a time when the facilitator and at least part of the circle recognizes that it is time for a change. That is the point when a change in attention, focus, or rhythm can happen. The group is waiting for something else to happen, sometimes consciously. They are in that position, ready to make a change, and they have empowered you to make that change. As the facilitator, you can create a facilitated orchestration that heightens the group's attention to the music it is creating, and then take the group to the next level.

Transition points in the group process appear many times during any particular drum circle event. They appear in the music after the group has reached a musical and emotional plateau, or after a peak in their musical performance. This means your circle has fully explored this particular rhythm or musical composition, and is ready to move on to another place.

Some of the more obvious signs of a transition point are when the energy of the group goes down, they begin to lose attention, the rhythm gets sloppy, and their technique begins to get mushy.

The transition point is a fulcrum, or leverage point where the on-going drum circle can be guided by you, the facilitator, through that point to another dimension in the music. Some of the changes facilitated could be a transition to a new groove, adding a new musical element into the ongoing piece, or bringing the piece to a close.

In a non-facilitated drum circle, this change can be that the rhythm falls apart and the drumming stops. If no one in the circle instigates some sort of change in focus at the transition point in the music, then the energy of the group does go down, the group does lose attention, and the rhythm does get sloppy. It is a phenomenon we call R.B. That's short for *rhythm burnout*—the group rhythm falters, and stumbles to a stop.

As the facilitator for the event, you want to be able to read the signals from the group, and utilize the transition points they give you before the circle reaches rhythm burnout. How important are transition points?

Transition points:

- define where the windows of communication appear; (Chapter 5)
- are a major element affecting your event format; (Chapter 6)
- are your opportunities to introduce body language; (Chapter 10)
- are where you do your pacing and leading; (Chapter 10)
- are where the elements to facilitate get used; (Chapter 11)
- are where the orchestration tools are applied; (Chapter 12)
- are what the orchestrational ideas revolve around. (Chapter 14)

Drum Circle Game: Transition Point

Using your drum circle, do in-the-moment drumming, listening for rhythm burnout. As each person senses that the drum circle is reaching the transition point, have them close their eyes, but continue playing to support the rhythm, and listen for the person who will change the rhythm to a new groove. The last person to recognize that the drumming circle has reached the transition point will be the only person with his/her eyes open. They initiate a new rhythm and dynamic into the circle. They can play a new rhythm louder than the other players are playing, increase the tempo, or make other changes. When the other players in the circle hear the deliberate volume, tempo, and rhythm change they open their eyes and support the new direction the drum circle is heading as the game starts over.

If the person who initiated the rhythm change at the most recent transition point finds themselves being the last person in the circle to close their eyes at the next transition point, they will initiate a new rhythm and dynamic into the circle. Once it gets going, they will close their eyes and continue playing to support the rhythm, listening for the person who will change the rhythm at the next transition point. That way no one makes the rhythm change at the transition point more than twice in a row, and when they do make the change twice in a row, they get to listen to their second rhythm with their eyes closed and then go into and through a new transition.

If everyone is not letting the circle drop the rhythm ball, then when is this exercise over? Never, or when all the players reach rhythm burn out at the same time.

Addressing the Circle

Windows of Vocal Communication

There is an art to knowing when, where, and how to address the players in a circle as they progress through an event toward a natural climax, closing, and completion. The place to speak is between each musical piece. I call that place a "window of vocal communication"—a space of time when one musical piece is complete before the next musical piece starts.

Less is more.

How you address the circle inside this window of vocal communication is determined by where this window occurs relative to the total event. Toward the beginning of the event you are helping define what the circle is and why you are here and where you as a group are going. But you want to spread that defining process over multiple communication windows. You want to keep the windows as small as possible. Three basic elements need to be in a window. First, include the wrap-up of the last piece played to define what the circle just did. Secondly, use that window to define where the circle is at the moment and where they are going. Finally, set up any metaphors, and any information that you need to give the group to prepare them for the next composition. Then, away you go into the next piece.

Since you are the facilitator, you are the one who defines the length of the window of that communication. If you let that window get too long, by talking too much, then you will get "Hey, let's drum" feedback from your community. It is one of the first lessons that you learn: people are not there to hear you speak. They're there to play!

Effective Speaking Style

A few hints are listed below that will help you develop an effective speaking style.

Less Is More

Be succinct in your communication, keeping the words to their essential minimum. The people have come to the event to be an active part of the entertainment. They came to play, and won't sit still very long while someone is standing in the middle of a drum circle delivering a long monologue.

Watch Your Attitude

Watch your attitude. This applies to both what you are saying, and how you are saying it. You want to enter a circle with an intention and attitude of service. Then your body and vocal language will reflect that attitude and help generate the rapport needed to successfully facilitate the event.

The danger of bringing an "I know and you don't" attitude into the center of a rhythm circle is that, whether you are aware of it or not, you are projecting in body language and vocal intonation a "holier-than-thou" attitude that separates you from the circle and can defeat your purpose for being there. Find your center of rhythmical bliss and share that with your circle.

Vocal Dynamics

Dynamic vocal range is a powerful technique to use in a drum circle. It can set the tone of the circle from the very beginning. With the proper use of vocal dynamics you can create a very intimate environment in a very large circle. If you start your drum circle by yelling at the top of your lungs while addressing the group, you have nowhere to go in terms of vocal dynamics. Do not just speak to them in a loud monotone. To communicate, sometimes you must speak softly to get them to listen. Experiment with the possibilities.

Metaphors

A metaphor is defined as "a figure of speech in which a term is transferred from the object it ordinarily designates to an object it may designate only by implicit comparison or analogy." WOW! I will tell you one of my favorite metaphors that I use in my community programs.

> *Everyone in the village has a role to play to make the village healthy, wealthy and wise. No role is any more or less important than any other.*

You are the village. The village is a living, breathing, economic, social, and spiritual entity that is interdependent on all the parts of itself. Everyone in the village has a role to play to make the village healthy, wealthy and wise. No role is any more or less important than any other. When people gather together to celebrate that living breathing entity they do so in ritual form, using music, dance, and song. Everyone has a part to play in the celebration and no part is any more or less important. So the people of the village play together just like they work together.

I call this metaphorical language. A lot of the messages I deliver are through the use of metaphor. Why? If you build your message in metaphorical language it can go as deep as any individual person wants to take it into their lives.

With metaphors you deliver the message, but you deliver it so that, like the water that seeks its own level, it gets the message into those places that are asking for it the most. The metaphors go to the place where the person's personal experience can use them the most.

Using the rhythmical event experience as a metaphor for creating harmony and community is a skill you can master. This skill goes beyond just facilitating the music to facilitating the population toward community consciousness.

Opening Addresses

The opening address establishes your relationship with the circle and sets the tone for the rest of the time you spend with the group of people with whom you are working. Below I list some of the basic points to address.

Welcome

Welcome is a very powerful word. Welcoming the group to itself is acknowledging that a community drum circle is about the community. Thank the people for coming and welcome them to their experience as a group. You can then ask them to turn, greet, and shake hands with their drumming neighbors.

Thank You

Thank the group or organization who is sponsoring the event. Acknowledge the people who help with the community outreach.

Acknowledge and thank any hand drum teachers or community elders in the circle for their contribution to building the drum community. Remember, somewhere in the program, to thank the group members for showing up and participating.

Community

You can put welcome and community together and say, "Welcome to your community drum circle." Let the people know that this is an experience that they are creating for themselves and that they create the community by being at the event. Tell them that to be able to have a community drum circle, they are needed. Otherwise you are just a facilitator. No matter what the reason is for the rhythm circle event being created by a specific population of players, the underlying result will be a synergizing of the people participating. Community values are reinforced by a successful rhythm circle event.

You Are Enough

Communicate to the group that whatever level of rhythmical skills they bring to the event is enough, whether they are rhythmically-challenged beginners or hotshot drummers. Ask for full-spirited participation with whatever skills and instruments they have to share. Whatever skills they have are enough and whatever instruments they have are enough, even if it is just their voices and their hands.

This is the place to let the circle know that each individual in the group is no more and no less important than any other person in the group in their ability to make this experience successful for the whole community.

Depending on the population you are addressing in the opening circle, all of the elements listed above can be brought together and addressed in a few short sentences, or can be divided up and delivered in windows of communication between the first few musical pieces you orchestrate.

Mistakes

Communicate to the group that the only mistake they can make in their rhythmical process is when they think that they have made a mistake and judge themselves for it. Any perceived mistake that is made is a learning moment. Sometimes the mistakes sound so good that part of the message from the learning moment is to repeat it over and over again and create something new with it.

Everything about mistakes applies to facilitators as well. You will learn from the unexpected situations you encounter.

"Welcome to your community drum circle. You are enough, you can't make mistakes," is a Haiku version that includes this idea in the introduction.

The next three elements, discussed below, can be addressed in the opening of a drum circle or throughout the process. How these elements are presented totally depends on the population that you are addressing.

Definition of Who We Are

Although every population is different, the reason that they gather together for a rhythm-based event has, as part of its universal foundation, the need to celebrate the community that the group represents. It does not matter if it is a group of doctors, teachers, or factory workers. A community experience where common values are shared is a bottom-line goal. Create metaphors that support and strengthen the basic mission statement of that group of people.

Why We Are Here

The definition of the purpose of the group can be short in the beginning and then can be used metaphorically throughout the event. In a community drum circle it could be simply to express ourselves as a community or to celebrate life, to come together to remind ourselves that we are a community through music, dance and song.

You could be addressing a population that is gathered for a three-day business conference, or a personal growth conference. A definition of purpose in this case might be to synergize the group to gather and exchange information, ideas, and spirit.

In a kids-at-risk program you might address the use of this experience to create more communication, more listening, and more trust amongst the participants.

Any group that comes together and participates in a rhythm-based event is drumming with intention. The more conscious the group's intent is, the stronger the result of that intention will be. Corporate executives drum together for team building, shaman study groups come together to create states of trance consciousness, and kids drum together for fun.

The purposes for the meetings and gatherings are all different on the surface, but the result of their rhythm circle is always the same whether they know it or not. The bottom-line result of any drum or rhythm-based gathering is synergy, and whether you bring the idea to the group consciousness or not, Rhythm Church is happening.

Where We Are Going—Long, Short, and Future Views

Three descriptions of where the group is going are: the long view, the short view, and the future view.

The Long View. The long view is the overview of the whole program. It is an aspect of the "why we are here" part of the presentation and can be addressed in the same sentence. You want to let them know what you hope to achieve by the end of the event.

The Short View. Let the group know what to expect as the event progresses. Reveal to them a little of what to expect, just before any new piece that you facilitate.

The Future View. "Future pacing" for an event is ascertaining what the group wants to get from the experience that you are facilitating. You want to let them know how to use the experience once they leave the event. It will help you to talk to the event coordinator that represents the group about how they would like to see the group synergy get focused after you pack up and leave.

Points to Address in Windows of Vocal Communication

During the course of an event you are educating your group about how to play with each other by describing the elements that make a rhythm circle work. You can add a new element into each piece you facilitate. This gives them an experience of that element functioning inside the music. You want to provide information, but you do not want to overwhelm them with too much. Address only one or two points at a time. That way you create small successes for the circle and they can experience and build from each added element.

Points to address during your windows of communication include the following ideas:
- How to create cooperation, instead of competition;
- How to play notes that create space for other people to play, rather than trying to fill all the space with notes;
- Creating an awareness of different pitches and timbral groups in the circle;
- Understanding how they are each one of the many parts that make up one whole song;
- The importance of listening to the circle as much as playing in the circle;
- Defining entrainment, and how it can work in a rhythm circle;
- How to respond musically in-the-moment rather than planning on what you are going to play;
- Being a part of the song rather than playing a neat part;
- The participants' physical relationship to their drums and emotional relationship to each other;
- The use of the drum as a voice of expression, rather than just a tool for rhythm grooves;

Closing Addresses

Some facilitators start their closing addresses in the window of communication just before the closing musical piece, to prepare the group for dispersal. Other facilitators do it all at the end of the program. I like to at least warn the participants that this is the last rhythm piece before the closing, and then possibly add one more closing piece.

Circle Calibration

Bring to the group's attention that there has been a change of state of consciousness of the whole circle from the beginning of the event to the end. Have them notice the difference. I call this calibrating the circle. I do this in personal growth rhythm circles by asking the participants to close their eyes and calibrate their state of consciousness. Then I have them open their eyes and notice the difference in their neighbors. In a community circle I have them notice that they were disconnected strangers when they started, and that during the event they have played themselves into a synergized community. If I haven't done it earlier in the program, I have them turn, greet, and shake hands with their new friends.

Thank You

Begin by thanking the participants for coming and making the event a success. Without them there would be no event. Then, thank all the people you thanked in the opening, including the group or organization who sponsored the event and the people who helped with the community outreach and the program itself.

Acknowledge and thank any persons who you might have showcased in the program, and especially any who might have taken an active part in the facilitation of the event.

Drumming is family friendly.

Upcoming Events

Find out about upcoming events in the local community before you go to the circle. You can ask them what's coming up next in the community. This may include announcements for drum and dance classes, drum circles, world beat performance events, and any other focused information that affects this community.

Future Pacing

Take this energy out into the world and do something positive with it, is the basic message I deliver to any group. As with the circle calibration address, I adjust the message to fit the consciousness and intention of the people in the group.

Sendoff

Let them know when it is time to leave. In some environments it is appropriate to let the die-hard drummers stay and play. Other times it is not. In any mixed-population rhythm event, where there are children present, it is appropriate to set an official closing, so that your population doesn't trickle out when it's bedtime for the kids.

"Welcome to your community. Thank you for coming to Rhythm Church. I hope you enjoyed the sermon. Good night."

Thank you for coming to Rhythm Church.

The parade

*Are you in
the bliss,
or is the bliss
in you?
YES!*

Event Format

As an experienced facilitator, I have pre-planned formats developed for facilitating rhythm circles for many different populations. I am ready, at a moment's notice, to adapt that format to meet the changing needs of the participants as they play themselves deeper into their rhythmical alchemy experience. My goal is the unfolding process of that event. As the facilitator I keep that goal in mind as I lead a circle through specific rhythm pieces, as we modulate our dynamics to a climactic ending.

Some of the basic elements in my formats are explored below.

Focused Intention

"Focused intention" is what I call what I do when I adjust my format in an ongoing rhythm circle, while at the same time keeping my vision of what the circle could be at its fullest, healthiest, and most successful moment. By creating small successes with each drumming segment I set up a basic foundation for a total group success.

Focused intention is a powerful facilitator's tool when you use it properly. It is the large overview that includes the facilitator's and the circle's goals welded into one purpose. You will want to use focused intention in all aspects of facilitation.

If you keep using focused intention throughout the event, you will avoid getting lost in small incidents that are not constructive, and avoid getting lost in the complexity of all the crazy things that happen in the midst of an ongoing drum circle. Instead, you will see ways of using these as opportunities to take you and the circle to the final goal. You can use focused intention to do everything with the intent of guiding the event toward an experience of common completion and fulfillment. In the rock-hopping story I related in Chapter 4, my focused intent was to end up at the mouth of the stream swimming in the Pacific ocean. The dance with the rocks dictated how I got there.

Understand that when you are facilitating, in the middle of the circle, you're in a very powerful position. You want to use that power to serve your group with the deepest humility. Hold your vision, goal, and purpose of service in your sights at all times, always trying to ascertain where these people can go, even though they are not yet there. You can guide the circle to a more advanced place, based upon the information that you get from the people in every changing moment. That information will determine the technology you can share with them to get them to the next level of their musical relationship with each other. You can do this with focused intention.

Begin with Small Successes

By creating small successes with each drumming segment, you set up a basic foundation. While you are facilitating the circle, you are also educating it, through its own experience, about the basic elements that make a drum circle work. You can reinforce this education by pointing out these elements during your windows of communication throughout the drum circle. Explaining and exploring the more fundamental elements in the beginning segments of the program will set up a more solid musical and rhythmical experience for your participants. After creating these simple successes you can fine-tune your circle. Then you can explain and explore the more subtle elements that make a drum circle work.

By adding one or two drum circle elements, such as pulse and tempo, into the consciousness of your participants at each progressive window of communication, you pile one small success on top of another. I itemize these elements in Chapter 5 under Points to Address During Windows of Vocal Communication. Adding awareness of each of these elements increases the quality of the music and drumming being created. As the drum circle continues, you can then apply them in the next musical piece. Throughout the program you are fine-tuning the community's ability to hear all the varied parts of itself playing together.

Modulate the energy, the spirit, and the rhythms of the group to a final climax in which everyone in the group experiences a mutually-created peak experience.

Facilitate the simplest rhythms needing the least amount of drumming expertise in the beginning of the program.

Address the group in a way that educates the group through metaphor about what functional elements are required to get closer together in the rhythmical spirit of the group experience.

Small pieces of information add up to a continual string of small successes for the community as the rhythms become more intricate. Every time you instigate another activity that will teach them something else about their experience, you empower them to be more musical together without you. Once that begins to happen, you no longer need to pay attention to that particular musical aspect of the drum circle facilitation, as they have learned it and are facilitating it themselves into their music. That will free you to add another aspect of the technology that will take them to an even higher plane of experience, perhaps musical, emotional, and spiritual.

Integrate everyone's talents to create the spirit of community. You want to modulate the energy, the spirit, and the rhythms of the group to a final climax in which everyone in the group experiences a mutually-created peak experience.

Middle Times

The attention span, focus, and energy level of a community drum circle usually lasts around two hours. That formula works if yours is truly a diverse community, meaning that there are families with kids, as well as young single adults, and senior citizens. There is a natural excitement and sound modulation that happens in the beginning of the circle as it begins to discover itself through your facilitation. That excitement begins to level out about an hour into the community drum circle event. I call this the "middle time." This middle time may occur after several introductory pieces and may include several rhythms.

The middle of a drum circle presentation can be seen as an emotional plateau, when the group has settled into a solid groove. The drum circle participants develop that deep drum trance and the inertia of the groove is almost like a perpetual motion machine feeding itself. This middle time of a drum circle is also an opportunity for you to fine-tune the dynamics of the circle. You can create a piece that is soft in volume and that emphasizes graceful and subtle aspects of the music, by directing the people in your circle to listen to and play with each other softly. It is also a good time for you to move away from the center of the circle, thus encouraging the circle to depend as much on itself as you. This gives you more time to assist participants, encouraging them, giving individual attention, support, adjustments, and acknowledgments.

The middle time in the circle is a good place to acknowledge and possibly showcase any teachers in your circle. You can invite another teacher to facilitate a piece with the community. In other words, share the facilitation space.

This middle plateau is also a place where you can give the hands of the drummers a longer rest than they would have during a window of communication. You can do this by facilitating a group hand and finger stretch. Another way to rest their hands is to create a vocal piece, song, or chant with the group that you later facilitate into a drum piece.

In the middle time, you want to create space for a good deep breath in the circle, facilitate a change of pace in the event, and do some minor adjustments and fine tuning of the group. Your circle will then be ready to be encouraged to modulate itself toward a closing climax.

Finale

As the program you are facilitating approaches its conclusion, you want to be in the center of the circle less and less, and you want to play more with the group, as part of the circle, rather than leading it. This does two things. It gives the circle more responsibility for listening to itself, rather than following you. This reinforces your original intent of leading the circle to lead itself. Secondly, it shows the circle that it doesn't always need you. This frees you to participate as a musician, fulfilling another of your basic intents, which is to create a drumming circle with whom you can play.

Whenever possible I try to give myself a little leeway about the length of the event. Then, as I read the group's energy, I can bring the event to a close when they are ready to stop, regardless of whether it is before or after the "official" stopping time. That way we, the circle and I, mutually agree on when we are done, like in the finger dance exercise described in Chapter 4.

It's Over When They Say It's Over

This story unfolds as I facilitate a community drum circle at the opening ceremony of a four-day international alternative healing conference. It is the end of the evening and the two-hour drum circle was scheduled last on the program, following the keynote speaker, Baba Ram Dass. The circle started out well with high energy, as alternative healing people tend to be "percussion puppies." However, the transition points were coming up sooner than usual in the drumming pieces, as if the group's attention focus was weak. The quality of the music was exultant and everybody was having fun, but the group was coming to the closing of the event one half hour before the scheduled end. I couldn't understand why, if they were having so much fun, were they ending early? I had no choice but to follow and support the group I was leading, so we created a mutual finalé.

Most of the population disappeared in minutes. I immediately went looking for the program planners who hired me, to apologize about the shortened program. I found one who had participated in the circle. She let me know that this was the first night of a truly international event, and that two thirds of the people had flown in from all parts of the globe, and were experiencing jet lag. She was surprised that the people had lasted in the circle as long as they did, and thanked me for acknowledging the group's choice to finish early, successfully following the people who were following me.

Drum Circle Game: Passing the Solo

This game is for an all-drum circle, playing in-the-moment music.

Once you have started an in-the-moment music circle, and you have established a solid rhythmical relationship amongst the players, direct the group to lower its volume and maintain the rhythm at that volume throughout this drum circle game. The instructions for the game are as follows.

- A designated player stops playing, rests their hands on their drum head, and listens to the rhythm that is being created around them.
- When they are ready, they play a solo. When they solo, they are expressing their rhythmical spirit in relationship to the rhythm that is being played. Part of their solo could be dialoging around a specific part being played in the circle. They could also interweave their solo around and through the group song, as if the in-the-moment music was a forest, and the solo was a bird flying around and through the trees.
- After the soloist expresses herself fully, they stop playing, rest their hands on their drum head, and listen to the group song for a minute or two.
- Then they begin to play softly with the group rhythm, ready to support the next solo.
- When that person begins to play with the group, it signals the person on their left to be the next soloist. They solo, stop playing, listen with their hands resting on their drum, and the process starts again.

The solos can continue to be passed around the circle more than once until the whole circle is satisfied they have expressed their rhythmical spirit.

Arthurian Terminology

Some of the words I describe below are there to help you grasp my facilitators' discussions. Others are Arthurian terminology that express ideas and concepts particular to my facilitation, for which I had previously found no adequate words. Sometimes Arthurian terminology is a single word that describes a whole series of actions. Once you understand this terminology, I can describe to you in one sentence what would normally be three written pages of facilitation direction. As an example, "Sculpt and showcase the wood timbral group, while on the run." After you absorb the ideas presented in this chapter, you will be able to understand this sentence. Begin by simply reading these definitions.

I take no responsibility for the definition of my Arthurian words or their source. My elfself did it!

The Groove

"The groove" is the continuous repetitive cycle of the rhythms being played by a rhythm circle. That groove creates an identifiable melody line amongst the pitches of the drums and percussion. It is linear in time, and when all the individual rhythms are interconnected into a solid groove, you want it to go on forever. When the rhythms are not connected, and are fighting each other, you have no groove, just noise. You may want the noise to stop, and it usually does.

The melody line in a culturally-specific rhythm usually repeats itself over and over again with a minimum amount of change throughout the life of the groove.

The melody line in a community drum circle groove is constantly evolving as the different players adapt their rhythmical parts to the ever-changing dynamics of the drum circle's interaction.

Entrainment

"Entrainment" happens, for example, when a tall person and a short person walk down the street together, both of them unconsciously adjusting their stride to accommodate the other so they can walk together at the same pace and continue their conversation.

In some programs, I hand out drums and other percussion toys and explain a little bit about how a community drum circle works. I then count off to the group, and say "Go." The people just start playing and looking for rhythmical agreement. Sometimes the group finds that agreement and comes up with a rhythm song. But most of the time they stumble, fumble, and go nowhere rhythmically. I let the group start at rhythm burnout, and fall into chaos. I then stop them all in a comical fashion and explain to them that what they just created was what, at the university, we would call cacophony. But in jazz terminology what they created was what we call a train wreck. We all have a good laugh and I explain to them that there's a spectrum of musical synergy that describes a group playing together. The two opposite ends of that spectrum are the train wreck and entrainment. The only difference between the two is that in a train wreck everyone in the group is singing and playing their own part but not in relationship to anyone else. That creates a musical and rhythmical train wreck. But in entrainment everyone is singing and playing their own rhythmical part, but doing it so that they're having musical dialogue and playing in rhythm with the whole group. When that happens it creates entrainment. Creating a successful group entrainment is less about a person's rhythmical sensibility, and more about their willingness to dialogue, communicate, and collaborate musically with the other players. In other words, to get to entrainment you want to play with your head up, and your eyes, ears and heart open.

> To get to entrainment you want to play with your head up, and your eyes, ears and heart open.

Buddhist Festival Entrains with Community Drum Circle

As this story unfolds, I am in the Republic of Taiwan in the middle of an ongoing community drum circle sponsored by a local drum shop and Remo Drums. We are outside the store on the sidewalk of a main street in the city of Taipei in the Republic of China on the island of Taiwan. We are 50 people, half kids, half adults, playing our hearts out and having a wonderful time.

Around the corner, from a half a block away, comes a flatbed truck with speakers blaring vocal chanting. It drives slowly up the street toward the drum circle. On the flatbed truck are two Taiko drummers beating a huge four foot high double-headed Taiko-like drum. Coming around behind them is another flatbed truck with blaring speakers, and on that truck is a group of percussionists playing Taiko-like drums and gongs. Following that truck is a third truck full of a chorus of chanters and horn players sitting around microphones, singing the Chinese chants that came blaring out of the speakers on all the trucks. More flatbed trucks full of drums, gongs and chanters follow the first three trucks around the corner. It is a Buddhist holiday celebration and all the participants on the trucks are dressed in orange robes.

As the rolling percussion parade proceeds to head directly toward our drum circle, I get the attention of the first Taiko drummers by holding my drum high in the air and jumping. I entice them to beat along with the rhythm that the drum circle on the sidewalk is already playing. They look surprised seeing this westerner waving at them from the middle of some sort of percussion ensemble, while jumping up and down to the beat being created by the circle. By following my body as they drive by, the drummers on the first truck slowly change their rhythm to entrain with ours. The other drummers in the second flatbed truck hear the change in rhythm and respond in kind along with the chanters in the next truck, and the next, and the next, and so on. As this parade of over 30 flatbed truckloads of drummers, chanters and horn players pass by our rhythm circle, they adjust their rhythms to meet our rhythms. It is an ongoing challenge to entrain a group of first-time beginning-beginner community drummers together with a moving parade of flatbed Buddhist percussionist in the middle of a Chinese culture. Needless to say I lose five pounds in sweat, but we all have a wonderful time.

> *As this parade of over 30 flatbed truckloads of drummers, chanters and horn players pass by our rhythm circle, they adjust their rhythms to meet our rhythms.*

Circuitry

When you drive a car, shifting gears, you are using your driving *circuitry*. You are accomplishing a vast number of calculations, body commands, responses, and moves, all automatically, to fit the situation. It is the *circuitry* of all of these acts that you've done over and over again that allows you to shift gears while driving without paying a lot of attention to the basic mechanics of accomplishing these movements.

When you pick up a spoon, direct it over to a bowl of mush, scoop up some of that mush into the spoon, and get it to your face, you have just completed a complicated series of calculations, body commands, and mental adjustments to accomplish the goal of eating. But what your brain says is "eat" and within that you do all of these things to accomplish that goal. All these adjustments and actions are attributed to the *circuitry* of eating.

"Drumming circuitry" develops from the constant repetitive use of certain strikes and patterns that become automatic, so that when somebody asks you to play a certain rhythm, your body has the circuitry to repeat the pattern and create the rhythm on demand, without a lot of struggle or thinking about the process.

A facilitator utilizes circuitry to facilitate a group and achieve their goal. As an example, the word "showcase" consists of a half page of instructions in Chapter 12. Doing the showcasing exercise over and over again will develop your facilitating circuitry and your ability to showcase.

Whether you are eating, driving, drumming, or facilitating for the first time you must develop physical and technical skills to achieve a smooth result. You develop any of these skills through repetitive action. As you repeat these actions over and over again you develop the neuron pathways to initiate a series of commands. The commands and resulting action, over time, create the circuitry that encompasses one complete act.

Student Crisis Mode

"Student crisis mode" happens when someone is being overly challenged to produce something that is beyond their rhythmical expertise. If you ask someone to play a rhythm that is beyond their technical abilities in a public drum circle, you place them under performance pressure. That could put anyone into student crisis mode. A beginning-beginner drummer who is given an ethnically-specific rhythm or a part that is more challenging than their rhythmical expertise allows them to execute will go into student crisis mode. Their bodies will tense up and their breathing will be shallow. They will experience a certain amount of personal stress trying to achieve something that is out of their reach.

As a drummer, you can go into student crisis mode if the rhythm you are playing has been sped up past your ability to effectively, comfortably play it and still get the proper sound out of your instrument.

Indications of student crisis mode, in any one person or in a whole group, are shallow breathing, tense shoulders and concerned faces. If you could see their toes inside their shoes they would probably be curled.

Student crisis mode is part of the process in any drumming class. Avoid it in your community rhythm circle. It's one of the big no-no's!

Facilitators' Crisis Mode

If you are a juggler, then juggler's crisis mode can be caused by having more balls in the air than you can handle. "Facilitators' crisis mode" is the feeling of being overwhelmed with too much information to handle and too many decisions to make at any one time. You have too many balls in the air. Breathing helps.

Sincerious

Sincerious is the act of being sincere and serious at the same time, but not so serious that you lose your elfish attitude.

Percussion Puppy

"Percussion puppies" are people who love to express themselves rhythmically. They're not necessarily serious percussion enthusiasts. A percussion puppy is a person who will play anytime, anywhere, for any reason, with any person, if it has anything to do with percussion, rhythm, and drumming. A serious percussion enthusiast can also at the same time be a sincerious percussion puppy.

Percussionitis

Percussionitis is a highly contagious and incurable disease. The only known way to relieve it is to scratch it. The only known way to scratch it is to play. The best way to scratch it is with friends.

You know that you have percussionitis when you find yourself tapping on your desk with your pencil at the office or tapping on the dashboard of your car with one hand, while listening to the radio, and driving down the road with the other hand. You know that you have advanced percussionitis if, while driving down the road, you find yourself steering with your knees and playing with both hands on the dashboard. You know that you have advanced percussionitis when the clothes in your washing machine shift out of balance in the spin cycle and you can't decide whether to play with the rhythm the washing machine makes with your hands on top of the washer, or to dance to it, or to turn the washer off and adjust the load.

The REMO Percussionitis Meeting

This story unfolds at the REMO Drum Company marketing management meeting in Los Angeles, California. It was one of my first visits to REMO, and we had been discussing the possibility of them choosing to have me design a drum for them and their potential endorsements. There were six of us at the meeting, including marketing and sales department heads and artist representatives. We were all sitting around a table. As the subject matter in the meeting moved from my involvement with REMO to more mundane business matters, people began to lightly tap on the table top. Some people tapped with a pencil, some with a pencil and one hand, and some were playing the table with both hands. The rhythm was quietly being played under the conversation about market share and research and development. The group was so perfectly entrained with each other that an information clipboard was repeatedly being pushed across the table and received in perfect timing with the rhythm being played. Their focus was so intent on the meeting that I could not tell if any person at the table was consciously aware of the rhythm that they were creating. Understanding proper drum circle etiquette, I was determined to join them without disrupting the process, or being too obvious. I began to tap on the edge of the table with my fingertips very softly, supporting the basic groove created by the group. I looked down at all the hands dancing on the table and felt satisfied that I was in harmony with the group groove. I decided to raise the volume of my playing to join into the rhythm. Just at that moment the whole group stopped playing and looked at me. The room was totally silent for 20 seconds. All hands were frozen in midair. Then someone said, "Nice riff, Arthur." The business and rhythm meeting continued, with me as one of the players.

> The rhythm was quietly being played under the conversation about market share and research and development.

These people were more than executives for a major U.S. drum company. Their table tapping was the unconscious manifestation of a group of people with an advanced case of percussionitis. That was the moment I decided to become part of the REMO drum family.

Modulation

When you *modulate* the volume, up means that you get louder. When you modulate the volume down you bring the volume down. Modulation in a rhythmical-based event is a process involving emotion and energy as well as volume dynamics.

Emotional modulation refers to your ability to shift the emotions in an event, starting from a regular social level, and bringing them up to performance level, and then to an excited level and finally to a climax level. That's one example of emotional modulation. In some drumming populations a rhythmical event will even start deliberately in the other direction, at a highly exciting level. Slowly but surely, as everyone gets their "yayas" out, fulfilling their need to excitedly express themselves, they modulate down to an emotional level where everyone is ready to play the one beat trance beat, a continuously-repeating simple one-beat pattern. They ride that pattern off into a group trance state.

Synergizing

Synergizing is the act of creating a tangible feeling of camaraderie amongst the participants of a program.

Rhythmasizing

Rhythmasizing is the act of using rhythmical-based events, musical or interactive-game based, to ground the participants in their bodies, and create group entrainment. For example, you can use a rhythmically-based event in the middle of a day full of highly-cognitive meetings, so the participants can get out of their chairs, move around a little, and take a "mind break." Rhythmasizing need not involve instruments. You can rhythmasize a group using clapping, or vocal or movement games.

Just one note—a *rhythmasizer* is someone who *rhythmasizes*.

Windows of Communication

A "window of communication" is that quiet space between two drum grooves, when one rhythm piece is over and everyone has stopped drumming. You can use that window as a place in your drum circle presentation to communicate verbally to the participants in the circle. It is a place to speak to the group to prepare them for the next piece, or provide metaphors that facilitate better musical or community development. It can also be a place to facilitate hand and body stretching.

Sculpting

Sculpting is a way of identifying various combinations of people in your group. You may choose a section of a circle, a group of individuals in the circle, or a single player in the circle, using body language and some vocal language. When you are sculpting, you are communicating to a group or a person in a specific manner that gets their attention so they can receive your instructions.

Exercise: Sculpting Three Vocal Parts

Use all vocals with the participants standing in a circle. From the middle of the circle, sculpt the circle into three parts. Give the first part of the circle their vocal part to sing into the circle. Make it a simple pulse-oriented vocal part to create a musical foundation with which to build the other two parts. While the first sculpted part of the circle is singing, turn to the next part of your sculpted circle, and give them a more syncopated vocal part to sing that relates to the first part you taught. Listening to the song created by the first two vocal parts, turn to the last third of your circle and add a third vocal part into the song. You can leave the song as it is now, or else turn to the first group that you sculpted and add to or have them elaborate more notes in their basic pulse part. Listen to and enjoy your creation for a minute or two. Then stop the group and let someone else come into the center of the circle and sculpt three vocal parts. This is also a good three-point radar exercise.

Orchestrational Spot

The "orchestrational spot" is the place where the facilitator chooses to stand in the circle, usually in the middle, to give directions.

Call and Response

A "call and response" is when the facilitator plays a particular rhythm pattern as a *call* to the group of players. The players *respond* by repeating the facilitator's call, starting on the first note of the next rhythm cycle.

Call to Groove

When some of the participants of a rhythm circle are not playing, the facilitator can do a "call to groove" to get them to start playing their instruments all at the same time. This is usually accomplished by the facilitator as they count "in time," the first three pulses in a rhythm. They then use the rest of the time in that rhythm cycle to encourage the players to start playing at the beginning of the next rhythm cycle. "One, two, lets' all play," is one version of a "call to groove."

In Full Groove

"In full groove" refers to times when all the participants in a rhythm circle are playing together with all the instruments.

On the Run

I call facilitating while the drum circle is in full groove "on the run." Certain orchestration and facilitation techniques can be instigated in an ongoing rhythm. The phrase "on the run" usually appears in this book after a particular facilitation direction has been given. It indicates that the particular facilitation action is taking place while the group is playing with all the instruments, in full groove. An example would be sculpting a group to prepare them to receive a particular facilitation command, while on the run.

Stop Cut

"Stop cut" is a body-language facilitation instruction that directs a sculpted group or individual or the whole circle to stop playing at a certain given point. It is usually preceded by an attention call from the facilitator and can be done so that the whole group stops playing at the same time.

Exercise: Sculpting A Vocal Song On the Run

For this exercise, pointing at a player indicates that you want them to "continue to play." Begin this exercise by having one person create a pulse-oriented rhythmical sound with their voice. Then ask everyone in the circle to contribute their individual vocal sounds to make an in-the-moment group song. Get in the middle of the circle, listen to the song, and pick the vocal parts that you like. Ask the players of those parts to "continue to play." *Stop cut* the rest of the group. This uncovers the vocal parts that you have chosen, as they continue to sing their parts. By using the stopcut, you uncover the particular song that you have *sculpted* out of the circle while "on the run." After listening to the song that you created, call the rest of the group back into the groove with a four count.

At that point everyone who wasn't singing, who listened to the singing group, has a new perspective into the song. They do not necessarily need to sing the exact same part they sang before they were stopcut, nor will most of them do that. This creates an ever ongoing, evolving rhythmical song during the exercise.

You have just done the exercise. You join the circle by going to another person who's singing in the circle and relieving them of their place in the circle. By relieving that person of their place in the circle, you choose them to be the next facilitator to run the exercise. This "sculpt a vocal song" exercise continues until everyone has taken a turn sculpting one song.

Rumble

Call *rumble* into a circle and the circle responds by stopping the rhythm song and going into musical cacophony. You are leading a cacophonous rumble that sounds like the rumble of thunder. Rumbling is one of the basic facilitators' orchestrational tools.

Showcasing

Showcasing happens when a facilitator acknowledges an individual or group. Sometimes this is done by sculpting in a way that gives them a chance to solo, or, as we say, to shine.

Rhythm Dork

A "rhythm dork" is a person who believes they are rhythmically challenged. They are usually trying to play the rhythm with their bodies in response to mental commands, rather than playing the rhythm with their bodies as a kinesthetic dance with their hands on the drums. The result is that their strikes on their instrument are late or out of time. Their minds are overwhelmed by the rhythm that surrounds them and they put themselves in an emotional crisis mode.

True rhythm dorks are very rare. I would typically find perhaps one rhythm dork, out of the hundreds of students I taught at UCSC each year.

True Rhythm Dorks Are Rare

Most people who think that they are rhythmically challenged are just trying to play the rhythms from their head, having their mind tell their body when to hit a particular syncopated pattern rather than letting their body just dance the pattern on its own. The result is that they are always hitting late and behind the beat. If I find a person like that in a rhythm circle then I always have them sit close to a *djun-djun* player, as the big bass boom will help their bodies feel the beat.

Once they discover that rhythm is not about cognitive knowledge but about a kinesthetic dance, in time they bypass the brain circuitry and become drummers.

Out of the hundreds of students a year that I taught at the university, there would usually be one that I could truly classify as a rhythm dork. They could not feel where the pulse was, and they depended entirely on their brain to tell their body where and when to hit which, of course, would mean that they would always be behind the beat and in constant student crisis mode.

With these people I would refund their class fees directly out of my pocket, and tell them that I would let them take the beginning beginner class for absolutely free the next quarter if they took this money and went to an African or African-inspired village dance class with live drummers, which in Santa Cruz is easy to find.

I told them to focus on the simple body part isolation warm-ups in the beginning of the dance class. For the choreography part of the class, I told them to focus on their feet in relationship to the drums, and let the rest go, not to worry about all the heavy choreography moving across the floor, flaying their arms and their bodies to the drums in syncopated contortions. Often, rhythm dorks to whom I made this proposal took the money and did a dance class for a quarter, came back and had the basic kinesthetic sensibilities to learn how to drum. Now their body was listening to the heartbeat and they had a physical reference point from which to play. One of those persons came back to my classes and wouldn't leave for four years. She became a member of a local ethnic-arts performing group, and went on to Africa to study drum and dance.

In some of my community rhythm circles I have everyone hold up their front feet (their hands) and say, "Drumming is dancing, and dancing is drumming."

> Drumming is dancing, and dancing is drumming.

Marian Oliker's African-inspired dance class

Do the drummers
make the dancers dance,
or do the dancers
make the drummers drum?
YES!

Facilitating in Specific Populations

Any group of people creating a rhythmical event together using drums and percussion to express their collective musical spirit is utilizing basic universal principles of entrainment and synergy. The reason why particular people gather together will usually define what kind of specific population they are, and what kind of rhythmical event you can design to meet their needs.

Drumming can be used in almost any population as a tool for unity, when it is presented in a metaphorical context appropriate for the culture of that group. For instance, you can use team-building and organizational-change metaphors in a corporate event with executives, and save the cosmic consciousness metaphors for the personal growth percussion puppies and trance dance drummers. Some of the specific populations that are being served by drum and rhythm-based events are described in this chapter.

Open Community Drumming

I use the open community drum circle as a model, throughout this book, for facilitating rhythm-based events, because the facilitation tools, techniques and principles that are utilized in a community drum circle can be adapted to facilitate specific populations.

The open community drum circle presents the greatest challenge to some facilitators because an open population sometimes includes people from all of the specific populations listed below. A good example of an open, walk-in population can be found in almost any restaurant that you might visit. Next time you are in a restaurant imagine standing up and facilitating a rhythmical event with the people playing percussion with whatever they have at their tables. Cameron Tummel, my friend and Village Music Circles teacher and facilitator, contributed the following story about doing just that.

Tableware Evangelism

by Cameron Tummel

The 1997 Hawaii Facilitators' Rhythmical Playshop was an informative, magical time. During our week together, the mixed group of people from all over our planet spent hours upon hours cooperating to achieve our goals: to play and to facilitate rhythmical music. By the end of the week, our group of newly-met friends had melded into one big, happy, rhythmical family and we were chompin' at the bit to get out into the "real world" and use our freshly-honed facilitation skills.

Picture, if you will, an idyllic open-air restaurant on the shore of a tropical sea. The moonlight sparkles and dances on the water, and the tropical air wafts casually into the restaurant, flowing luxuriously among the large fans and ferns. Couples and friends and families enjoy their food and their togetherness, warmth and laughter fill the air…

and a group of "Arthurianized" facilitators discreetly enter and then occupy a central table in the restaurant…

Amidst our drinks and food a while later, the Shaker Man casually remarks, "You know what would be my bliss right now?"

"What might that be?" I ask, wiping the last few droplets of tropical marinade from my plate.

"I would love to see this *whole restaurant* playing music together!"

"Well if it were ever going to happen, this is the group of people to do it…"

Moments later, someone starts to tap out a playful little pattern upon the edge of their glass. Immediately the contagious rhythm is picked up by another set of tableware, this time to the tune of a plate, fork and saucer. Glasses, pitchers, spoons, bowls, all come to life in our eager hands. The music is beautiful, and it grows. Our group of well-fed rhythmical evangelists takes hold of that groove quicker than Guinean *djembe* players, and the magic of the music takes us all. I look across the table at the Shaker Man and say, "Here we go…"

> *Polyrhythms dance from the butter dish to the salad bowls and back again, changing and evolving as they grow, spontaneously creating and adding notes and sounds to our chorus of tableware.*

A symphony of clinking, chiming, ringing, cascading patterns fills the air. Polyrhythms dance from the butter dish to the salad bowls and back again, changing and evolving as they grow, spontaneously creating and adding notes and sounds to our chorus of tableware. It is fantastically alive, and we are with it. Our entire table gets transformed from inanimate lumps of metal and glass and ceramics into a glorious, joyful celebration of the beauty of sound and rhythm.

By now the volume of the music has grown to a considerable level. Having fifteen percussionists in one place at one time tends to produce above-average decibel levels. But this isn't noise, this is the universal language, this is music. And as our music becomes louder and louder, more and more people in the restaurant begin to notice. Without looking up (or missing a beat) I ask Shaker Man if the tables around us have noticed. He informs me that they most definitely have. I ask if the other people around the room are paying attention. He assures me that we have their attention. And then, as if I need any further convincing about the readiness of the situation, the people from a nearby table get up, place their hands upon each others' hips, and proceed to form a dancing "conga line" around us with smiles and laughter all around.

Armed with my butter knife and dinner glass, I rise from the table while playing. I grin at the other facilitators and signal them all to "keep playing." I take a deep breath and turn to the tables beside us, encouraging the people to pick up their own "instruments" and join in. Awkward as I may feel, I can't help myself. The music is alive right there in that restaurant, and the only thing to do is invite everyone to enjoy it. About one-third of the people whose evening meal has been interrupted by our rhythmical circus are resigned to sit and watch. But the other two-thirds of the people at those tables are ecstatic to be empowered with the chance to join in the fun. By the time I visit a half dozen nearby tables, other facilitators are up and on the move. Look out Waikiki, facilitators on the loose!

Believing as I do that music is for everyone, regardless of background or level of experience, I then take my trusty butter knife and dinner glass across the floor of that great big restaurant and proceed to engage the other groups of dinner-goers. By connecting with two large groups of people at the far sides of the room, my intention is to spread the music among us all. When all of the people at those two big tables eagerly join in the fun, I stop at a few other tables to encourage anyone and everyone who wants to play. Imagine my bliss-filled revelation when I turn to look back toward the table where it all started and discover that the *entire restaurant* has become enveloped by the joy of spontaneous, rhythmical music!

Cameron Tummel

So what do you do with an energetic ensemble of over a hundred players? "Soon as they're cookin', start sculpting!" is a very Arthurian way of saying that when the group is ready for more, give it to 'em. I know there are at least twelve to fifteen of us who are so attuned to each other that any facilitation cues will be well-received and supported. I also want to give our piece of music a zap of something really special. So…

With theatrical, slightly exaggerated gestures I point at myself, and then point at the group, point at myself, then the group. Thus I indicate a call and response format. The facilitators are smiling, they are ready.

Holding my glass up high, I pause to find the proper place within the music, and then play a simple one-measure-long pattern. Then I listen to their response, while clearly indicating that I am listening. Good response. I follow their response with another simple call, and listen for the new response. This response is even better, because now many of the players are aware of this new element of our musical game. By the third call, I know the group is with me because I can hear the silence they leave me when it is my turn to give the next call. The fourth call is excellent; they are ready for it. To keep our game interesting, I increase the rhythmical complexity of the call pattern. They give me their interpretation of the pattern, and our sequence continues. I lead a few more call and response sequences, and their responses are enthusiastic expressions of the fun we are all having. For the final sequence in this round of call-and-response, I want them to "return to the groove" rather than continuing to mimic my patterns, so when it is my turn to give the call I shout, "Ready and let's all play!" Our chiming, clinking, musical circus jumps back into its musical groove. It is a beautiful sequence, and very empowering for

The music is alive right there in that restaurant, and the only thing to do is invite everyone to enjoy it.

the group to hear itself unified in a single voice. I walk around a bit, enjoying our music.

By now we have completely taken over the restaurant for at least fifteen minutes, and it seems the time has come to return the people to their regularly-scheduled dining experience.

I return to the place where I had led the call and response (my orchestration spot), and again give the non-verbal gestures for "Hey, heads up everybody, we're going to do another call and response sequence!" I could also hear the music getting tired (transition point), so it is time use this sequence to wrap it up. I hold up my knife and glass.

The call-and-response sequences are clean, the players are together, and I increase the complexity of the rhythmical pattern each time. For the final sequence in our masterpiece, I choose the popular pattern known as "Shave and a haircut, two bits" ("Dun da-da-dun-dun, DUN DUN!") It feels as if every single note being played in that room is perfectly in unison. The sequence is superb, and it seems like the happiness of the players is a tangible feeling throughout the room.

As fate would have it, the final note of the final call and response sequence which I am leading upon the beautiful and very delicate rim of my dinner glass proves to be a little too enthusiastic for the poor little glass. With a climatic crash, the glass shatters upon the final note. I am filled with an exuberant feeling of completion, and am simultaneously filled with the terrifying thought that everyone might try to mimic my example. Fortunately, both the restaurant staff and I are relieved when nearly everyone manages the sequence without the instrument-damaging finale.

The room erupts into a spontaneous roar of applause and laughter, as our musical magic comes to a close. While still having most of the attention of the group, I thank them all for playing, inform them about the free community drum circle the following day, and thank them all again—tableware evangelism at its tropical finest.

Kids

Drumming is a fun, high-energy kids' activity that gives immediate gratification and feedback while encouraging self expression.

Kids just want to have fun. Whether the purpose of your presentation is educational or for community building, putting lots-o'-fun into it will increase you chance of success. To transmit the message you want to deliver to the kids, bury it inside a fun activity.

> Kids are our most powerful teachers.

Only do this if you are going to have fun yourself. If you are really enjoying what you're doing, they will know it. You can't pretend. The kids will give you back exactly what you give them. They want you to express your bliss and share your spirit.

With their independent spirits, and their courage to express themselves, kids are our most powerful teachers. This is why I expect every training associate that apprentices with me to find a group of kids and work with them on a regular basis.

Go out and find some kids and start playing. Hint, there is a kid in all of us.

The State Fair Water Jug Band

Jeff Salt is a dedicated drum-community facilitator in Salt Lake City, Utah. Every time he brings me into town to serve his community, he also sets up some school or kids-at-risk program for me, as drum-tithing. One summer Jeff volunteered me to do a kids' program at the Utah State Fair. The response was so overwhelming that even though Jeff owns a percussion shop, he couldn't supply all the drums needed for the project. So he went to a local drinking-water distributor and they gave him plastic water jugs that were not re-usable.

A plastic water jug makes an excellent-sounding drum when you cut off the neck, and leave a four-inch hole at the top. You can turn it upside down and use its bottom as the playing surface. For this program we used five-gallon jugs for the low pitch and two-gallon jugs for the high pitch.

The Utah State Fair organizers gave us a performance tent on the fairgrounds for all of the kids' day events. The school system bussed in forty kids at a time to play together with me. Each specific group of kids bussed in were all about the

A fun time was had by all.

same age, and in the same grade. One circle I facilitated would be fourth graders and the next would be tenth graders.

While facilitating these water-jug drum circles all day I got the chance to observe the different energy and social dynamics exhibited by the different age groups. The fourth graders were not afraid to squeak, squeal, and express themselves. They were ready for whatever I had to offer them. The eighth graders automatically separated themselves in the circle, with boys on one side and the girls on the other. A lot of the boys were doing any silly thing to get the girls' attention, and the girls just ignored them. The high school kids coming into the circle acted bored and, at first, skeptical about what the drum circle was supposed to be. I think they were waiting for me to give some sort of anti-drug message or some other adult message.

> *No matter what age the kids were, upon the last note played on each closing rumble, they would scream and yell with glee.*

No matter what energy each age group brought to the circle, the results were the same. Once the kids settled down, and focused on creating a group experience, they would go into a light drum trance that would only be broken by the group rumble at the end of each rhythm groove. No matter what age the kids were, upon the last note played on each closing rumble, they would scream and yell with glee. A fun time was had by all.

Kids-at-Risk

There are officially fifteen million at-risk kids in America. In my opinion, in this day and age, there is no such thing as a kid not at some sort of risk. It does not matter how safe your community is; risks, such as broken homes, drugs, gangs, and child abuse permeate our total social environment.

> *A rhythm-based event is a natural way to provide a young person with an opportunity to creatively channel and release the pent-up emotions and frustrations that usually accompany the process of growing up.*

It is a natural part of our social evolution for a teenager to rebel against the established norm. It is important to make a distinction between the positive, constructive rebellion that a healthy teenager naturally has, and destructive rebellion. This understanding will affect how you present your event to a particular group. To help you make that distinction, I suggest that you do a rhythm event inside an alternative high school, or a continuation school, where the kids are working out that distinction for themselves, before you work with a kids-at-risk group.

A rhythm-based event is a natural way to provide a young person with an opportunity to creatively channel and release the pent-up emotions and frustrations that usually accompany the process of growing up.

Three Cultures

Nestled in the foothills of the Sierra Nevada mountains in California, just north of Sacramento, is an small mining town. It was slowly turning into a ghost town until it started to become a bedroom community for the Sacramento metropolitan area.

The town's high school counselor called and asked me to come and do some troubleshooting in a unique situation. For generations, the population of the high school was mostly the children of the Anglo-Saxon miners. In the late nineteen-eighties the high school's dwindling population was slowly being replaced by African-American kids, whose middle-income families moved out of Sacramento's inner city. Then there was a large influx of Vietnamese children into the high school, from a group that moved into the area with the help of the Federal government.

The counselor said that it wasn't a gang situation, "yet!" But there was a growing tension amongst the different cultures in the high school population. The African-American kids who had brought with them the tough-inner city slang and attitudes had begun to hang out on the athletic field behind the gym. The Vietnamese kids spoke to each other mostly in their native tongue, and were keeping pretty much to themselves in their close-knit inner-tribal culture. Their hangout was around the science building. The miners' kids had commandeered the cafeteria quad, and were feeling defensive about what they saw as two invading cultures coming into what was once a homogenous community. Because some fights had erupted, the counselor feared that turf wars were soon to come.

Human tripod putting trust in the center

The high school gave me the gym for the day to do five drum circles, each with about a hundred kids. The cultural populations at the school were fairly evenly divided, so I requested that they send me equal numbers of each of the three cultural groups each class period.

The bell would ring, the doors would open, and the kids would walk into the gym and see a pile of percussion toys in the middle of the floor. The kids had recently received "unity through diversity" lectures and they expected the same from me. You could cut the tension in the air with a knife. As I told them to form a circle around the percussion, they would sort themselves by culture, so that there were three separated curved lines of kids surrounding the percussion instruments. As this opening ritual repeated itself five times during the day, I began to realize how deep the problem was. Not only did the kids form three separate groups around the instruments, but four out of five times they formed in the same basic physical configuration in the gymnasium. The African-American kids had their backs to the bleachers on the west wall. The Anglo-Saxon kids lined up with their backs to the north end of the Gym, and the Vietnamese kids had their backs to the main gym entrance to the east. After the kids formed their circle in this same configuration twice in a row, I brought this to the attention of one of the teachers. With surprise, the teacher noted that each group had consciously or unconsciously grouped themselves in such a way that they were protecting their designated hangout territory on the campus. If the gym walls were not there, the African-American kids' backs were facing the Athletic field, the Anglo-Saxon kids were protecting the cafeteria quad, and the Vietnamese backs faced the science building on the other side of the campus.

The fact that they separated themselves into three groups served my purpose well. I gave each group a vocal part that depended on dialogue with the other two parts to be performed successfully. They had to listen to each other to connect all the patterns into a total vocal song. Then I passed out bells to one group, wood instruments to another and shakers to the third group. They each played the part they had sung on their instruments.

When they finished playing their song with percussion, I asked them which part they thought was the most important. They all responded that their part "ruled." I then asked each group to play their part separately. Each group failed to be able to play their part without the other two parts playing as a reference for where to fit.

I said, "Let me show you how it works." I invited one person from each group to come to the center of the circle, one African-American, one Vietnamese and one Anglo-Saxon, making sure that all three kids that I chose were the same height. I had them face each other, reach out with both hands and connect with each of the other two kids' hands at face level to form a tripod. While they were still touching hands I had them step one step backward. This forced them to lean their weight into each other as they formed a human tripod. They were now literally holding each other up by leaning into each other. I then told them that in order for all of them not to fall down each had to trust their weight to the other two people who were leaning into the circle and holding them up. This trust amounted to all three people leaning into the center of the circle to stay stable.

The kids got more excited, dropped their attitudes, and for the most part, forgot the culture of the person standing next to them, and just had fun.

After I sent the three kids back to their respective groups, I then translated this physical metaphor into a musical one, saying that they had to gift their parts into the center of the circle and listen to the whole song to play their individual parts successfully. They had to trust that the other two parts would be there for them, and then they could play their part to the other two parts to make a whole song. If they did this correctly, they would hold each other up musically so that the song would not collapse and fall apart.

I told them that they thought their particular part sounded like it "ruled," because they were *ganged up* with people who were all playing the same part, and that to hear the whole group song that they should disperse the circle, and regroup so that they were each standing next to two people who did not have the same type of instrument as them. The whole circle dispersed into chaos as the three separate groups of kids reformed themselves with equal numbers everywhere in the circle...bell, shaker, wood block...African-American, Anglo-Saxon, Vietnamese...

When we played the song again in this new mixed configuration, it had a depth and wholeness to it that it didn't have when we played as three separate groups in the circle. I asked the kids if they noticed the difference in the quality of the music. They did. Then I asked them, "Was any part being played any more important than any other part?" They said no. After I made that point in all five rhythm circles, I proceeded to work with the circle as one body, using value-based community-building metaphors between each piece. As we moved into drums the kids got more excited, dropped their attitudes, and for the most part, forgot the culture of the person standing next to them, and just had fun.

There was an assembly at the end of that school day. It was a welcome back rally for an Anglo-Saxon athlete who had been injured in a football game a few weeks earlier. Attendance was optional. Given the racial tension in the high school, the faculty predicted that only the Anglo-Saxon kids, thirty percent of the population, would attend. The counselor who brought me into the school said that the attendance level at the assembly would be my "litmus test" as to how my community building drum circles worked. Attendance was seventy-five percent of the school population.

Tough Love

The Foundry School is a tough-love school located in the inner city of San Jose, California. It is named after a type of steel plant that reclaims discarded scrap metal by melting it down, pouring the molten metal into new forms, and then tempering and reshaping it into usable materials.

The Foundry School is a last chance for kids from the inner city who have been neglected or abused, who are beyond-control youth, who are delinquent, or law violators. They have been kicked out of junior high, high school, or continuation school one too many times because of drugs, fighting, gang-related activities, etc. The kids must voluntarily make it through the Foundry program to get back into the school system. These kids have a lot of incentive to make it, because for most of them school is a lot safer environment for them than the streets or their home situations. These kids have gone beyond risk to experiencing the dangers of the world-at-large. These are kids who have been "risked."

The school focuses as much on life values as academics. A major player and teacher in the foundry is John Malloy. John and his staff's hearts have to be as big as their mission and as strong as steel to give these misshapen kids what they need to help them re-shape themselves into happy, healthy, and productive souls in their own community. I call it "tough love!"

As part of my tithing to the Church of Rhythm, I visit the Foundry regularly. I do my program when they are integrating the new students into the veteran population. The first two weeks are the toughest for the new kids as they find out that they are responsible for making it through the Foundry program with a proper attitude and by participating fully.

John Malloy uses my rhythm circle as a metaphor to show how everyone is equally responsible for the success of the group. I tell them, "You are the village and no one is any more or less important than anyone else in accomplishing the village's goals."

In a rhythmically-based event it is easy to see who is putting their spirit into the exercises and who is not, and the veteran students "call out" the new kids who are holding back or exhibiting a negative attitude. They let them know that they dislike their disruptiveness, lack of participation, etc.

After each program John has the students write to me about their experience. Here are some of their comments.

"Drumming together benefited our group so much because it was our first day and we needed that lesson about doing something as a community."

"When I first came here, I was very uneasy about this group and felt uncomfortable. After you were done with us, I did not feel that anymore. I felt closer to everyone as we made something together."

"I sometimes have anger inside of me, so when I was able to play your drums it released me of my unnecessary moods."

"The drumming changed me by forcing me to work as a part of a group to accomplish something."

"No matter how much you want to go at your own pace, you must stay in the group rhythm to be successful. I noticed that my part was very important to the beat."

"I was at peace with my mind, body, and soul. Well, at least I got to be at peace for one day."

"When you first came I thought you were a crazy old man. I thought about how you brought us together without bullshitting us in any way. I respect that."

"I didn't know till now that you could open up somebody's heart with the drum."

At the end of one of these Foundry programs, one young man came up to me and said "I knew that I would bash in somebody's head today. I did not know who or why. Even though I didn't want to get kicked out of the Foundry, I just knew it would happen, so I bashed in your drum head instead. Here it is and thank you." With that statement he handed my broken drum to me and walked away. My heart filled with joy as I realized that I had given someone an opportunity to break my drum head instead of someone else's head.

The drum circle is a lesson about doing something as a community.

Challenged Populations

The vibration of a singing drum is a kinesthetic massage that calms the mind, the body, and the spirit. It permeates its immediate surrounding environment with a physical vibration that bypasses any challenge that someone might have, be it mental, physical, or spiritual.

Bypassing the Brain

Jason walked into the middle of an outdoor community drum circle in full groove. Standing in the center with his eyes half closed and unfocused, his head rhythmically twisting to the left and back, he was wringing his hands together in a particular fashion. I have worked with groups of autistic children before, and this young adult was expressing those body symptoms. His caretaker tried to bring him back into the drumming group and have him sit down. I encouraged her to let him stay in the center. He was obviously getting a drum massage and liking it. His rhythmical head-twisting entrained with the group pulse and stayed with it for the rest of the time he was in the circle. Carol, his caretaker, said Jason moves his head to certain music that he likes to hear, and only when the vibration works for him. She taught home and daily-living skills to the developmentally disabled, and in this outing for Jason they discovered the drum circle. Carol deciphered Jason's hand movements for me as his language. While standing in the middle of the circle he was saying with his hands, "Pray. Love. Having good time."

Carol got Jason to sit down with a drum in front of him. At first he would sit with his hands resting on the drum head, feeling it vibrate to the beat of the drums being played around it. Every once in a while he would bounce his hands on the drum to the rhythm of the circle, and then stop and rest his hands on the drum head or speak to Carol with his hand signals. Carol was playing a drum as well and was constantly encouraging Jason to participate. His playing spurts increased until, by the end of the event, he was constantly playing with the rest of the circle and staying with the group beat.

> *Jason moves his head to certain music that he likes to hear, and only when the vibration works for him.*

Carol came up to me after the closing. She said that even with all her expertise it would have taken her months to get Jason to play the drum, let alone play it for any consistent amount of time. She believed that the vibration of the drum circle attracted him, and his prolonged immersion in the ongoing drum circle gave his body the information it needed to play. I agreed, also feeling that the drum circle massage gave Jason the kinesthetic support he needed to keep his focus long enough to participate. Jason is proof that rhythms soothe the brain, and that the body plays the rhythms. God bless you Jason. Play, Love, and have good life.

Let Your Body Be Your Ears

Under a California educational training program, my "Rhythm Playshop for Kids" was placed in a catalogue as a choice for middle school programs. The State would give each school a budget, and each school would spend their budget by choosing different presenters and performers out of that catalogue. I would get a call from the program office with a list of dates, schools, classrooms, teachers, and times to appear for that month. I would show up at the school an hour ahead of time, and then find the appropriate classroom and teacher. Then I would find out how to adapt my program to fit their specific needs, set up the drums and percussion, and play with the kids.

I arrived one morning at what I soon found out was a "special" school. I walked into the classroom to find thirty kids who were partially hearing impaired

And the deaf shall hear...

or totally deaf. My kids' format usually started out with vocal calls and responses. I knew that my voice could not reach them, but that my drum could. I had my interpreter sign to them to let their bodies be their ears, and then proceeded to do call and response with all drums. Once we understood that we could talk to each other with our drums, I pretty much did the same program that I would do with any class or kids' group.

Mentally-Challenged Players

Although I'm not actively involved in the Mormon Church at this time (I'm currently serving the Church of Rhythm), I was raised with a solid Mormon background and foundation which serves me well today, with ideas such as family values, community service, and tithing. Tithing in the Mormon Church means that you give 10% of your energy and your income back to the church. I still do that, except that I'm giving my 10% back to the Church of Rhythm. While in Singapore on a Southeast Asia REMO drum tour, I was asked to visit a group of mentally-challenged children in a "special" school in Singapore. I thought, "Ah, here's a chance to tithe back to Rhythm Church."

I told them I would be more than happy to visit the school. I told them I needed to know how many kids that they wanted me to work with, in order to collect enough percussion toys and instruments for them. Their response was, "No, no, Mr. Hull. These children are mentally challenged and we don't expect them to participate. We'd like you just to go there and play for them and show them your exuberance and your elfishness."

I have watched a masterful music therapist repeatedly work with triply handicapped blind children in rhythm-based events, with excellent results. I knew the possibilities, so I said, "I'll be happy to do that provided that we also are able to have enough percussion toys available for the children regardless of whether they're going to use them or not." The people said, "Fine, no problem," and we gathered the instruments we needed.

On the way to the Yio Chu Kang Garden School in Singapore, my host kept reiterating the fact that I should not be disappointed if the children that they present to me are in different states of mental focus and attention. She said I might get some of the kids to participate, but not to be disappointed if I don't get a fully participating drum circle for any length of time. She told me if I wanted to do a drum circle they would provide me with children who they knew could participate. It was obvious that her expectations of the mentally-challenged children, their attention span, and ability to participate was not high.

> Because the drum membrane vibrates, and goes directly to the body, bypassing the brain, the children's bodies responded.

We arrived at the school. I set up the chairs in a circle, piled all the toys in the middle of the floor, and they brought the children in and sat them in chairs. There were caretakers for the children, so that they wouldn't fall off the chairs or hurt themselves, and indeed the children were mentally challenged to various degrees. I became my best elf self, played my drum, danced around in the middle of the circle, and got their attention. Because the drum membrane vibrates, and goes directly to the body, bypassing the brain, the children's bodies responded. We got all excited together. As I jumped around, I put the drum down, picked up other percussion toys and started playing around with them. When I put a toy down to pick up another one, I would put them closer to the children and then finally I would just play a toy and put it in a child's lap or be playful with a child and almost give it to her, and then not give it to her, and then almost give it to her until she grabbed it out of my hand.

Once we all had percussion toys in our hands, we made a ruckus with everybody in full cacophony until I began to create call and response in the group. The children would wait for me to speak to them with my instrument, and they would speak back to me. We got to the place where we could sing sounds together, and clap our hands together, and play our instruments.

All the kids, to varying degrees of focus, as predicted, were creating their own little drum circle. The caretakers had scheduled a twenty-minute session with the kids, thinking that that was the longest extent of time that they could spend doing any one particular activity. Except for one small child who got scared of the noise, we stayed together in that room and played together for almost forty minutes. At the end, we put the percussion in the middle of the floor, sat in on our chairs and sang to each other. I decided to gently bring them out of their excited state by doing call and response with vocal sounds that would encourage them to breathe deeply. Long soft notes brought us a group sigh to close, and I returned the children back to their caretakers.

On the ride back to the hotel my host apologized for underestimating my abilities to work with the children. I told her that she did not underestimate mine or the children's abilities, she underestimated the ability of percussion rhythm to bypass the differently-functioning circuitry in the children's brains, and connect with the circuitry that is totally functioning in their bodies.

Personal Growth and Healing

People take many different personal growth paths, many of which involve rhythm and drumming on some level. Some people use the drum as a personal tool for developing trance or altered states of conscious. Other people come together and play as a group to achieve the same state of being. In some groups the drum is a supporting element in their personal growth process. In other groups, rhythm and the drum are the main elements for that process.

I have done Rhythm Alchemy Playshops™ in personal growth events and conferences. Most of them lasted only two to four hours. My longest Alchemy Playshop was a weekend-long artist-in-residence program at Esalen Institute on the Big Sur coast of California. So when people of the Omega Institute in upper-state New York called me and asked me to do a one-week, six-hours-a-day program, I said sure, thanks, hung up the phone and swallowed hard. I was not sure if I had enough material to sustain a one-week process. As it turned out I had more than enough.

Throughout the Omega program, to take the group process to the next step I would ask myself, "What does this group need from me at this time?" I found, in this program, that interactive rhythmical process is in itself individually metaphoric in a deeply personal way for each individual. After we had finished an exercise, like the finger dance, for instance, we would sit down, share, and process our experience. Each person had their own personal experience and personal revelation through an exercise. The more we shared, the more we discovered that the universal principles functioning in these rhythmic interactions brought us closer together each day, creating a foundation of trust for deeper sharing. The exercises we did and the rhythms we played became vehicles for exploring our relationships with ourselves and each other.

You can take a shaman's drum, or any drum for that matter, and play by yourself and have deep relationship with yourself through your drum. The drum speaks to your spirit, and sometimes from your spirit when you play it. The rhythmical dance you do with that instrument makes it become more intimately connected to you. The more you play it, the more it becomes a part of you. So with your drum you are able to express your spirit and send it out into the universe. That release is a healing act. Some drummers believe that while drumming, you actually give yourself the vibrations you need to heal that part of you that needs it. That part might be mental, physical, spiritual, or psychological.

> *While being a tool for unity, the drum can also be a tool for personal transformation and healing.*

When you take your drum to a rhythm circle and play it with your community, healing happens. It does not matter if the group's focus is purely social or ritualistic. If you come and drum, the healing is compounded because everyone else is putting their spirit into their drum, and their hearts are open. You get and give a rhythmical massage that is compounded by the number of people in the circle and the energy they are sharing with each other.

While being a tool for unity, the drum can also be a tool for personal transformation and healing.

My friend and fellow facilitator Don Davidson contributed the following story that demonstrates this.

Breath Like a Wheel
by Don Davidson

At a 10-day hypnosis intensive in London, England, I noticed that one of the most difficult skills to master for some people is how to pace your communications with the breathing of the person you are hypnotizing. Just like in drumming, there are so many things happening at once in hypnosis that conscious tracking of all the tasks can be overwhelming. And as in drumming, there is a point at which you must surrender to the relationship before it can move forward. So I took Arthur Hull's metaphor literally, and sought to create in the group a sense of being "one big body" so we could focus on breathing.

I asked the group of 40 people to form a circle sitting on the floor and gave each a percussion instrument or a small drum. The two lowest drums were placed at the top and the bottom of the circle and we called them the top of the inhale and the bottom of the exhale. So the circle

Don Davidson

together comprised one big respiration, a wheel of breath. With the two opposing pulses as markers, both in time and in space, the group proceeded to experiment—filling in their rhythmic messages at different points on the wheel. The result was a music like no other I have ever heard. It had a presence and a life of its own that was forever changing and yet spoke to a timelessness. I didn't anticipate that a majority of the group would begin to synchronize their own breathing with that on the wheel. We collectively created a profound altered state that brought a palpable charge to the whole room. The song was absolutely unstoppable and we played on in that groove for three quarters of an hour. We all left that night with a wholly new intimacy with the process of breathing.

It was for me a great validation of how drumming and rhythm are about wordless language, unspoken communication, and messages that are cooperatively created. The next morning I received what is still one of the most chilling compliments I have ever received when one of the participants said to me, "Who are you really?" The only answer still remains, "I am a drummer."

World Unity

The first World Unity festival site was a remote area high in the mountains, 50 miles south of the Grand Canyon in Arizona. It was a global gathering of artists, musicians, indigenous and religious leaders, the Rainbow Family Tribes, and the national hand drumming community. The intention was to come together to do healing among the different cultures represented. The festival was also the focal point for the first Drums Around The World event. It would be the largest drum circle in the world at that time. It would be facilitated by drum community elders such as Babatunde Olatunji and Hamza El Din. I felt honored to be asked to be master of ceremonies for the event. Over four hundred other drum circles throughout the world would be playing and praying for peace at the same time.

I arrived at the festival site to find well-established campsites hidden in the pines surrounding the Great Meadow. The Great Meadow was the focal point for activities. In its center was a peace pole with symbols on it and ribbons tied to it, with crystals and objects around it representing all the different cultures that had gathered here. This is where the main counsel meetings and ceremonies would be held.

After each ear-piercing thunderclap followed each blinding flash of lightning, we responded with our own drum thunder.

The sounds of the drums were constant and came from every direction. Everywhere I walked in the woods, I would find drum circles. Some were open drum circle jams where anybody could sit down and play with any rhythm they wanted on any instrument they had, as long as they supported the group. Other circles I walked into were culturally specific. There were lots of Afro-Cuban circles playing different styles of rumbas on conga drums. There were *djembe* circles playing rhythms from the Mandingo-speaking people of West Africa. I found two Ghanaian stick-drumming circles, a Jamaican-style *Niabingi* circle, and a Native American pow-wow circle. Throughout the camps, I ran into many impromptu drum classes and workshops. A Native American Seminole from the

Everglades of Florida, named Bantu was passing out his people's rhythms and songs. Madu, a Buddhist monk from Japan, was giving a Taiko drum lesson on any kind of drum that was available, including an upside-down cooking pot. I used a cardboard box. Muruga, a Serbian-Croatian percussionist, gave a drumming and chanting workshop at the wooden peace pavilion. This pavilion was dedicated to the people of Serajavo. When I ran across a group of drummers arguing over what part goes where in a *Merengé* rhythm, I ended up giving a workshop myself. All they needed was a rhythmical chiropractic adjustment. Out on the Great Meadow, forty drummers were playing the Liberian Fanga rhythm, with as many dancers practicing the welcome dance that went with the rhythm. They were preparing to perform it in honor of Babatunde Olatunji when he arrived the next day for the Drums Around The World event.

> *All the people in the camps poured out of the woods onto the meadow yelling, chanting, and singing in praise of such natural beauty.*

Late that afternoon, clouds suddenly appeared over the mountain tops and they dropped a deluge of rain, highlighted by lightning and thunder, on the meadow. The circles scattered under camp tarps and into lodge teepees. I ended up in the wooden drum yurt on the edge of the meadow, which was just a 6-foot-high latticework fence with a canvas roof. We were so jammed together in the yurt that we hardly had enough room to swing our arms to play our drums, but play we did. After each ear-piercing thunderclap followed each blinding flash of lightning, we responded with our own drum thunder. The storm passed as quickly as it came. Just before sunset the clouds cleared to unveil a bright solid rainbow arching up out of the woods and ending right in the middle of the meadow by the peace pole. All the people in the camps poured out of the woods onto the meadow yelling, chanting, and singing in praise of such natural beauty. There were thousands of people who had come here to create a drummer's paradise, and they did.

Women's and Men's Groups

I call women's and men's groups "gender-empowerment groups." The women's and men's circles are forums for therapeutic disclosure. They create a safe place for emotional release, healing and bonding, so it is no surprise to find drums being used in these circles to support their process.

For years, I've facilitated the drumming part of the opening or closing ceremonies for the annual California Men's Gathering conferences. At each opening ceremony, the presenters acknowledge the women's movement for pioneering the gender empowerment process and being a positive role model for the men's movement. My belief is this kind of work empowers the whole community.

It is also my belief that the drumming inside the women's movement has empowered more women to join open community drum circles and balance the gender population of these

Keio Ogawa leading a circle

circles. In the sixties and seventies the hippie thunder-drummer circles were typically dominated by males. The drumming was often rough and rugged, and the women had to play as loud as the men to participate and be heard. As the drumming in these circles has matured and improved over the years, the gender ratios in these events has evened. Thanks in part to the women drummers and the gender empowerment drumming groups, our community drumming circles know better how to listen to each other and play with grace and finesse. The gender population of most open community drum circles is now equally balanced between men and women. I find the same population balance in my Rhythmical Alchemy Playshops and my Facilitators Playshops. There are typically two or three men and women participating in these playshops who plan to take information, new ideas, and rhythm and drum games back to their gender-empowerment groups.

Trance Around the Sweat Lodge

I am at a wilderness men's gathering. The program planners had accidentally scheduled me to run a trance-drumming workshop around the campfire pit at the same time they scheduled a healing sweat at the sweatlodge next to the same fire pit. Enrollment for each program was full. I talked with the sweatlodge leader, and we decided to do our programs in conjunction with each other.

I warned my drummers that once we started drumming we would not stop until the sweat ceremony was complete. I asked them to think about the energy that they would be generating and using as we drummed together. I told them, as they drummed to meditate on a person or a part of their life that needed healing. I asked them to dedicate their drumming to that person or place in their life. I asked them to stay silent when we stopped drumming, as they released that energy, sending it to whomever or whatever part of their life it would do the most good.

We began to softly drum a pulse trance beat around the fire as the sweatlodge men silently wet themselves down and covered their naked bodies with thick mud. Then as they walked in a line, clockwise around the lodge, we got up from the fire, still drumming, and joined them. As they entered the lodge by crawling through the entrance hole, we drummers continued drumming and walked clockwise around the lodge three times before going back to the fire circle.

Whenever the men in the sweat-lodge started to chant to our rhythms, we would get up from the fire and walk slowly around the lodge...

The process had started. The two groups of men were doing their cleansing meditation in the wilderness, sweating from fire and steam in the dark womb of the lodge, and sweating from drumming in the noonday sun sitting next to the lodge.

I deliberately had everyone remove their watches before we started drumming, so as to keep time by the rhythm of the drums and the thoughts passing through our brains, such as "Why the heck did I decide to do this in the middle of the day? Its hot! My arm hurts from drumming. How long has it been? Who will judge me more if I stop drumming and walk away, my friends or myself?"

Whenever the men in the sweatlodge started to chant to our rhythms, we would get up from the fire and walk slowly around the lodge, playing our drums until they became quiet again.

As we drummers slowly lost ourselves in the rhythms, the rhythms slowly changed and evolved. The thoughts in our heads devolved to silence, and time stopped for us.

Suddenly it was coming to a close. Halfway through the drumming it had seemed that we had been playing for hours. But when the sweatlodge entrance flap flew open and men came crawling out of the sweatlodge womb looking like dirty newborn babies, it seemed that we had just started drumming. We drummers continued to play as the sweatlodge men silently washed and dried themselves off, got dressed, and joined us around the fire. When both groups were all together the drummers played softer and stopped.

There was silence for a long time, and when someone did speak, it was softly. Some of us shared our healing prayers and experiences. Some of us cried and hugged each other. We did things men don't usually do around men, and we felt better for it.

Corporate Groups

Rhythm-based events are used mostly in the corporate environment as team-building tools during management training programs, leadership academies, offsite meetings, and sales conferences. Inside these events, you may be asked to address, in metaphorical terms, such subjects as unity through diversity, organizational change, group vision or

A team-building circle with Pacific Bell

the corporate mission. By its very nature, an interactive rhythm-based event in these type of programs will result in stress reduction and community building amongst the participants.

You will find it very useful to understand the inner workings of the corporate world if you venture into facilitating rhythm-based events in that environment. I personally have had the experience of working as an outreach director for a research and development group that designed health maintenance organizations, as well as teaching a business communications course in that company. I combine my corporate and rhythmical expertise to create programs for specific corporate situations.

Diverse business entities use rhythm-based events. Listed below are the names of a sampling of the companies for which I have created rhythm-based team building programs: Sprint, Silicon Graphics, Australia Telecom, Kinko's, U.S. Dept. of Forestry, Clairol, Smithsonian Magazine, Levi Strauss, Microsoft, Kaiser Permanente, The Wall Street Journal, Canadian Public Works Dept., Motorola, American President's Shipping Line, Bank of America, Malaysian Human Resource Sector, Patagonia, Family Circle Magazine, Toyota, Bristol-Myers Squibb, Bethlehem Steel, U.S. Dept. of Agriculture, N.O.V.A., Canada Defense Department, Sun Microsystems, Pacific Bell Directory, Shell Oil, four Hospital Administrations, three Construction Companies, two Insurance Conglomerates, and an Apple Computer in a pear tree.

> *Sometimes they will list my session as a lecture in team dynamics, and then surprise the participants when they walk into the room, finding no chairs or lecture podium, just drums, percussion toys, and little old me.*

In the more conservative corporate meeting environment, the program planners like to use me as a surprise. Sometimes in the meeting program biography they will list my session as a lecture in team dynamics, and then surprise the participants when they walk into the room, finding no chairs or lecture podium, just drums, percussion toys, and little old me.

After doing more than sixty-five programs for Apple Computer and forty programs for Silicon Graphics, I can no longer surprise those particular corporate populations. There are now weekly lunch-time employee drum circles being held in the courtyard quads at both companies' headquarters, partially as a result of the Village Music Circle programs.

Anticipating the Rhythm of Change

Following is a descriptive write-up for a Fortune 500 company meeting that I facilitated. The write-up was created by two program planners who had hired me regularly for their offsite programs. To surprise the participants, they described in their program what I would do during my presentation, without mentioning drums or percussion. They entitled their program "Anticipating The Rhythm of Change" by Arthur Hull, expert in organizational training and teamwork, from the University of California, Santa Cruz. Their program description follows.

"Readiness counts for little without proper execution, but in large organizations, execution requires coordination and cooperation across disparate parts. This is often fiendishly difficult to obtain. Arthur Hull provides both theory and practice on structuring the work environment in a way that creates greater trust and respect among employees. Much of the session will concentrate on seeing and hearing things differently, paying keen attention, and experiencing what communication is really about. It is a unique demonstration of just how quickly and easily learning can take place when the conditions are made favorable."

"Arthur's unorthodox approach has provided guidance to numerous executives bent on sharpening their ability to coach, align, and execute complex tasks. But this is a topic that resonates with people outside the corporate environment. Spouses and guests are therefore warmly encouraged to attend."

I started the program at a podium in a standard meeting room with a projector next to me and writing boards behind me. After I was introduced, without the mention of drums, I told the participants that I had been brought to the meeting to challenge them in the way they think about a subject about which they already know everything there is to know. I told them that I would present to them the subject in a format that was totally out of their expertise, and most likely out of their lifestyle.

Then I led them out of the room and into the room next door where the drums and percussion toys were waiting. Some of them walked into the room and saw the drums, stopped in their tracks, looked around the room as if maybe they were in the wrong room, folded their arms, puffed up their chests, and started backing up to the wall. Two of the people who walked in and saw the drums, got excited, and walked over and started tapping on the drums, picking out a particular one that they would like to play.

I got the participants to form a circle and started my program by walking out of the circle, then back in, modeling the same body language with which the executives walked into the room. I modeled and demonstrated the guy who saw the drums, thought that he was in the wrong room, then realized the he was in the right room and was going to be expected to drum and reacted by putting up his shields, crossing his arms, and puffing up his chest. Then I demonstrated one of the guys who was now standing in the part of the circle that was closest to the drums. I walked over to the drums and tapped on them, then got back into the circle next to the executive I was modeling. I continued to look back at the drums, just like he had done, making sure the drum I picked was still behind me. We all had a good laugh. The laughter released the tension in the room and helped the executives drop some of their corporate physiology.

This program is not really about drumming. It is about relationship.

I then asked them not to worry because they thought they were rhythmically challenged, because the program would not be a drum class. I told them, "This program is not really about drumming. It is about relationship." With that I started my program.

Small Successes for All of Us

After facilitating many leadership programs, management trainings, offsite team-building, and sales conferences with Motorola, I thought that I had seen most of its corporate culture. Then, a particular Motorola program presented a number of new challenges for me. First, it was not going to be the upper or middle managers with whom I normally work. It was going to be the guys and gals working on the production line at a Motorola plant in Austin, Texas. Secondly, it wasn't an offsite program where the participants in some hotel venue were doing a series of meetings, which would include a team-building program with me. This team-building program was scheduled directly after their work shift, at what they thought was going to be their monthly managers' meeting, just before going home. Surprise! Surprise! Finally, this wasn't going to be a drum circle. The program was held in an auditorium where I would work with three hundred people at a time from the stage. I did all four shifts of the plant in two days, a total of twelve hundred plant employees.

I kept the standard Village Music Circle format, but adapted it to an interactive presentation between me on the stage and the audience.

I started the program with a fun vocal interaction game. Laughter was the best medicine for relieving the initial tension and the resistance that came up in the workers. We kept all of the instruments out of sight, and at each new part of the presentation, my assistants, the managers, would distribute the required percussion toys among the rows of participants. By the end of the programs we were all crowded together on and around the stage with a full complement of drums and percussion, in what I would call a drum donut, rather than a drum circle.

Of every 50 people who participate in a corporate team-building event I usually get one or two people who come to me and tell me a the similar kind of story, "My junior high music teacher verified my belief that I was a rhythm dork, by putting me in the dumb section of the chorus. This experienced erased that." Or "I was taught that women were to be seen and not heard so it was hard for me to hit the drum and make noise, but by the end of the program, I didn't want to stop."

Of every one hundred to two hundred corporate people I work with in these programs, someone will have a powerful personal experience inside the village drum circle event. They come see me after the program wanting to know whether and where there is a teacher in town, what kind of drum should they get, and so on and so forth.

> *Laughter was the best medicine for relieving the initial tension and resistance that came up in the workers.*

By coincidence, during the Motorola event described above, a personal growth program was happening at the hotel where I was staying in Austin. Babatunde Olatunji was one of the presenters in that two-day event. However, it was a problem that to see Baba you had to register for the whole weekend event. HappyShel, a local community facilitator and drum advocate, convinced the personal growth program developers to open Baba Olatunji's part of their program to the public, since it was celebratory in nature. It helped that Happy offered to have extra drums available for the participants from his Drums Not Guns organization.

Because the personal growth program planners opened Baba's event to the public at the end of each of the four teambuilding programs, I announced Baba Olatunji's availability at his workshop happening in town that weekend. At Baba's event I recognized at least ten Motorola employees that had attended my corporate team-building programs. That's par for the course, and gave me a very good feeling inside, that the work that I did in the corporations affected people beyond the corporate walls. I also realized by their comments, that as these Motorola employees drive home from work, crossing over the bridge in downtown Austin, they look down at the thunder drumming circle in the park below the bridge next to the river. Because of their Village Music Circle drumming experience, I believe that they now have a different, and more positive viewpoint of the drumming "hippies" under the bridge.

The Motorola managers liked the results of the program enough that they invited us back a few months later to do another program with twelve hundred of their plant workers.

Conferences

A conference is a gathering of people of like mind and interests. These people are usually gathering together to exchange information on a particular subject, while meeting other people from other parts of the nation and the world. Two uses of rhythm-based events in a conference environment are community building in opening and closing ceremonies, and workshops that deliver appropriate metaphors for that particular population.

> In the playshops I would create interactive rhythm-based exercises ...and let them verbally process their own experiences.

I had facilitated a few opening ceremonies at conferences before I found myself on the cover of *Yoga Journal* in January 1993, but after that particular publication came out, I found myself on the national conference circuit. I did more conferences in that one year than all the ones I had previously done combined. In that year I found myself at national conferences for many groups, including the following: Neuro-Linguistic Programming, Music Therapy, Noetic Science, the Association of Humanistic Psychology, California Peer Counseling, Spirituality in Business, four corporate sales conferences, three National Training Association conferences, two human resources conferences, and a Yoga Journal Conference in a pear tree.

The common element for most of these groups was that I knew almost nothing about them. When the program directors called I just said yes. By immersing myself into these diverse populations, I learned how to deliver interactive rhythmical experiences that had a metaphoric relationship to who they were and why they had gathered together at their particular conferences.

I developed the Rhythmical Alchemy Playshop™ in a workshop format that would accommodate almost anyone's needs. In the playshops I would create interactive rhythm-based exercises, then sit down with the group and let them verbally process their own experiences. Each group had a different perspective into these experiences, and talked about them, using semantics specific to their culture. Most of the time I would instigate the discussions, then sit back and listen. It was in these process discussions that I learned about these specific populations, each of their special languages for communicating, and how I might create more rhythmical exercises to help them continue on their path.

Birthing a Rhythmaculture in Noetic Science

This story describes the evolution of a community that changed from being rhythmical neophytes, to being a rhythmaculture community that uses rhythm and ritual in its gatherings.

This story begins at my first National Noetic Science Conference. Noetic science is the study of the connection between the mind and the body. The Noetic Science conference populations are a mix of scholars, scientists, doctors, healers, and personal growth people. This one was held near Washington, DC. I was scheduled to facilitate an opening night community rhythm celebration after the keynote speaker. I was also scheduled to facilitate a Rhythmical Alchemy Playshop later during the three-day event.

Along with the other presenters, a photograph of me, facilitating a drum circle, was included in the registration packet brochure. Under the picture was information about what a community rhythm circle is and an invitation to the participants to bring drums and percussion toys to the opening night celebration.

When I got to the conference I discovered that many of the people there had not read the brochure, did not know what a rhythm circle is, and did not bring any drums or percussion toys. While I had brought one hundred drums and percussion toys for the playshop scheduled for later during the conference, these instruments would be enough for only a fraction of the population who might attend the opening night ceremonies. Additionally, when I checked my Playshop registration, I found that it was only one-third full.

Luckily for me, I was scheduled to do three guerrilla fillers during opening day of the program, before the evening celebration. A guerrilla filler is a short audience rhythmasizer that I do for five minutes just prior to a scheduled speaker. I facilitate a short, fun audience participation event from the speaker's podium. It entrains and focuses the group and helps them settle down in their seats in preparation for a presentation from the speaker. From my bag of guerrilla filler tricks, I engaged the audience by facilitating interactive vocal games, hand clap parts, or hand movements while they were in their seats. By the end of the three guerrilla fillers that day, I had introduced the majority of the Noetic Science conference population to my facilitation skills and elfish spirit, and had also educated them about what a community rhythm circle celebration is, and how to find or make found sounds from things available in the hotel, so they could participate in the evening celebration.

> *From my bag of guerrilla filler tricks, I engaged the audience by facilitating interactive vocal games, hand clap parts, or hand movements while they were in their seats.*

Before coming to the conference I had contacted some of the community drummers in the area and invited them to come and assist me. I had cautioned them that they would be playing in a community that would be mostly beginning-beginners playing mainly percussion instruments, and that I would be using the community players as shills in the audience to help keep the groove locked together. I knew that Sule Greg Wilson lived in the area, so I invited him to the event.

Sule Greg Wilson is the drummer, historian and author of the book *The Drummer's Path— Moving the Spirit with Ritual and Traditional Drumming.* He is a traditionalist, whose focus is culturally specific. An important message of his book is the importance of respect for and acknowledgment of the African cultures and traditions that are the foundations for the birth of rhythmaculture in North America today.

That night at the first Noetic Science Community Drum Circle, Sule walked into a ballroom full of people representing nearly every culture on the planet, playing a non-culturally specific rhythm jam, on every type of found-sound object the group could scavenge from their rooms at the hotel. The ensemble included a few drums, percussion toys, lots of upside-down plastic trash cans, coke cans with hotel ashtray rocks in them, a pair of metal shoe horns, a brief case, a half-filled carton of chocolate malted-milk balls, two sandals slapped together, coffee cups, and spoons, etc. Sule brought to the circle his *djembe* and a *djun-djun*. He had a choice to make—to play either on top of the percussion groove with his high pitched *djembe*, or else to help solidify the groove by playing the double-headed *djun-djun* drum with a stick. He pulled out his *djun-djun* and played support grooves all night long. With the help of Sule and the Washington drumming community, the opening rhythm circle was a rousing success. As a result, my Rhythmical Alchemy Playshop, scheduled for the next day, was full.

Showcasing found sounds

I was invited to the next two annual National Noetic Science Conferences held first in Chicago, Illinois, and then in San Diego, California. There were people at these conferences who had been exposed to my drum circles at a previous conference. Some of them had returned home and gotten involved with their local drumming community, expressing themselves and bonding with and healing each other through rhythm.

...upside-down plastic trash cans, coke cans with hotel ashtray rocks in them, a pair of metal shoe horns, a brief case, two sandals slapped together, coffee cups, and spoons...

The conference programmers added multiple rhythmical alchemy playshops to their programs as I integrated rhythmaculture into their community. Many more people showed up at each successive conference with drums and percussion, prepared for the opening night community rhythm celebration. As the community became more rhythmasized, the celebrations became more powerful expressions of its collective spirit.

At the end of my third Noetic Science conference, the conference programmers asked me what could we do next year to top it. My answer was to bring Babatunde Olatunji to the next conference as keynote speaker. So that is what they did.

A conference event is typically closed to the public except for registrants who pay for the whole event. Sometimes you cannot attend a conference unless you are a certified member of the organization. I get around this by arranging with the conference planners beforehand, to allow a group of community percussionists to come to the conference and participate in the opening rhythm ceremonies as assistants. I deliberately leave open the number of assistants allowed to participate, so that I can accommodate the number of local community drummers that choose to join the celebration.

My fourth National Noetic Science conference was being held at the Boca Raton Resort near Miami, Florida. As with many of my conference programs, I let the local drumming network know about the opportunity to play in a community-building drumming ceremony for a specific population. This time it was a chance to play with Babatunde Olatunji, as well.

I have followed Babatunde Olatunji around for years as his student, recording with him, supporting him in keynote presentations, and performing with various versions of his Drums of Passion band. Until this conference, though, Baba had not had seen me in my element. I was looking forward to showing Baba how I had developed what he had taught me. When I got to the conference they also told me that I was to introduce him to the conference at his keynote address. I was thrilled. This was an opportunity to publicly thank and acknowledge Baba for his mission as I introduced him to the four-year-old Noetic Science rhythmaculture community that I had helped build.

Baba's mission takes us beyond the rhythms, dances, and songs of Africa, to their ability to bring communities together to express the joy of life and love.

The population of the Noetic Science conferences had increasingly grown over the past four years and I found myself at the podium facing two thousand people at the opening ceremonies. After Baba's keynote address I was scheduled to lead the participants in a musical conga line from the auditorium to the ballroom on the other side of the conference complex where Florida drumming community members were already warming up the circle.

I introduced Baba. "It is a privilege to introduce Babatunde Olatunji. This man influenced me many years before I met him. Once I did meet him, he slapped me around, straightened me up, and set me on his path. His heart is full of his message, his spirit, and his mission. He has been on his mission since he came to the United States to become a diplomat for his country, Nigeria, Africa. He has become a world-recognized ambassador for the spirit of Africa, and all its cultures. His mission takes us beyond the rhythms, dances, and songs of Africa, to their ability to bring communities together to express the joy of life and love. It is a pleasure to introduce Babatunde Olatunji to you, because as soon as I've finished introducing him, I will be able to play with him."

Rhythms and transitions flowed effortlessly, like a boat sailing down a fast river.

When Baba gives a keynote address he holds Rhythm Church. He talked from behind his drums in the windows of communication between musical demonstrations that we did for the audience. Toward the end of his presentation he got the audience vocally involved.

The audience was full of people who had brought their drums and percussion instruments, prepared for the conga line percussion parade to the drum circle celebration. His audience vocal participation piece turned into a audience drum piece with a song.

At the conclusion of Baba's keynote we started a solid groove. While Baba took a break, I led his rhythm congregation, marching through the convention site to the big open ballroom to join the Florida drumming community that was already in full groove. As we walked into the ballroom we meshed our marching groove with the Florida community groove to start the celebration circle.

This was the Noetic Science community's fourth rhythm circle with me as facilitator. They could read and follow my kinesthetic language as well as I could read where they wanted to go with their music. The finger dance had been well established between us as we played. Rhythms and transitions flowed effortlessly, like a boat sailing down a fast river.

Halfway through our rhythm circle celebration, Baba appeared at the edge of the circle. While playing in full groove, we opened a path for Baba, leading from the outside of the circle to the center so that Babatunde Olatunji and his entourage could make a royal entrance. He took his sweet time getting to the center of the circle, slowly building the excitement. When he reached the center, we brought the Baba entrance rhythm piece to a closing rumble.

Baba addressed the congregation with metaphors focusing on community and love. "Love is a lifetime process," said Baba.

Baba addressed the congregation with metaphors connected to his keynote presentation, focusing on community and love. "Love is a lifetime process," said Baba. He kept his windows of communication short, between the rhythm pieces. He facilitated three rhythmical pieces, which included calls and responses, vocal chants, and showcases of the best dancers. As the pieces progressed, Baba modulated the circle upward in volume as well as with technical and emotional dynamics. We closed the evening by co-facilitating the Noetic Science drummers into the heartbeat rhythm where the silence between the notes is just as important as the notes themselves. Babatunde Olatunji masterfully facilitated the circle's music into magic.

I sit at the feet of the master.

Music Therapy and the Well Elderly

Drumming is an invigorating aerobic exercise. It heightens the physical senses while at the same time it awakens the sleeping spirit of any person of any age.

The American Music Therapy Association is a well-organized and recognized group of therapists who have been using music as therapy in conjunction with other American

Drumming at the American Music Therapy Association Conference

Medical Association sanctioned healing practices. In the last five years they have begun to integrate rhythm therapy into their music therapy.

The American Music Therapy Association, through their Rhythm for Life project, studied the positive effects of rhythmic drumming exercises with Alzheimer's disease patients. They obtained some interesting and positive results. They are actively involved in using rhythm-based events with what I call the well-elderly population.

I have worked with groups of well-elderly adults, and have seen in just one session a marked improvement in their attention spans, emotional states, and their energy levels.

Barbara Reuer and Barbara Crowe, two well-known and respected music therapists in the U.S., have written what I feel is a very useful and informative manual entitled *Best Practices in Music Therapy*. It utilizes group percussion with strategies for promoting volunteerism in the well older-adult population. The manual is available through the American Music Therapy Association in Washington DC.

For information on drumming with the well-older-adult population and Rhythm for Life, contact the American Music Therapy Association. Contact information is available in this book in the Resources List, with both a phone number and an email address provided in Internet Resources.

Career Considerations

As you can see from the general listing of the specific populations above, there are endless possibilities for the uses of the technology in this book. I know many people who have created inspiring careers serving these special populations. All these people have something in common. They were performing their rhythmical services for their community long before those services turned into careers. They were following their bliss.

If you are just starting out, my advice to you is to think of what you are doing as community service rather than as career development. If you start by following your bliss instead of your career goals, then eventually, as you serve it, your bliss will start serving you.

If you put career goals on top of your list of priorities as reasons to facilitate, then you might also create a filter over your vision that makes you see the growing community of facilitators as competition for market share. They are really just a community of facilitators.

This point of view is sometimes called scarcity consciousness. It can only make your work harder and your successes less fulfilling. If you are in scarcity consciousness, you might also see your own unique service and gift to the community as a franchise to be protected by putting up walls of limitations that eventually limit only yourself. Keep franchise and scarcity consciousness low on your priority list. Although in this day and age it is common sense to trademark your organizational identity, just remember that you can't trademark the spirit that your service gives. You either use it or lose it.

Here are some criteria for deciding if you want to facilitate rhythm-based events as a career move:

- Am I already doing this on some level?
- Would it be an extension of following my bliss?
- Would I do this if I didn't get paid?
- Is there a compass in my life directing me down this path?

A community of drum circle facilitators at the Percussion Arts International Conference

	Kim Atkinson	Christine K. Stevens	
Paulo Mattioli	Keio Ogawa	Kalani	Sule Greg Wilson
Randy Crafton	Arthur Hull		

*Is the quality and quantity
of the spirit that you give out
the quality and quantity
of the spirit you get back?
YES!*

Babatunde Olatunji addressing the 1997 Facilitator's Playshop in Hawaii

"Whether you realize it or not, we are engaging in a cultural revolution. We are doing what our political counterparts are not. We are bringing all people together. We are bringing people from all levels of life, understanding, and background together. That's the wonderful thing about drumming."
—Babatunde Olatunji

The Mission

If you have gotten this far into the book, have completed the exercises and played the drum circle games, then you obviously have done so with a focused intention and an idea of why you are working with this book. This means that you probably know what you are going to do with the knowledge that you are gleaning from the experiences we are creating together. It tells me that, driving that focused determination, is a personal mission or intent of which you may or may not be aware.

Babatunde Olatunji blessed our 1997 Facilitator's Playshop by flying to Oahu, Hawaii from New York at his own expense. He hung out with us for the last two days of the program, and was our special guest at the closing inter-island drum circle at the Waikiki Beach Band Shell. Although I felt honored by Baba coming to my Facilitators' Playshop program, I knew he was there to juice, inspire, and bless the next generation of facilitators attending the program. At our evening welcoming celebration for him, one of the first things Baba said to us was, "Whether you realize it or not, we are engaging in a cultural revolution. We are doing what our political counterparts are not. We are bringing all people together. We are bringing people from all levels of life, understanding, and background together. That's the wonderful thing about drumming."

Since the ultimate goal of facilitation is rhythmical service to a population, there is an implication that behind the action of facilitation, there is a focused intent and purpose. Examining and becoming more aware of that intent will give you a strong foundation on which to build your skills. It will also help you solidify your goals as you go further down your path.

Answering the three universal questions in relationship to your facilitation goals can help you solidify and clarify your intent.

- Who are you?

- Why are you here?

- Where are you going?

Here is my personal example.

Who am I?
Besides being a father, husband, community member, musician, and teacher, I find at the core of my being a rhythmatist that sees, hears, feels, and relates to the rhythms that permeate the world around me.

Why am I here?
To follow my rhythmical bliss and share it with others by facilitating human potential through rhythm dynamics.

Where am I going?
Based on the evolutionary development and growth of rhythmaculture in North America, I think Babatunde Olatunji's vision of a drum in every home will come true early in the next century. In my quest to help make this happen, my path has changed and adapted itself to meet the needs of this ever-growing and maturing rhythmical community. From student and performer, to instrument maker, teacher and facilitator, I believe my next role in this community is to mature into a mentor to the people who will take our growing rhythmaculture to its next step.

At each Facilitator's Playshop intensive, I ask the participants to take some personal time to think about these three universal questions in relationship to what they want to do with the information they glean from their experience with me. Who are you? Why are you here? Where are you going? Then they write a one-page mission statement, and bring it to a group discussion. Here are excerpts of some of those mission statements:

- **To promote intercultural dialogue**, rapport, acceptance and understanding by bringing the drum to all the people easily and effortlessly.

- **To nurture a new American tradition of drumming** for the common people, with respect and dignity, and in a way that allows people to continue on their own after I leave.

- **To help grow a community of rhythmically-enabled people** across the country and beyond, that come together from time to time to re-create an environment where people work together to create love, joy, understanding, tolerance, and confidence in humanity's ability to live in harmony.

- **To empower people to create community for healing and fun**, while helping people realize themselves, while breaking down barriers...in the process of creating rhythmaculture.

- **To filter and balance all involvement through the heart.** To do what I love, and love what I do.

The mission statement that Sule Greg Wilson handed in at the Facilitators' Playshop he attended is as clear and concise as he is. With his permission I reproduce it here in full.

My Mission
by Sule Greg C. Wilson

My mission is to bring awareness of Spirit to people.
To do that, I drum, dance and sing and
Speak to people in groups, schools, audiences and one-on-one.
My mission is to bring comfort of Self to people.
To do that, I listen, teach, show.
I teach because that is my road.
My mission is to impart unto people a sensitivity of rhythm, of
People, of their own bodies, their times, their history.
My mission is to clear myself of crap that I may be a clear vessel,
and parent to be listened to, or followed.
My mission is to gain insight—the tools and techniques;
To pass awareness, sensitivity and hope to people.
With confidence and awareness of a greater
World, people grow and make a
Better Self and a
Better World.
For Us All. Ashé.

Sule Greg Wilson

Village Music Circles Mission Statement

The company, Village Music Circles™, sends out instruments and facilitators to use the village music concept as a tool for unity in schools, corporations, conferences, and communities. Like any company, Village Music Circles has a mission statement. Here it is:

> "Village Music Circles is committed to the role of rhythmical evangelism. Rhythm is a universal language that cuts across all cultural and social barriers. It permeates all aspects of our lives. When a group of people who are of common mind and purpose come together and harmonize with each other through song, music, and percussion, they create a synergized force that solidifies group vision and purpose. Village Music Circles is dedicated to making this happen, by using drumming as a tool to create unity."

Don Davidson, one of our Village Music Circles associates, submitted the following mission statement.

Statement of Mission
by Don Davidson

My mission is living a passionate commitment to bridging diversity though drumming, whether it be the separate voices of a polyrhythm, parts of a person, elements of a community, or cultures around the world. I seek to convey the joy of joining the left hand with the right, the head with the heart in the music I play, in the students I teach, and in the method of empowering groups to learn as one. I work to impart the values of humility, respect, and collective creativity in honor of my family, and in honor of the grace and wisdom of my teachers. My hope is to spread that wisdom of communal forms risen from Africa to generatively influence how all people live on the earth, and how we treat each other. And I want to impart the language of rhythm so I have many more friends to play with.

Community, Fun, Spirit, and a Better World

My mission as a community drum circle facilitator is to create the sensibility of a community experience in a drumming circle. It's as simple as that. My personal golden rule is to create fun, of course, with a minimal amount of anxiety for the advanced player and beginning-beginner drummers alike, and the maximum amount of pleasure and community spirit for all.

> *My deeper mission is to help people get in touch with their own rhythmical sensibilities and spirit.*

My goal as facilitator in a rhythmical event is to guide the group to a place where everyone who's playing, no matter what level of musical or drumming experience they have, meets at the same time and place inside the drum circle rhythm they are playing. My intent is to facilitate rhythmical spirit within the group in such a way that all levels of rhythmical expertise can be accommodated at the same time. The people may not be much better drummers after the rhythmical event, but they will be better drum circle players.

One of my objectives, in a rhythmical event, is to make myself obsolete as a facilitator by guiding the people in the circle to a place where they won't need to be facilitated to play together. That's what I call leading the people to lead themselves.

> *When people get in touch with the rhythms that permeate their everyday existence, it positively changes their overall experience of life.*

While the circle is facilitating its own musical and technical expertise, my end goal is to facilitate the spirit the circle hands me through its music. Doing so will allow me to play music with a fully-functioning rhythmical community!

My deeper mission is to help people get in touch with their own rhythmical sensibilities and spirit. When people get in touch with the rhythms that permeate their everyday existence, it positively changes their overall experience of life. That makes a better world for all of us.

Circuitry Exercise: Three Questions, One Answer

Sit in a quiet place and take some personal time to think about these three universal questions in relationship to what you want to do with the information you have gleaned from this book. Who are you? Why are you here? Where are you going? Answer the questions for yourself and then write a one-page mission statement. Bring it to your facilitators' study group for discussion.

Tools and Techniques
of Facilitators

The following chapters contain information that can help you develop the specific technical skills that are useful for facilitating rhythm-based events...and of course there are more Arthurian stories!

Body Language and Dynamics

You can learn to use body language to communicate to your rhythm circle, conveying specific information with your body dynamics. Establish your body and vocal language styles early in the facilitation of your circle. This body-language communication is essential inside the circle, because during much of the event time everyone will be drumming and unable to hear your vocal commands.

Develop very simple, succinct physical body-language signals that are easily readable from a distance. Then be consistent with these signals throughout this event with this group. Avoid changing them, to avoid confusing the circle.

Hand and arm gestures need to be succinct, specific, and a little larger than normal. Make the moves from the bottom of your feet and the base of your spine, instead of from your upper chest. Making moves from your upper chest portrays a physically ungrounded state that is a part of body language that gets communicated to the circle. It is better to communicate to the circle with your feet firmly planted, and your knees bent slightly. When your signals come from the base of your spine, even the large hand signals, your communication is grounded and conveys your authority. To ground myself before starting a drum circle I sometimes do a little Tai Chi or stretching.

I describe specific body language for each facilitators' orchestrational tool in Chapter 12.

How Do You Say "BeeDeep" in Japanese?

A growing company, in Silicon Valley, California, has worked with Village Music Circles regularly. They were also working with a Japanese company that makes a particular dinkle-dork component that fits inside their product. They purchased and absorbed that small Japanese company into their own, and flew all of its upper and middle managers from Japan to California to spend three days learning how this American company gets managed. Part of the program was a team building event with me.

This company rented part of a private park near their headquarters for the Village Music Circle's team-building exercise, and then had a barbecue afterward for the participants. They bussed people from the company to the park, and I waited for them, all set up for the program. I greeted them as they got off the bus and we started the program.

When the bus arrived for this program the director ran up to me and explained that, after the Japanese executives arrived, the company discovered that only 3 of the 30 people spoke fluent English. While a few more could understand a little English if I spoke slowly enough, the majority of the group would not catch any verbal input that I might have. That being the case, she gave me these options:

- Pack up and leave them to have their barbecue and receive full pay.
- Create a fun event with the group without doing the standard team-building format and without metaphor focus.
- Attempt to do the program as planned and experiment with what happens.

I chose the third option and proceeded to run the program pretty much as I would do with English-speaking people. I used the Japanese translator at the beginning, in the middle, and at the end of the program to apply the team-building metaphors to their drumming experience. The rest of the program was all body language and sounds. I chose to not speak a word of English during the program, and only used Arthurian verbal gibberish and street mime body language to direct the group. The sounds I used were in direct relationship to the moves and directions I was giving the group but had absolutely no cognitive context. I would entice one side of the circle to say "Bee-dee-be-deep" in unison, singing to the other side of the circle, who I enticed to respond with "Honk Honk Honk" sounds, in such a way that the two sides were dialoguing in rhythmical patterns: "Bee-dee-be-deep," Honk Honk Honk." Once we had created that small success, I added more sounds into the group song until we had a four-part interlocking song. After they got their vocal song connected, I passed out percussion instruments that represented the particular sounds they were singing. They translated their four-part song onto percussion instruments.

> *I chose to not speak a word of English during the program, and only used Arthurian verbal gibberish and street mime body language to direct the group.*

I proceeded to run the standard team-building format, with the same amount of success as if they all spoke fluent English, directing them with cognitive words. It was such a success that half of the group stayed after the team-building program and jammed out with the drums during the barbecue.

During the barbecue, one of the English-speaking Japanese executives came up to me and said, "We have just finished having a conversation with each other and I have been sent to ask you a question. We have decided that the language you were speaking to us was Portuguese. Is that correct?"

Vocal Calls

Sometimes during a window of communication, or when there is a lull in the proceedings, the group loses its focus. Private conversations and mini-rhythm jams start amongst the participants.

When you are ready to facilitate the next piece, and need to get the group's attention to re-focus the circle back to the event, a simple non-verbal vocal call such as EeeeAuahEeee!!!! to the group will start the re-focusing process. Some, but not all, participants will respond to your call by calling back to you. EeeeAuahEeee!!!! This alerts

Give me your voices.

other unfocused participants that there is a group event happening that they can join. With each vocal call that you make to the group, more and more people respond until the whole group is responding to your call as one body.

When that happens it is time to start the next part of the event. Sometimes it takes only one call and response, sometimes many. It depends on your relationship with the group and how unfocused the group is when you start the call. "EeeeAuahEeee"!!!! is just an example. Have fun making up your own.

In a kids' circle the call "sticks up" works well. When the kids hear that call they hold their sticks or hands up in the air until everybody's hands are up and the whole group is paying attention.

When the kids are holding their sticks up in the air, they cannot hit their instruments. The "EeeeAuahEeee ," call works well in a kids' group, and is more fun than "sticks up." The only problem is that sometimes the kids have too much fun with it.

The Physical Circle

If a rhythm circle is made up of points (meaning people), equidistant from the center of the circle, then it is the facilitator's responsibility to ensure that everyone is sitting or standing in the circle so that they can see and hear each other equally.

I have seen many circles come together spontaneously, with no one taking responsibility for its actual physical formation, so instead of a circle it becomes amoeba-shaped, and the quality of the sound and playing suffer because of it. The physical form of the circle itself is the responsibility of the facilitator.

A circle of people is a physical representation of the kind of energy that you as a facilitator want to create. Each person has an equal place in the circle and can see and be seen by everybody, can hear and be heard by everybody, and has an equal opportunity to participate in the celebration, and to contribute to the music.

In larger circles there are ways to formulate the physical structure of the circle so that you can compact a group of people into concentric rings that are at different levels, seated on the ground, seated in chairs, and standing, so that you can bring the people closer together, while they can still see and hear clearly. I call this type of circle formation a "sound bowl."

Creating a Sound Bowl

A sound bowl is a layering of players, at different height levels, as they are placed further away from the center of the circle. In a large circle, placing all the players shoulder to shoulder will spread them too far across the circle from each other to play effectively with the other side of the circle. Creating a sound bowl of people will solve the problem.

Here is how to do it. First, invite the kids and people with percussion to sit on the floor with the *djun-djun* players in the middle of the circle. Then, arrange chairs for the conga players, and other "chair people" leaving some open spaces in the circle for people to go in and out of the center of the circle. Finally, encourage the standing players: people with congas in stands or strapped-on *djembes* and *ashikos* to distribute themselves equally around the outside of the chair circle. This creates an acoustically-functional sound bowl which is capable of accommodating hundreds of people.

Sound bowls are great for kids' groups, no matter how big or small the group, because of their kinesthetic properties. It is easier for the kids to feel the rhythm through the excitement of drum playing than it is for them to hear it.

Kids' sound bowl

A Lesson Learned

I facilitated a rhythm festival at the Omega Institute in upstate New York, along with several wonderful musicians. We had a large variety of different drummers and participants in this program showing up from all over the east coast, and we planned a large closing drum circle celebration at the end of the three-day program. All of the teachers co-facilitated the circle, but no one took responsibility for forming the shape of the physical circle as the participants entered.

As the participants came into the large main building at the Omega Institute, they created their own drum circle with people sitting in chairs shoulder to shoulder to each other all the way around the edge of this ballroom. This left an enormous space in the middle from one side of the circle to the other. The sound connection, let alone the visual connection, was lost because of the distance between players. To compound the sound logistic, all the players of double-headed bass drums, mostly *djun-djuns*, set themselves on one side of the circle, thus attracting all the loud *djembes* to that side of the circle like bees to honey.

The rhythms would not stay solid and locked no matter which facilitator was facilitating the circle. People were so far apart from each other that it took time for the sound of the drums to travel across the circle. Everyone was constantly going out of time. That event truly took all of our facilitators' skills to generate a successful rhythmical event, and it taught us all a lesson.

That circle taught me an important thing about rhythm circle logistics. If all the *djun-djuns* are on one side of the circle, then all the *djembe* drummers will gravitate to those *djun-djuns*, as if they are playing in a traditional West African style dance class formation. That means that the loudest drums, the *djembes* and the big bottom drums, are all concentrated in one segment of the circle. That makes the volume of the circle heavy on one side as the rhythm spins. As a solution, you can place *djun-djuns* and bass drums equidistant from each other in a smaller circle in the middle of your big circle. If it is a small circle, place them equally throughout the circle.

I created a sound bowl at the last drum circle at the end of Seattle, Washington's World Rhythm Festival. I put a thousand people in a circle with an outside edge about the same size as the circumference of the circle created by the 300 people at the Omega Institute. Facilitating the 1,000 drummers who were snuggled in a 10-layer sound bowl donut was much easier than trying to facilitate 300 people in a cosmic Saturn ring. Moral of the story: take responsibility for your circle logistics or you will make a lot of work for yourself later during the event.

Drum Call

A "drum call" punctuates the beginning of any rhythm circle. It is the opening of the event, the forming of the relationship between the circle and the facilitator, defining the beginning relationship between the circle and all the parts of itself. The quality of the music produced by that circle will be less dependent on its musical expertise than on its relationship with itself and the facilitator.

Listen.

A drum call warms up the circle, giving you, as the facilitator, an overview of the circle's dynamics, power, and emotional dimension. It gives you an opportunity to assess the circle's ability to play with itself and respond to directions.

Because you have a walk-in population in a community drum circle, you must be flexible as you develop your circle. The drum call helps give you that flexibility as people begin to arrive.

You can use the single pulse as the drum call groove. Using this pulse in your drum call creates an easily-identifiable rhythmical foundation for the beginning player to find if they get lost in the group groove. The pulse leaves enough room for lots of experimentation and interpretation.

You, as facilitator, are responsible for the circle's physical arrangement. You can easily direct that aspect of the circle as the people begin to arrive and the circle begins to form. This physical formation of the circle can help or hinder the circle's relationship with itself, as I explained in The Physical Circle above.

Using a drum call, you as facilitator begin establishing rapport with the group, welcoming and relating with individuals as they enter the circle. By doing this, you begin the ongoing process of reading the circle and its potential, so you can better serve the group's needs.

A drum call is the place to begin to teach the circle the vocabulary of the body language that you will use to orchestrate the music. Your clear, precise, consistent use of body language will begin to build the circle's trust in you.

A drum call is a natural phenomenon, in established drum communities like Santa Cruz, Dallas, Seattle, Salt Lake City, Atlanta, etc. People come together to be part of a community drumming circle, and they just start playing and listening to each other. A drum call usually happens as the first few participants begin to gather and drum with each other while waiting for the rest of the group to arrive. Rarely will a group just come in and sit in front of their instruments waiting for the facilitator to tell them to start.

Sometimes a group of friends on one side of the circle will play and another group will play on the other side, starting something a little different. If the two groups are not quite in touch with each other, the rhythm or the pulse being played in the circle may falter or be mushy.

As the facilitator, you go into the center of the circle and get their attention with your body and instrument and give a physical pulse that the whole group can use as a rhythmical lock. Look at one side of the circle and pull on or point to your ear while pointing to the other side of the circle. Then use the same body language on the other side of the circle. When the circle gets in the groove, you can walk out of the circle to attend to your other drum call duties.

Within less than two minutes inside the circle, and without saying a word, you have just introduced yourself as their facilitator, educated them to expect body language as a means of facilitation, adjusted their pulse, and told them all to listen to each other. You have empowered them to take some responsibility for keeping the music going because you left the middle of the circle. This lets them know that you won't always be facilitating in the center of the circle.

Hopefully, by the time you get their groove solid, you will have at least one *djun-djun* player in the circle who will be your pulse keeper. That will give you time to greet people as they come in, and time to adjust the physical circle. As you welcome additional *djun-djun* players, guide them to the center of the circle and convey to them their responsibility to develop an intimate relationship with each other. They become the heartbeat foundation for the whole circle. You can give extra percussion toys and drums to people and children who come in empty-handed. You might admire someone's homemade percussion toy or drum, or you might help someone tune their drum, etc.

An important part of being a facilitator in a community drum setting, especially if you are coming in from out of town, is setting up your relationship with the community before you even start facilitating. The more one-on-one relationships you can get with the people that walk in, the more you can create rapport with the whole body of the community.

During "drum call" you organize the circle, help them establish a pulse groove, welcome them *and* all this time you have on your drum circle radar. You attune your hearing to the drum groove of the circle. Occasionally, you will hear and feel the groove start to wobble, as if the spin of the rhythm plate is heavy on one side, so you come into the center of the circle and make an adjustment. You get their attention, and lock in the pulse with your body language, reestablishing yourself as facilitator. They are already starting to understand the vocabulary of your body language. Once you get the pulse going, you leave the center of the circle. You can continue your facilitator's welcoming process until the majority of the drum community has arrived, personally empowering the circle of participants to make their own music in the drum call. They don't need you in the circle constantly facilitating them. Leaving the center gives you more facilitating room to do fun things with them later. Let "drum call" last until the full body of the community has arrived, and you are ready to bring the groove to a close and welcome them to their community drum circle.

> *The group is now in a circle, warmed up musically, educated about your body-language style, and in rapport with you and each other.*

When you complete the process described above, you will have completed the first musical piece, which I call drum call. You have created mutually-supportive communication dynamics between you and the community and facilitated its first groove without saying a word.

The group is now in a circle, warmed up musically, educated about your body-language style, and in rapport with you and each other. You educated them without stopping their music and talking to them about the body language that you are using to give them orchestrational directions. They can understand your body-language communication because you showed them your basic body vocabulary, simply, clearly, and concisely throughout the drum call. You can now build and expand this vocabulary as the drum circle continues.

The Orchestration Point

The orchestration point is the center of the vortex. It is an important facilitation technique to know how to use this vortex, the middle of your circle, as a place to give directions and receive information.

You can physically mark the center of the circle for a group by only giving vocal and body commands from that place. When you walk into the middle of the circle, and direct the group from that spot, you establish a point of power for communication and direction. If you want to give communication directions with body language, first go to that established place in the circle. If you want to move around in the circle while orchestrating, go first to the orchestration point and then initiate body communication. Then, when you have the attention of the group, you can begin to move about the circle.

As you step into the orchestration point, the circle knows you are going to do something that communicates directions to them. Stay away from that point unless you are addressing the whole community. Avoid walking to the orchestrational point when you have nothing to communicate, because in doing so you create ambiguity in your relationship with the circle. Consistency in action and physical vocabulary is an important aspect of creating trust and rapport with the people with whom you are working. When the orchestration point has been established and you walk up to it, you are literally stepping on a button that communicates to the group "Okay, I'm about to facilitate a new action or element into this composition."

The orchestration point is the center of the vortex.

Every time you use the orchestration point properly, it adds power to that spot. By the end of a drum circle event, just by walking toward that spot, you will have the complete attention of the whole circle.

When you use a riser, or a small stage, in a large circle, that becomes your orchestrational spot. Go away from your orchestrational point while working with individuals or parts of the circle, so that when you do return, that action becomes a sign that you are about to give vocal directions or body commands to the circle.

The center of the circle is a major power point. Use it judiciously and with great respect. If you find yourself confused, and need to stop and think about what to do next, do your thinking off to the side of the circle. The group is now attuned to your body language to a high degree. If you walk out onto the orchestration point with confusion or an attitude, that is what you will get back. The circle, while following your directions, is also molding your energy, so be aware of what type of energy you provide. Project confidence, joy, and enthusiasm.

Entering and Leaving the Circle

If the circle is grooving along just fine and you don't need to give them any directions, then get out of their way. Stepping out of the middle of the circle empowers the circle to enjoy their groove and realize their own successes.

Use the orchestrational point to denote action. When you stand there, the circle assumes that you are going to give an orchestrational direction that will add to what is already happening in the music, or that you are going to change the groove altogether. When the circle sees you standing on that spot, their attention and focus is directed toward you at an intense level, as they are anticipating a change. This heightened level of attention cannot be maintained for very long, so as a facilitator, you need to step on the spot, give your directions and get off the spot and out of their way. Be careful not to

abuse the control and power given to you by the circle, by overusing the orchestrational point. When that happens, the feedback you will get from your circle will be facilitator burnout. If overused, the orchestrational point will lose its power to command attention, and the circle's response to your facilitation commands will be sloppy, as not everybody will be paying attention.

Know when to get out of the way of the group's learning process. Empower the circle to take responsibility for the groove simply by stepping off the orchestrational point, and even leaving the circle, while being ready to jump in and help when needed. When you use the orchestrational point sparingly, the group will give you

Know when to facilitate and when to play.

more focus and attention when you do use it. This gives you time to work with individual people, or time to take a breath and listen to what needs to happen next. Sometimes what needs to happen next is nothing. If so, then get out of the way and let what's already happening continue. If nothing "needs" to happen and you still want to "do" something, then find a place in the circle, sit down and play with the group, until it is time to be a facilitator again.

Sometimes, you as facilitator can give yourself facilitator burnout. The cure is to ensure that the circle has good momentum in its groove, then get out of the middle of the circle, put your radar and facilitator's circuitry on hold, and breathe.

Planning Windows of Vocal Communication

Windows of vocal communication are more than just a place to talk to the participants of a program. They are an opportunity to use metaphor to communicate ideas as well as provide practical instructions. Whether the event is for well elderly, kids at risk, executives, or an open community, the message of the event is delivered in the same two ways, hopefully in balanced proportions to each other. The experiences created by the participants in the musical portion of event, directed by the facilitator, hopefully uses three-fourths or more of the event time. The information delivered in the windows of vocal communication by the facilitator, hopefully uses less than one forth of the event time.

What you do inside a single window of vocal communication is determined by where this window is relative to the total event. To determine how to deliver your message over the whole event you need to know how many rhythmical pieces you want to facilitate during the event, and then count the number of windows of vocal communication between pieces. Then, add two more windows, one for the opening address and one for the closing address.

Jim Greiner

I've watched my friend and fellow facilitator Jim Greiner do a two-hour drum circle with only three windows of communication—an opening address, a window of vocal communication in the middle of the program, and a closing address. That means he facilitated two musical pieces, each one ongoing for about an hour, using the transition points in those pieces to change volume dynamics and tempos, without bringing the piece to a close. Jim says, "The longer we stay on a pattern the deeper we get into the rhythm, our instrument, and ourselves."

Determine how to weave your message smoothly throughout the program, using the total number of windows of communication. An example program format may have the following windows of communication: opening, groove, window, groove, window, groove, window, groove, closing. Remember that in each window, besides delivering a part of your message, you will also want to close the last piece, and set up the next one. The windows of communication will help you as you plan a good event format using your focused intention.

Warning—a rhythm circle in full groove is a living breathing animal with a mind and an intent of its own. It is important to be in alignment with your circle's energy and state of being. Then the event will unfold mostly, but never quite exactly the way you planned it. It is the surprises in a rhythm circle that make it a fun adventure for you as well as your circle of players.

Creating Small Successes

The idea of creating small successes is a powerful teaching and facilitation technique. When utilized properly in a rhythm-based event, small successes set up a rhythmical foundation in each participant that encourages and empowers them to go out into the world and express themselves rhythmically, with less inhibitions.

It is important to consider how much information you present at an event. Otherwise, you may overwhelm the participants with more information than they can handle, putting them in student crisis mode. Putting a beginning-beginner drummer, or someone who is drumming for the very first time in student crisis mode when they attend what is supposed to be an entry-level rhythm expression event can reinforce in some of them the belief that they really are rhythm dorks. This can discourage them from trying to express themselves rhythmically again. As a rhythmical evangelist, the thought of discouraging a person from trying to express themselves rhythmically, during an event that was advertised to do just the opposite, is rhythm church heresy.

Accessibility is the key in community-based rhythm events. Giving accessible tasks in baby steps that create small rhythmical successes, and then compounding them into larger rhythmical successes, is the key to convincing a rhythm dork that there is no such thing as a rhythm dork.

Pacing and Leading

"Pacing and leading" is a technique used by facilitators when they are reading that their group is at a transition point or a completion point within the process.

I use the word pacing to mean matching your energy to the energy of the group—matching your rhythm and dynamics (volume, speed, emotion, etc.) to the rhythm and dynamics of the group. Then, you can lead the group from where you matched them to another tempo, dynamic, or groove. You lead them through a transition to somewhere else.

As facilitator you can see, hear, and feel when this point in the group process happens. It appears many times during a drum circle and is a fulcrum or leverage point where the ongoing drum circle can be guided by you using the technique of pacing and leading.

If you stand in front of a herd of buffalo and point in the direction that you want them to turn, you will get trampled. Instead, you ride alongside the herd, pacing their speed and direction, and then gently nudge them in the direction you want them to go. In a drum circle event, when you want them to stop, instead of standing in the middle of the circle and holding up your hands, causing a train wreck, you pace the circle, and then sometimes even lead them to go a little bit faster, so that you get everyone's attention before taking them to a finish.

Avoiding A Stampede

This story unfolds on a Saturday summer morning in a park in Salt Lake City, Utah. The public-sponsored radio station, KRCL was having its annual KRCL Day In the Park festivities. It was my first time back in Salt Lake City since I was a young boy growing up only thirty miles away. The drum circle was going to be the opening celebration to start off the day. I had been brought in by Jeff Salt, a percussion shop owner who is a drumming community networker in the inter-mountain area. I initiated a drum call with the first group of people who showed up. Some people brought large homemade double bass drums with mallets, so I put them in the middle of the growing circle. Then I went around the circle establishing rapport, bringing the kids forward while developing a solid circle, as more and more people arrived. The circle grew to two hundred people. I would hop on the small platform in the middle of the circle, and re-focus the rhythm as more people joined the group. Then I would hop off and let the drum circle maintain its own rhythm.

Jeff, as master of ceremonies, was going to introduce me. He came up to me and said, "It's time to start the program. I'll stop the rhythm and introduce you." Jeff stepped onto the platform and was in the process of raising his hands up into the air to stop the people from playing. I've seen this done before, and knew exactly what was going to happen if he did that. It's like standing in front of a stampede of wild horses. I grabbed Jeff and stopped him, just before his hands went all the way up into the air. I said to him, "Let me stop them and then you come up to the platform and announce me."

A rhythm circle in full groove is a powerful force that has its own inertia. Its rhythm is galloping along at a linear pace and you cannot stop it on a dime unless all of its parts are fully aware of your intent. If you stand up in the middle of a circle without first getting the whole group's attention, and then you put your hands up like a school crossing guard stopping traffic, they are going to rhythmically run you over. Some of the people would see you and stop, while a lot of the people who weren't paying attention to the center of the circle would not see you and stop until they noticed that the people around them were not playing. Even if it was me that jumped up on that platform and raised my hands up to stop the group, the result would be a messy ending to what was once a solid groove, not a good way to start a program.

> A rhythm circle in full groove is a living, breathing animal with a mind and an intent of its own.

I hopped up on the platform and started looking around at the people playing in the circle. I put out my hands, encouraging them to speed up just a little bit. As the tempo started picking up, heads started popping up in the circle and folks followed the energy until the whole community was focused and grooving together. I then brought the tempo up a little bit more, until I was sure that I had everyone's attention, and then brought the group to a simple rumble. To end the rumble, I jumped up in the air, and as my feet hit the platform, their hands hit their instruments on the last note. There was instant silence. I jumped off as Jeff jumped onto the platform and started the KRCL Day In the Park festivities with welcomes and introductions.

Working With What They Give You

Adapting to the situation in an ongoing drum circle is a kind of flexibility that you want to develop as a facilitator. The drum circle is a living, breathing entity that is interdependent on all the different parts of itself, and there are many factors and elements functioning in the drum circle at any given moment. It is an expression of spirit, emotion, excitement, and fun. Individual people are expressing themselves while contributing their spirit to the whole song. The energy in the circle that you help to create is itself a spontaneous, vibrant manifestation of the spirit of the people. It is ongoing, ever-changing rhythmical alchemy. The energy of the circle lends itself to spontaneity of expression by individuals.

If your radar is on fully and you are operating from your motivation to serve the needs of the circle, then these spontaneous expressions in the circle are gifts that the circle is offering to you, to showcase or to use as a way of feeding spirit back to itself.

Spontaneous expressions are stepping stones in the mutual musical dance created by you the facilitator and the group you're facilitating. However, if you are facilitating the circle from the point of view that you are controlling the circle, then these spontaneous sound acts and vocal emissions and movements appear to you as blocks that get in your way and limit your control. A controlling facilitator sees these kinds of situations as getting in the way of their ability to control.

A person who is facilitating with his or her heart open and radar on fully will see these situations as indications to get out of the way to help the circle go where it is going. You can adapt where you are going to the situation as it changes, and it is always changing. The ability to adapt to the changing situations that are ongoing in the circle and to lead by following and supporting these situations indicates your facilitating maturity.

As an example, as a circle is playing, on the run, someone in the circle starts a chant, and leaves space and chants again. One way to adapt to this is to encourage the people around the chanting person to join in on the chant. It could be words or sounds; it makes no difference. If only one side of the circle is chanting, listen to the other side of the circle for a response. And if you hear a response, then support that and encourage people to respond with the person who is responding to the opening chant. If there is no response with which to play, then create your own response and facilitate it as a call and response between the two halves of the circle.

Clavé Closure

This story unfolds at the Olatunji Drum Dance and Pray for Peace in Washington DC, a wonderful gathering with Baba Olatunji and the fulfillment of one of his dreams. Part of my assignment at that event was to do what I call "guerrilla fillers." I was assigned to interact with the audience between acts. On the stage were different acts and different groups of people who were going to perform for the audience throughout the day. But the audience was special. It consisted of almost a thousand drummers and percussionists who had in their possession their own drums and percussion toys. During any lull between the acts, they would immediately start jamming and drumming. My job was to glue them together between acts by facilitating them from the stage, musically, vocally, or drummage-wise until the next act was set up and ready to perform. Then I would bring the audience celebration to a close and re-focus them back to the stage for the next performance. Needless to say, I was having a lot of fun.

Bob Bloom, an excellent hand-drum teacher and facilitator from the east coast, was stage manager and was also going to do a guerrilla filler prior to introducing a particular act. When it was Bob's turn to do his guerrilla filler, he was still managing back stage, and before he could get in front to facilitate the audience, three different drum circles had convened, and were already in full drummage throughout this audience. The drum circles were not in touch with each other. They were separate little circles in a large mass of drummers, vortexes of drummers were joining each of the circles, creating different and opposing rhythms. The audience was turning into a three-circle, disjointed drumming monster. I grabbed Bob and told him his assignment was to go out there and facilitate a closing for the event that the audience had created.

Bob Bloom

Bob Bloom walked up to the mike and found a 2/3 *clavé* element that was involved with the largest of the three drum circles. Bob had a mike and the PA system directed toward the audience, so he began to sing, in conjunction with the *clavé*, a calypso song, "My grandma and your grandma, aiko aiko onde...," and got the part of the audience not playing to sing along with him. That forced the other two drum circles to begin to play with the largest drum circle and the rest of the audience, and soon Bob had all three drum circles and the full audience all singing and playing along with his calypso song. At that point Bob called a *clavé* break to the group, over the P.A. system. The whole audience responded as one with a *clavé* pattern and stopped. On the next beat Bob introduced the next presenter.

> *Bob Bloom took a dominant musical element from the playing audience and used it as a glue to bring the whole group together musically.*

Bob Bloom took a dominant musical element from the playing audience and used it as a glue to bring the whole group together musically. He then used that same element to bring the whole group to a close. The bottom line is that Bob, using what was offered to him, masterfully paced the group, and then led them to a synchronized groove where they could all have a successful closing together.

Drum Circle Game: Layering in a Rhythm

Do this exercise with your all-drum circle first, and then, immediately afterward, with your all-percussion circle.

- Designate a starting player. That person starts the rhythm song.
- The person on the left of the starting player listens to the rhythm and then adds whatever rhythm they think would be appropriate, to support, harmonize, or complement the rhythm being played.
- The person to the left of the second player listens to the rhythm song created by the two players, and them joins in by playing whatever rhythm they think would be appropriate, to support, harmonize, or complement the rhythm being played.
- The next person in turn listens to the song as it is being created, and adds their rhythmical contribution to the piece.
- This process continues until each player in the circle has layered their rhythmical contribution into the composition and there is a complete rhythm song.
- After everyone has layered their part into the rhythm, and has enjoyed the composition for awhile, the person who started that particular rhythm makes a call and leads a group rumble to a closing.
- The person to the left of the last starting player starts a rhythm, and continues this exercise.
- Take turns until everyone has had a turn starting a rhythm into which everyone else in the group layers. No two songs will be the same.

Individual Adjustments

Once your circle is playing together and gaining momentum, you will find that you, as facilitator, have more time for paying attention to individual people. You will find time to give a minor adjustment to someone to protect them from themselves as they learn drumming technique. You'll find the time to encourage a small child to play in the community or to see that they need a stick to hit a drum.

Avoid getting stuck spending too much time trying to fix a player who is not listening to the rest of the group and out of sync with the rest of the community, or playing against the grain. If you walk up to that person with your back to the rest of the circle and spend too much time with them, you can lose your focus with the total groove of the community. Players who are rhythmically getting in the way of the ongoing circle groove usually are doing so because they have gotten so excited about their own playing that they have forgotten about playing with everyone else in the circle. As the facilitator your job is to help them re-focus their playing toward supporting the total song, without making them wrong.

One way to get a person's attention in a circle is to walk up to them and give supportive gestures and directions that will help them get on track with the groove. At the same time, while you have their attention, back up into the middle of the circle, slowly but surely they will get their head up out of their drum and into the group's playing by focusing on you. This not only adjusts their focus into the community's groove, but helps refocus the players around them who might have been affected by the player you just readjusted.

Spinning Plates and Passing Out Parts

Spinning plates refers to an old European circus act where a performer would balance plates on top of pointed sticks by spinning them. As long as the plates had spinning momentum, they would stay balanced on the sticks. As soon as the plates lost their momentum they would wobble, lose their balance, and crash to the floor. The intention was to keep the plates spinning while adding more and more spinning plates on more sticks without any plate losing its momentum or spinning off of the stick. To do this, every time the performer added another spinning plate onto another stick he had to give other plates a little spinning nudge on the edge to keep them spinning and balanced. He had to be aware of all the plates' balances and spinning inertia, and notice which ones he needed to adjust to keep in balance.

This metaphor refers to what a hand drum teacher is doing in the middle of an ongoing drum circle that is his or her class. They are teaching culturally-specific rhythms that consist of different drum and percussion parts being played at one time. All these parts together create a prescribed song or drum circle arrangement that is being taught to the group. The teacher has control of the song and the group.

Most of the time, in a community drum circle, the parts that constitute the song are created by the individuals in the circle. Instead of having control of the group like a teacher does, the facilitator has the responsibility to read where the group wants to go and where they are capable of going, and then help get them there.

From a drum teacher's point of view, every part that is being shown and played in the drum circle class is, in effect, a spinning plate. In a community drum circle the part each participant is creating, playing, and changing is evolving as the total drum circle song itself is changing and evolving. If you tried to lead a drum circle by trying to spin all those individual parts, the small plates, you would go crazy. But facilitating a circle is not about spinning individual parts.

As facilitator, view your drum circle as one big plate. Think of the group as one body. Knowing where to nudge the circle to keep its momentum going helps you spin the big plate. Finding and adjusting any irregularities in the circle that can be gently facilitated into alignment with the rest of the circle is spinning the small plates. This keeps the groove happening.

When, as a facilitator, you choose to pass out specific parts in the circle, give those parts in a way that does not pressure the participant to try to produce something that is out of reach of their expertise. Avoid putting anyone in the circle in student crisis mode. (This is one of the reasons why I discourage facilitators from passing out culturally-specific parts in an open community rhythm circle.) Give participants the parts, giving them your blessing to feel free to play the part according to their own abilities and inter-pretations. This empowers the community to create rhythmical alchemy based on the simple rhythm format you provide.

Each part is a plate to spin. When you have two or more specifically different parts going in a circle, then you are spinning as many plates as you have parts. By keeping two or more parts going in a community drum circle, you are spinning the small plates at the same time as you spin the big plate, the community groove. Choose carefully how many plates you decide to spin in your circle at any one time. With too many plates spinning at one time, you might be putting yourself in facilitator's crisis mode.

Seattle World Percussion Festival

Elements to Facilitate in a Drum Circle

The elements to facilitate in a drum circle are the nuts and bolts of the music that exist in any drum circle environment, from thunder-drumming circles to culturally-specific classes, and all points between. The elements are the pulse, rhythm patterns, tempo, timbral group, pitch, time signature, vocals, movement, and spirit. By identifying these elements to the participants in your circle, you educate them. When you facilitate these elements in an ongoing circle, you provide an opportunity for participants to experience them. Through their experiences, the circle can take ownership of these elements and utilize them to create the music on their own during the event. This empowers you as their facilitator to add, identify, and facilitate more elements into the experience. As players utilize more of these elements, the circle becomes self-facilitating. This gives you more time to focus on facilitating the orchestration, dynamics, and spirit of the event that is being created by the group's music. You are leading the people to lead themselves, and when you do this, they will give you an orchestra to orchestrate.

World Percussion Orchestra

At the World Percussion Camp in eastern Illinois, I found myself in the middle of a drum circle with a very special population. Some of the best instructors of hand drums, marching bands, orchestrational percussion, and trap drums were teaching 300 college and high school percussion students from throughout the United States. As we were warming up, I came to the full realization of the potential of this particular group. Within this closed environment, I found highly capable and responsive percussion-oriented students. REMO Drum Company had provided lots of instruments with the proper mix of timbral groups, and the college had shared various hand drums. I had full access to a percussion orchestra.

That evening, we created together a very special event that would be remembered by all of us. Because of their ability to listen and respond, I could do two or three cycle calls and responses instead of doing a standard one cycle call and response. I got powerful responses back from them. Instead of doing just slow, medium and fast speeds, we explored middle grooves and dynamics. Instead of taking the group volume down dynamically for a minute, I took the group down for a full five minutes and worked inside a soft volume with 300 drummers listening to each other, playing delicately and gracefully. As I challenged them more in relationship to their musical and rhythmical abilities, they challenged me more in relationship to what orchestrational finesse I could add to the previous level that we had achieved together. By the end of the evening I felt more like an orchestra conductor than I had ever felt before in my life.

Pulse

The pulse is the heartbeat of the community drum circle. It is an important element, responsible for creating agreement amongst the players; it needs to be supported and reinforced by the *djun-djun* and bass drum players. Although the pulse is a universal rhythm that can be facilitated by itself, you will find it functioning in every rhythm pattern you facilitate. (It is where you tap your foot.)

The community pulse is a living, breathing beat, set by the relationship of the rhythmical alchemy created by everybody participating. This organic beat varies with the energy and emotional dynamics of the circle, and can only be facilitated and directed, not forced or imposed.

Rhythm Patterns

You can present repetitive rhythm patterns to the circle, and they can use them as blueprints for improvisation with each other. I discuss these universal rhythm patterns that are used in most community rhythm circles in Chapter 13, Universal Grooves. These rhythms are the basic foundation from which the different elements listed in this chapter are facilitated and utilized to create the rhythm circle experience.

Tempo

Tempo is the speed of the rhythm, usually dictated by the speed of the pulse (or foundational rhythm) being played in the circle. Generally, tempos can be slow, medium, or fast, just like the pitches on drums can be low, medium, or high. But there are many different speeds available to a drum circle, depending on its playing and listening ability.

The common denominator speed of a circle is the speed of the rhythm when the whole circle plays its best. This common denominator speed varies with each circle, and with each rhythm in each circle. Usually as a circle plays together, their rhythmical connection strengthens, and the common denominator speed gets a little faster in each progressive groove.

Timbral Groups

There are five basic timbral groups in most drum circles. They can be divided and sub-divided many different ways, but these basic timbral groups include hands on skin, sticks on skin, sticks on wood, sticks on bells, and shakers. You can use and identify these timbral groups in different ways to help the circle hear itself better and pay attention to the other timbral groups being played in the circle

Within each timbral group there are many different timbres. As a good example consider the hand drums. A drum such as an *ashiko* or a *djembe* with a goat skin head can be tuned to the same pitch as a cow skin drum, but their timbres will be entirely different because of the structure and thickness of the skin and the shape of the drum. Similarly, you can compare timbres of different wood blocks that might have the same pitch but a different timbre because of the material and design of the particular wood instrument.

Pitch

Within any one timbral group, such as hands-on drums, and within any one of the sub-groups of those hands-on drums such as hands-on *congas* or *ashikos* or *djembes*, you will find instruments tuned to different pitches. They are commonly divided into low, medium, and high pitches, but they can have as many different variations of pitch as the number of drums available in a circle. The same thing applies to the timbres of bells and wood blocks and to a lesser extent, shakers.

Volume Dynamics

Volume refers to how loud or soft the circle is playing at any given time. Volume is an element within the circle that can be facilitated and, as with pitch, can be divided into low volume, medium volume, and high volume, with many variations between, based on the group's ability to listen to itself and to participate.

Time Signatures

A time signature is a musical notation for representing how a rhythm is structured. Common time signatures in our culture include 4/4 and 6/8. 4/4 refers to four notes per measure where each note is a quarter note. 6/8 refers to six notes per measure with each note being an eighth note. It is not critical that you understand music theory to continue from here!

4/4 Time Signature

The most frequently played time signature in open community rhythm circles is straight 4/4, the time signature of much of our contemporary music. Because it is so prevalent in our music, it is the most accessible time signature for our western musical sensibilities. That means it is easier for us to feel 4/4 time signatures. All of a 4/4 rhythm's smaller parts can be divided by even numbers, such as 4th's, 8th's and 16th's. I consider the 4/4 time signature to be a square rhythm. It is easy for us to play because we do not have to pay as much attention to the time signature, and this leaves time and focus for us to pay more attention to what we are playing. All the rhythms in the universal grooves chapter are based on the 4/4 time signature, except one. That exception is the 6/8.

As a notational device for this book, I use numbers to represent pulse notes and dots to represent the notes between the pulse notes. In all 4/4 rhythms, each dot represents a 16th note (and there are four pulses in a measure.) For example, 4/4 looks like this: 1•••2•••3•••4•••1•••2•••3•••4•• etc.

6/8 Time Signature

In Arthurian terminology, if a 4/4 time signature is a square rhythm, then a 6/8 time signature is a round rhythm. It is sometimes called the triplet rhythm. Beginning-beginner drummers hear it as a waltz gone crazy. Example notation for 6/8 rhythms is 1••2••3••4••1••2••3••4•• etc. where each number represents one of four pulses, as well as one of the eighth note triplets, and each dot is an eighth note triplet.

When different rhythmical relationships coexist simultaneously, such as 4/4 and 6/8, a polyrhythm is being played. The 6/8 and 12/8 time signatures are different ways of looking at the same basic polyrhythm foundation. The length of a musical cycle determines whether you hear a rhythm as 6/8 or 12/8. Polyrhythms are common in most African cultures.

First Night Santa Cruz drum circle

You can find the 6/8 time signature being played in drumming circles when the population is predominately people who are studying culturally specific rhythms. I would not hesitate throwing a 6/8 rhythm into the seasonal Santa Cruz It's Beach drum circle celebrations because the majority of the population are students of mine or of Don Davidson. I refrain from facilitating a 6/8 rhythm at the annual First Night New Year's Eve Community Drum Celebrations in downtown Santa Cruz because many people who come to drum there are not yet experienced drummers. They are families out for a good time.

Most facilitators who successfully instigate a 6/8 rhythm in a mixed population drum circle, do so by reinforcing and emphasizing the four pulse in the rhythm to give the beginner players something to hold onto as the more advanced drummers play around with the syncopated bell patterns and the triplet upbeats.

Other Time Signatures

The further away we get from 4/4, the closer we get to the deeper aspects of other cultures' rhythmaculture. At the same time it can be harder for a non-musician to participate and have fun. Not only are the uneven pulse counts of the 5, 7 and 9 pulse time signatures hard for a beginner player to follow, but culturally-specific sensibilities emphasize the pulses differently.

Until your body learns to feel these different rhythms by repeatedly playing them, continually counting the pulses will be the only way that you will be able to maintain the beat. A beginning-beginner player playing an odd time signature for the first time will be spending more energy counting than playing. That's not too much fun.

I would suggest that you avoid facilitating odd-pulsed time signatures in an open community rhythm circle, unless you are confident that you can do it without either turning the experience into a class, or else causing the majority of your population to go into student crisis mode.

Where Is The One In The Master's Magic?

This story takes place at the Berklee College of Music World Percussion Festival in Boston, Massachusetts. Why they call this a Percussion Festival I do not know. I would call it a seriously intensive percussion program. To qualify for the one-week program, you must audition for the level of class you want to take. "Why so strict?" you might ask. The answer is that the teachers are more than just teachers. They are the world-renowned drum and percussion masters in their field. If you took a beginner class they would treat you like a beginner, but if you took the advanced class they would kick your rhythmical butt.

I regularly facilitate an outdoor community drum circle for this annual event. We do it in a small park next to the college in downtown Boston. There is a strong hand-drumming community in this city, thanks to Jimi and Morwen Two Feathers of Earth Drum Council, so we usually get a good public turnout.

At this particular event most of the Haitian, Afro-Cuban, and Latin masters drummers from the program came to participate and gravitated toward each other in a section of the circle. Walfredo Rayes, Sr., Horacio "El Negro" Hernandez, Jose Eladio, Robert Vizcaino, and Giovanni Hidalgo were among this group of world class players. Any one of these people could carry on a performance on their own. It is a special treat to hear one or two of them play together on the same stage. To have this group of master drummers playing together in this drum circle was too great of an opportunity for me to pass up.

I had just handed my circle over to a bunch of rhythm magicians whose intent was to play with each other between the notes in the magical places in the rhythm.

As the circle was in full groove, I signaled the master drum group to keep playing so I could showcase them. Then I stopped the rest of the circle. They were playing a good mix of instruments, *congas*, timbales, *clavés*, bells, and a big bass drum, so I let this ensemble entertain us with their mastery for five minutes before I returned the other players in the circle to full groove. After closing the piece with a big group rumble, I thanked the masters, introduced each one of them to the circle, and then asked the master group if they would start the next groove.

That was a big mistake. On the first rhythm cycle someone in the group started playing what I call the standard 6/8 short bell on a cow bell. The 6/8 short bell is a highly-syncopated pattern that has inside it the 3/2 *clavé* pattern in triplet form. To the untrained ear, this syncopated pattern has no relationship to the pulse. Without a pulse reference you could hear the start of the pattern in three different places. In one of these places you could be hearing the pattern backwards. You might think that you were starting your rhythm part at the beginning of the pattern, but you would actually be starting in the middle.

The Berklee College of Music Percussion Festival

Facilitator's panic set in. The second rhythm cycle started but no one joined the bell player as he repeated the 6/8 short bell without accompaniment. I fought back my panic with the hope that when the bass drum player started playing what should have been a pulse-oriented pattern, he would establish a rhythmical foundation for the percussion students and advanced players. If that happened, after all the masters started I guessed that I could then give the beginner players a simple pulse-based triplet to follow. Then off we would go into 6/8 rhythm land.

I held my breath, while on the third rhythm cycle the bass drummer started a pulse pattern that revolves around the 6/8 *clavé*, rather than grounding it. I watched the advanced players as they tried to understand the relationship between the bell pattern and the bass drum pattern. I saw their mouths fall open as they understood that. Yes, the bass drum player was playing a pulse, but it was a six pulse floating through the bell pattern, rather than a four pulse grounding it.

I realized that I had just handed my circle over to a bunch of rhythm magicians whose playing agenda was entirely different than the one I had intended. It was obvious that the masters drummers' intent was not to play a simple 6/8 rhythm to help me get the community circle started. Their intent was to play with each other between the notes in the magical places in the rhythm. A 6/8 rhythm can be hard enough for the beginning beginners in the circle to follow, but without some basic grounding rhythmic patterns it would be impossible.

My last hope was Jose Elado who was on the *congas*. If he were to play a bass-orientated melody line on the two drums in front of him he would have given the others in the circle something with which to start.

No way Jose. Just before the fourth rhythm cycle started, Jose handed a cohort the bigger lower-tuned *conga*, and with an expression on his face that looked a lot like a kid let loose in a candy store, he started using the higher-pitched *conga* drum, called a *quinto*, to play a lead part over the rhythm already established. He played sparsely, using only the magic notes.

Living inside the 6/8 rhythmic spider web created by the master drummers were at least three different pulses.

I gave up. On the fifth rhythmical cycle I looked over at Jose's friend on the bottom *conga*. I held my hands out to him in a body-language gesture that said "your turn." I knew full well that whatever he played, it would not have the grounding four pulse that I wanted for my circle to use to find a way to start playing. Sure enough, he played a three pulse instead of a four pulse.

We looked for the beat in the masters' magic. By the sixth rhythmical cycle all the other players in the master group jumped into the rhythm with their percussion parts. Somewhere in this last layer of percussion, a four-pulse bell part was being played, but it was too late to be a reference point for the rest of the players in the circle. That was because living inside the 6/8 rhythmic spider web created by the master drummers were at least three different pulses, a three pulse, a four pulse and a six pulse. I would notate this experience as the following:

6/8 three pulse: P • • P • • P • •

6/8 four pulse: P • • P • • P • • P • •

6/8 six pulse: P • P • P • P • P • P •

It was magical. The circle stared in awe, mesmerized by the magical rhythm spell created by the masters. Because of the roundness of the 6/8 rhythm, the tones of the drums were interwoven around each other into beautiful melody lines, and the timbres of the percussion created an intricate pattern of color.

A few players tentatively tried to join into the magic groove, but it was obvious that a lot of them did not have a clue of how to fit their pattern into it. The potential for a train wreck was high. I ran into the middle of the circle and jumped into the air, landing on the ground on the first pulse of the next rhythm cycle. I call that marking the pulse. As I continued to mark the first pulse of each sequential rhythm cycle the players in the circle began hitting that note on their instruments. That gave some of the players the information they needed to begin playing with the master group. Hearing them play gave me some hope, but this groove was not out of hot water yet.

I added another jump into each rhythm cycle in a way that gave a more solid rhythmical foundation to the three-fourths of the circle of players who were still lost. Now the people who were not playing the groove were marking the fourth pulse of each rhythm cycle and the first pulse of the next. This set up a strong enough foundation for at least one half of the players to join into what was still a shaky 6/8 groove.

My biggest problem was that the rest of the circle population did not recognize that we were playing in 6/8 and would not know what to do if they did. My hope was that they would just keep on marking the pulse with me as the rest of the players solidified the groove. My wish was that they would only mark the pulse with their instruments and not try to join into the 6/8 groove with the only rhythms they knew, which were all in a 4/4 time signature. I didn't get my wish. Upon hearing the pulse, half of the participants jumped into the 6/8 groove with 4/4 rhythms. 6/8 and 4/4 grooves mix together like oil and water and unless you are an advanced player, mixing these two time signatures together is almost an impossibility.

Whenever you mix 6/8 and 4/4 rhythms in a community rhythm circle, the result will almost always be a train wreck. That is just what happened at this particular drum circle. It took less than eight rhythm cycles, in less than one minute, for the masters to create a magical 6/8 groove. Then the other participants in the circle struggled for three or four minutes trying to join that groove. Once the shaky rhythm turned into a train wreck, Giovanni Hidalgo walked toward the center to the circle to stop what was left of the groove. The train wreck completed itself and the groove was already dead before Giovanni reached the middle of the circle.

It was magical. The circle stared in awe, mesmerized by the magical rhythm spell created by the masters.

Giovanni spoke to the group saying " Let's get it together here, and follow the beat." I heard somebody mumble under their breath "What beat?" Someone else in the group said "Arthur, where's the one?" I took the question as an opportunity to do what I would have, could have, should have done in the beginning to this groove. As Giovanni walked back to the master group in the circle, I announced to the group that this would be a 6/8 rhythm in triplet form, and for the beginner drummers to wait and follow me once the groove got started. The minute the 6/8 short bell started, I instructed the bell players to copy that pattern. Then I had the *djun-*

djuns play the four pulse so that I had my circle foundation. Once the groove was established with the intermediate and advanced players, I played a simple bass-oriented triplet on a drum for the beginner players to model and away we finally went, to 6/8 rhythm land.

As the groove reached its fullness I once again showcased the master group by having them continue to play as I stopped the others. This uncovered the magical master groove. Since they had been playing that groove with the master group, people had a pulse reference with which to appreciate the masters' magic. The circle now also had a sense of where to return when I called them back into the groove before bringing the 6/8 piece to a close.

The tones of the drums were interwoven around each other into beautiful melody lines, and the timbres of the percussion created an intricate pattern of color.

There is a lesson for you, as the facilitator, in every train wreck.

Vocals

Vocals express the spirit of the community. As facilitator you can add them into a rhythm while the rhythm is being played. Sometimes vocals are a spontaneous expression of the group.

Vocals can also be initiated by you as the facilitator separate from the rhythm during a window of communication as you start a rhythm.

You can sing a rhythm vocally to communicate rhythmically and help people fully internalize it, making it easier for them to play it.

Movement

Movement is a natural extension of the musical expression of rhythm. There is an Arthurian question floating around the drumming community: "Does the drummer make the dancer dance, or does the dancer make the drummer drum?" The answer, of course, is Yes!

Even the uninitiated curious who stick a foot in the door of a dance class with live drummers, to see what all the racket is about, will begin to tap their feet or nod their head to the rhythm being played, if they stay around long enough. Whenever I'm facilitating an open outdoor event, a group of curious on-lookers come up and surround the drum circle. When I get enough of these people they constitute what I call my peanut gallery. I first get these people engaged in the process by enticing them to clap their hands in any pattern they want. Once the peanut gallery is a participating

Movements are a spontaneous part of a rhythm event. Find the moves, model them, and pass them around.

part of the rhythm circle, it is easy to find someone doing some sort of hand or body movement. I then entice the rest of the people in the peanut gallery to model that person and join in. Soon the peanut gallery becomes our dance ensemble. Movements are a spontaneous part of a rhythm event. Find the moves, model them, and pass them around.

The Disneyland Drum Snake

This story unfolds at the closing drum celebration of an alternative healing conference at the Disneyland Conference Center in Orlando, Florida. REMO Drum Company supplied hundreds of drums of different types, and as part of the program the participants got to take one home. Wow! This became a high energy drum circle full of drum virgins playing their own drum for the first time.

A *conga* line of dancers formed on the outside of the circle. They playfully followed each other, snaking around the circle of drummers, playing their instruments. A spontaneously-forming line of people dancing in a *conga* line to rhythms around the circumference of a drum circle is as natural an occurrence as ants dancing around your picnic blanket. As the *conga* line snaked its way around the circle it attracted more and more of the drummers from the outside of the circle to join the line. The population of drumming dancers in the *conga* line became much larger than the population of drummers standing around the facilitator's platform. Had this mass of hundreds of drummers marched in a straight line somewhere, it would have turned into a rhythmical mess and a logistical nightmare for the facilitator, but they were marching and dancing around themselves in a large circle so that the rhythmical song was ever-changing and always together.

The whole circle became a self-facilitating rhythmical snake that was biting its own tail. All I could do was stand on the platform, enjoy the music, and get dizzy watching them dance around me.

Spirit

Is spirit an element that can be identified and facilitated in a rhythm circle? Most facilitators say that you can hear spirit being manifest in the quality of the music that is being produced by a group.

Spirit begins to appear as the music forms into a cohesive group vision manifest in sound. As the community gels musically, this spirit element functions within the drum circle. It's readable.

Look for spirit with your three peripheral listening tools—vision, hearing, and feeling. Use that inner ear that you have developed by listening for the infinite amount of information that exists in the silence between the notes in the music.

What tells you that spirit is present? The quality of the music produced in the circle depends on the quality of relationship the participants have created with each other. You will find that the exchange and expression of spirit is part of the glue that creates that connection. When it's there you will know it's there. When it's not you'll know it's not.

The stronger the connection, the better the music, the more palpable the spirit. The stronger the spirit, the better the connection, the more palpable the music. The stronger the music, the better the spirit, the more palpable the connection.

Can you facilitate spirit?

You cannot dissect and manipulate spirit with a facilitator's instrument, but you can read it, acknowledge it, reflect it, and give it back to the group that gave it to you. The stronger your facilitation, the better the music, the more readable the spirit.

Facilitator's Orchestrational Tools

In this chapter I present orchestrational tools that you can use to facilitate the elements described in Chapter 11. These elements exist in the music whether you facilitate them or not. When you identify and facilitate the pitches and timbral groups in an ongoing circle with the tools in this chapter, you become the conductor, orchestrating the musical event.

Remember, as facilitator, to recognize that a transition point in a drum circle musical piece is a time for instigating changes in the groove. Among these changes could be a transition to a new groove, a closing, or some facilitated orchestration that heightens your group's attention to the music they are creating so they can take it to the next level. These tools are listed and explained below. They depend on body-language signals directed to the participants to orchestrate the circle. A description of each body-language signal accompanies each tool.

Arthurian Admonitions

Body-language signals are a lot less complicated than they look on paper. Take your time learning them. Practice being succinct, precise, readable, and consistent in your body-language signals. These are the goals.

To put any of the body-language signals into your facilitator's circuitry, I offer you this simple Arthurian rule: "the slower you do it, the faster you'll learn it."

If you are afraid that you will look the fool trying body-language signals with real people, then you can perfect your facilitation circuitry by setting up your dolls, teddy bears, coke bottles, or tin cans in a circle and practicing the dance. It worked for me.

Believe me when I say that it is a dance. Any body-language signal that you communicate is a full body contact dance with that body of people that we call a rhythm circle. The more you project your self and your spirit into your body communications, the easier it will be for the circle to read your intent and purpose, and the more responsive they will be to your facilitation. Good luck!

CD Example

You will find CD headings throughout the remainder of this book. Any comments under a CD heading refer to one or more of the musical pieces on the enclosed CD. You will discover that any subject, tool, or technique that has been discussed in a section preceding the CD reference will be found as an example in whatever musical piece is mentioned.

Sculpting

Sculpting is the act of identifying a specific part of your circle. The act of sculpting signals a particular group to prepare to receive new directions. You may choose to sculpt a section of the circle, a person, a specific group of people (for example, just the kids or all the women), a timbral group (such as bells, or wood, or drums), or a type of drum, such as the *ashikos* or *congas*.

You can use sculpting throughout a program. It is one of the most basic facilitator's tools and is used often in musical pieces.

You can usually sculpt using body language directed to the circle while it is in full groove. Sometimes you can vocalize your sculpting during the window of communication between grooves. Sometimes you vocalize and use body language to sculpt while the group is in full groove.

Sculpting half the circle

Sculpting a Section of the Circle Using a Body-language Sequence

Lets say, for example, that you want to sculpt one third of your circle to facilitate a new element into it. Do the following actions.

- Picture the circle as a pie with you standing in the middle of it. You are the pie cutter and your hands and arms are the knives.
- Divide the group in your mind first, so that you know what section of your circle you are going to sculpt.
- Make the first cut in the circle with your right hand. Outstretch your arm, shape your hand like a meat cleaver, and use it to make an up and down chopping motion. You are cleaving a line between a group of people, so make eye contact with those people as you chop.
- Keep chopping and making eye contact until you are satisfied that they know who is on what side of the line you are making. The first time you do this it may take three or four chops to communicate what that signal means. By the third time you have sculpted the circle, they will have learned your body language, and it may only take one chop to communicate to them where the line is.

- When you are satisfied that you have established the first line that marks off the section you are sculpting, maintain that line by holding your right hand cleaver out with a straight arm and pointing at that line.
- Maintain the right hand position as you bring your left hand up with your index finger in pointing mode. Your left hand pointer is now parallel to your right hand chopper, so that you are pointing at the first person on the left side of the established line.
- While maintaining the right hand cleaver position, begin to move your left hand pointer away from right hand, pointing with your eyes as well as your finger at the people that you are including in your sculpted section.
- Stop your left hand when it gets to the place in the circle that represents the total group of people that you want to include in the your sculpted section.
- With your left arm outstretched, form your left hand pointer into a meat cleaver. You are now standing with both arms and hands outstretched, and between them is the section that you just sculpted.
- With your left hand meat cleaver, make the same chopping motions into the circle as you did with your right hand, until you are satisfied that you have established the left line of your sculpted section.
- With both arms outstretched and using your hands as cleavers, make simultaneous chopping motions, cutting one third of your circle into a piece of pie. From the sculpted section's position it looks like you are going to hug them all.
- You now have one hundred percent of people's attention in that sculpted section. They know that you are about to facilitate them, and they are ready to respond.

This whole process I just described takes only a few seconds in a real-live drum circle situation, but in a practice session with your study group, take your time.

You can use other body-language signals to select all participants using a particular type of drum. Hold up the drum and point to it, showing it to the whole circle. For percussion instruments, like bells, do the same thing. Hold up a bell and point to it. To sculpt individual people, I point at them. It's as simple as that.

Attention Call

"Attention call" body language gets the whole circle's attention while they are playing and prepares them for an indication or command that you will be giving them. To signal for attention, hold out your arm with your index finger pointing out over the heads of the people in the circle. You walk around the inside circumference of the circle one or two times until you are satisfied that you have the attention of the majority of the

Heads up!

group. With that attention focus you are ready to facilitate the whole circle.

Avoid giving them an attention call without following it with a facilitation signal. If you do, you become the facilitator who calls wolf, and your leadership will be less clear.

On the other hand, if you are consistent with your attention call and facilitation throughout your program, then by the end of the event you will hardly need to raise a finger to get their attention.

Vocal Attention Call with Body Language

If the circle is small enough, or if I have a microphone with a P.A. system, then I will give a vocal "HEADS UP" call to the circle while giving the body-language attention call described above. I say "heads up" because the biggest reason most people miss a facilitation cue is because they are looking down, with their heads bent over their drum.

Stop Cut

The "stop cut" signal is a physical indication given by you as the facilitator to the group to stop either the whole drum circle groove or else a particular sculpted part of the circle. Several body-language examples of stop cuts for facilitators are described in the next section.

> Any body-language signal that you communicate is a full body contact dance with that body of people that we call a rhythm circle.

The stop cut is usually made while the music is happening. You will want to give the signal on the first note of a particular rhythmical cycle. The designated sculpted group immediately responds by hitting the note indicated by the facilitator as a stop note. The stop cut can be directed at the whole drum circle, stopping it on a dime, so to speak, or it can be directed to a particular timbral group or pitch group within the drum circle that has been sculpted. These people will be prepared for some direction from the facilitator.

Start of stop cut

End of stop cut

Stop Cut Body Language

The stop cut action is universal, but the style is individual. Watch any orchestra conductor. I'll give my four favorite examples.

- **Arthurian style:** To start, I cross my arms and hands across my chest, palms down. Then, I make a quick cutting motion from the chest out to the sides. Sometimes this happens in the air with a stop jump. (These are described in the next section.) The bigger the circle, the higher the jump. I'm fun to watch with a thousand-person drum circle!

- **Jim Greiner style:** Jim is a Latin Percussion endorser, who created an excellent video called "Community Drumming for Health and Happiness." To start, Jim crosses his hands above his head in front of him. Then he makes a quick downward-cutting motion from above the head, across the chest, downward and out to the sides of the hips.

Mabiba Baegne

- **Mabiba Baegne style:** Mabiba Baegne is a beautiful Congolese drum and dance teacher on the West Coast of the U.S. To start, Mabiba holds her hands up in the air over her head, with her palms open and facing forward. To make the stop cut, she quickly reaches forward and grabs the air in front of her, pulling her closed hands to her chest.

- **Reggae McGowen** is a drum maker, teacher, and community drum circle facilitator on the island of Hawaii. To start, Reggae makes a right hand and fist above and in front of his head. He then brings it down to waist level while his elbow juts out behind, keeping the fist, and simultaneously bringing up the right knee.

Reggae McGowen

CD Example

While listening to the CD, you will know that my attention call to the players was successful if the music cleanly and succinctly changes grooves, direction, or dynamics. You will also know my attention call to the players was not successful if the tempo gets mushy during a musical transition, or if somebody was not paying attention and played through a stop cut. I take full responsibility for any musical mess on the CD, and I share with my rhythm circle friends the glory for any musical magic created on the CD.

You can hear when a stop cut signal is being given because most of the players drop out on the first beat of a rhythmic cycle to reveal a certain timbral group or type of drum being showcased.

You can also hear when stop cut signals are being given at the end of the musical pieces, especially if there's a rumble.

Continue to Play

When you have sculpted a segment of the circle you may want the rest of the circle to "continue to play" whatever they are playing while you work with your sculpted group. It is important to give the non-sculpted part of the circle a continue-to-play signal before you facilitate the sculpted group, or else the whole circle might just stop when you do the stop cut. I point my index fingers at each other in front of my chest and move them around each other in a circular fashion as my continue to play signal.

Continue to play.

Call to Groove

"Call to groove" is usually a silent body-language command from the facilitator, directed to any part of the drum circle that is not playing, to start playing at the beginning of the next rhythmical cycle. I use the call to groove during a showcased sequence to get the part of the circle not playing to start playing again or else to get a whole group to begin to play. After a call and response, I use the call to groove to move to another rhythm.

Call-to-Groove Body Language

From the center of the circle, I hold up my hands and count the pulses leading to the beginning of the next rhythmic cycle with my fingers. At the first note of that next rhythmic cycle I quickly lift my hands from my chest, palms up, into the air, and the group starts playing.

You can also use this counting technique to prepare for a stopcut.

CD Example

When you listen to some showcased timbral group or drum on the CD with little or no rhythmical background, and hear the other members of the drum circle suddenly jump into the rhythm, it is usually because I have just given the group a silent call to groove.

Vocal Call To Groove

You can vocally count the group into a rhythm while using body language. Three examples of the verbal count that accompanies the fingers are "one, two, let's all play," "one, two, here we go," and "one, two, play the groove." To initiate a groove after a call and response sequence, I use the vocal call "one, two, make up your own."

CD Example

You will hear a "one, two, here we go" as I layer in the percussion on top of the opening *djun-djun* groove in "The Clavé." An example of using the vocal call "one, two, make up your own" after a call and response sequence is at the beginning of "Make Up Your Own To Surprise Groove."

Exercise: Sculpting a Rhythm Song

This exercise can be done with all drums, all percussion toys, or mixed instruments. In this exercise you will be using the facilitator tools described above. Take your time practicing with these tools to build your orchestration foundation inside your study group.

Get in the middle of an in-the-moment circle while it is playing. Listen to the song being played and pick instruments that you like. Signal the players of those instruments to continue to play by sculpting them for showcasing, and giving them a continue to play signal. Stop cut the rest of the group. This uncovers the instruments that you have chosen. As they continue to play their parts, you uncover the song that you have sculpted from the circle while on the run. After listening to the song that you created by sculpting, call the others in the group back into the groove with a silent four count, or any of the call-to-groove vocal calls.

Everyone in the group who has stopped playing has listened to the showcased group, and now has a new perspective of the song. When they begin to play again, they will not necessarily play the exact same part they played before they were stop cut. This creates an ever-ongoing, evolving rhythmical song during the exercise.

This completes one cycle of the exercise. You join the circle, going to another person who's playing in full grove. Relieve them of their instrument, choosing them to be the next facilitator to run the exercise. Continue this "sculpt your own song" exercise until everyone gets a chance to sculpt at least one song.

CD Example

You will find that the basic orchestrational tools mentioned above are used frequently in almost every musical piece on the CD.

Accent Jumps

I jump into the air and when my body hits the ground the players hit their instruments as one note. This is the same body motion as you use for stop cuts, except you jump! These "accent jumps" are a facilitator's tool that can be used in many situations.

- In closing a piece you can mark a final note at the end of the final dynamic rumble.
- After a full stop you can mark the pulse, leading your participants back into a full groove.
- You can use accent jumps to mark the pulse during an ongoing musical piece, after sculpting specific instruments, and then have those instruments play accent notes along with your jumps, while other instruments are still grooving.
- You can mark the pulse with a sculpted section that's being showcased.
- As an attention focus during a window of communication, you might jump and wait for a mirrored response from your group. Then you will have the group's attention more fully.
- You can create accent patterns with the group using accent jumps.

Christine Stevens' accent jump

CD Example

Accent jumps are used throughout the CD to facilitate different aspects of the music, but they can most easily be identified in the music at the end of "Highlife" and "6/8."

Accent Stomps

Kim Atkinson

You can use accent stomps along with accent jumps. By stomping your feet you can mark spots in time with the group. You raise your feet one at a time, waiting for the group to notice, and then stomp down heavily. I use accent stomps to signal and accent more syncopated rhythms than the evenly spaced notes marked by accent jumps. Kim Atkinson and Sule Greg Wilson are two facilitators who use accent stomps with grace.

Call and Response

"Call and response" is a powerful and versatile facilitator's tool. The facilitator calls by playing a pattern within one rhythmical cycle and the circle responds by modeling the pattern, repeating it as well as they can in the next cycle.

Call and response possibilities include:

- To start or stop a drum circle groove,
- As a musical transition point to re-focus the group or possibly guide it to a new groove,
- As a dialogue tool with which the facilitator can empower individual participants to speak their spirit with their instrument into the drum circle and get a powerful response back from that circle,
- As a musical call for attention in a window of communication.

The Call and Response Sequence

You play a pattern, and the circle responds by modeling the pattern, repeating it in the next cycle. You start the call and response at the beginning of a rhythmical cycle, and the pattern typically fills that cycle. Then immediately point at the circle at the beginning of the next rhythmical cycle, indicating the spot in time for the response. The group responds by playing back whatever pattern has been called. You can conduct the response by playing the pattern you just played in the air during that response measure, thus indicating for the circle where the strikes are in the pattern. Alternatively, you can dance the response. Instead of playing in the air during the response measure, use other parts of your body and dance to the circle's response to your call pattern.

Start your calls with simple patterns, adding more intricate and interesting phrasing as you progress in the call and response groove. You can add volume dynamics in the patterns. Remember to attend to the circle's ability to respond to you. If you let your drummer's ego show off during your call and you play beyond your circle's ability to model and respond, you will create panic, crisis mode, and chaos in your circle. This will defeat your purpose for being there, which is to inspire and empower.

A cowbell is a good instrument to use for giving the call at the beginning of an event. It has two distinct sounds and it is easy for everyone in the circle to see your stick movement. In my all-kids programs I use the cowbell as the call and response tool before moving on to the drum.

Using the cowbell for call and response.

A complicated call and response segment with drums can challenge someone beyond their level if they are beginning-beginner drummers. Such people may not be familiar with the technology of accessing the three basic drum sounds. This can create student crisis mode and frustration in that person.

If, as a facilitator, you hear the circle's response to your calls as mushy and out of time, then your calls might be too complicated, creating crisis mode in your whole circle. This can undermine the trusting relationship you are trying to create with your circle, and usually is an indication that you might be showcasing your drumming expertise, rather than listening to and serving your community. Keep your calls simple in the beginning of an event. Let accessibility be the mantra running through your facilitator's mind as you do call and response.

If you are using a hand drum as your call instrument, it is better at first to facilitate the call and response piece from the edge of your circle so that your back is not facing anyone. This way everyone can see your hands for modeling. For larger circles use bigger hand movements.

At the end of your call and response sequence you can stop calling, thus effectively ending that part of your program. Alternatively, you can call a rumble for an end, or start a transition piece or another groove. Some of the many ways to set up and use call and response in your circle will be explored later in the book.

CD Example

You will find me using call and response in "Make Up Your Own To Surprise Groove," to start the piece and at the end of the piece, I use call and response to change to the "Surprise Groove." I also use a *clavé* call and response at the end of "Vocalage."

Exercise: Vocal Call With Instrumental Response

Use a mixed-instrument circle for this exercise. Do the call and response sequence (described in the previous section) from the center of the circle, using your voice to make fun and creative sounds. Singing a rhythm enhances your communication and allows your participants to fully internalize the rhythm. Vocalizing the rhythm also allows the group to interpret and play it easier. Any sounds you can sing rhythmically will work. They can then play the rhythm on whatever instruments they have. You can sequentially provide several different calls and listen for their responses.

This completes one cycle of the exercise. You join the circle and choose someone to be the next facilitator to run the exercise. Continue this vocal calling exercise until everyone gets a chance to sing at least a few rhythms.

Preparation for the Call and Response Sequence

When I want to use a call and response sequence inside an ongoing musical piece, I usually preface it with a body-language attention call to the whole circle. I do this by pointing to the instrument that I'm playing, then pointing to my ear and then pointing to the group. Then, I start my call. Later in the program, after they have learned my body language, I can simply hold up, or point at the instrument that I will use in the call and response sequence and they will be ready to respond.

Exercise: Facilitating Call and Response

 Using an instrument, take turns in your practice circle facilitating the call and response sequence four or five times and then passing the facilitation responsibility to another member of your practice circle.

Drum Circle Game: Passing "Call and Response" "On The Run"

The first person in the circle uses one rhythm cycle to call, playing a pattern encompassing one cycle, saying whatever they want to say on their drum or instrument. At the first note of the next cycle the group responds to that pattern, reproducing it. The person to the caller's left is next to make a statement within the 4 pulses of the next cycle. Starting on the first note of the next cycle after that call, the group responds to that person...and so on and so forth as you go around and around you go...and where you stop only the practice group knows. Pass the call and response among the group, like a tag team, without dropping a beat.

The Rumble

The "rumble" is a versatile facilitator's tool with many uses and variations. A rumble happens when everyone goes into musical chaos and makes a group noise.

The rumble can be a facilitated element by itself, or it can be used to make the transition to another groove. Additionally, a rumble can be a sculpted element facilitated inside an ongoing rhythm, or can be used as a musical call for attention in a window of communication.

Dynamic and tonal rumble waves are discussed in detail in Chapter 14, Orchestrational Ideas.

Rumble Body-language Signals

I start the rumble in different ways, depending on the group's size and temperament. Sometimes I call a rumble by waving my hands frantically in the air and yelling to the circle "RUMBLE." Other times I signal for the group to rumble by energetically rumbling on my drum while the groove is going. I stop a rumble with a stop cut, or go from the rumble to somewhere else with a call and response sequence.

CD Example

I use rumbles in a variety of ways to bring "Drum Call," "The Clavé," "Vocalage," "Highlife," and "6/8" to a close. You will find a rumble being used at a transition point to create a new groove in "Highlife." A rumble starts the piece called "Magic Chicken."

Tempo Up

"Tempo up" refers to raising the tempo of the group during a groove. This facilitation technique provides a way for you to increase the group's focus and excitement as well as their attention level. Raising the tempo at a transition point is a quick, easy way to give the whole circle a little focus nudge, thus spinning the big plate to steady the groove.

Tempo up is sometimes reinforced when the facilitator points to their drum, and then leads the group with his or her drum to the desired tempo. I sometimes increase the tempo of the group by dancing in the middle of the circle, and the players follow my body movements to the increased pace. Tempo up can be used in a transition spot within the music when it seems the group is ready for a change of pace.

I've seen some facilitators create a new rhythm groove at each transition point, thus creating as many as seven or eight musical pieces in a two-hour event. I have also seen a facilitator use tempo up and down at every transition point—sustaining focus, interest, and excitement in one rhythm groove for over an hour.

Attention Call for Raising the Tempo

While facilitating large circles of two hundred people or more, I let them know that a tempo up signal is coming by walking up to the orchestration spot (in the center of the circle) and ceremoniously bending over and touching that point on the floor with my index finger. Then I slowly raise my hand up to the sky, following my pointing finger with my eyes, head, and body. After that I proceed to implement one of the tempo-up body-language signals described in the next section.

By the end of an event, if I have led the circle to lead themselves properly, I walk up to the orchestration spot, do the attention call to up the tempo and then step back, without leading them to a group speedup. I slowly turn around the inside of the circle, with my arms held out in front of me and a questioning look on my face, waiting for them to take themselves as one body to the next tempo level. They usually do.

Tempo-Up Body Language

Three different versions of tempo-up body-language signals that I use are described here.

You can point both fingers up in the air, marking the pulse just a little ahead of the group until they catch up to the tempo that you are marking.

Alternatively, point one finger up in the air holding it steady while using the other to mark the speeded up pulse, pointing at the circle at the same time.

Finally, you can hold both hands in front of you, either pointing your fingers toward each other, or else with your hands open, and mark the speedup with a circular motion. On the first pulse make the circle in time to the rhythm by bringing your hands down and around, toward you, then complete the circle by bringing your hands up and around to stop at the starting point in front of you before beginning to mark the next pulse. Increase the tempo by moving your hands faster than the current pace.

Remember your pacing and leading techniques and be careful not to get too far ahead of your group rhythmically.

CD Example

 I use tempo up in five of the pieces on the CD. They are hard to miss. "Drum Call," "Make Up Your Own to Surprise Groove," "The Clavé," "Highlife," and "Heartbeat."

Tempo Down

"Tempo down" refers to decreasing the speed of the groove. Lowering the tempo is harder to do than raising the tempo and it requires a lot of focus and cooperation from the circle to bring the rhythmical pace to a slower level without having it fall into chaos, or losing the momentum of the groove. Prior to slowing the pace of the groove of the group, I caution my *djun-djun* players to follow my body as closely as possible.

Tempo Down Body-Language Signal

Marking the pulse with my whole body, I point down to the ground with my fingers, just behind the pulse of the group.

Exercise: Tempo Dynamics On The Run

Using a mixed-instrument drum circle in full groove, stand in the middle of your circle and experiment with facilitating up and down tempo dynamics. After doing this, bring the group to normal playing tempo, and choose another person to do the exercise by pulling them into the center of the circle and taking their place in the circle.

Bringing the volume down

Volume Up and Down

Volume dynamics are a lot of fun to facilitate, and successfully changing their volume lets the group know that they can play a powerful groove together quietly.

Volume Up and Down Body Language

To raise the volume, raise your arms up and over your head, with your palms turned upward, as if you were lifting an invisible object.

To lower the volume, lower your arms from over your head, with your palms turned downward, as if you were pushing an invisible object down toward the ground.

Exercise: Volume Dynamics On the Run

 Using a mixed instrument drum circle in full groove, stand in the middle of your circle and experiment with facilitating up and down volume dynamics. When you're done bringing the group back to normal playing volume, choose another person to do the exercise by pulling them into the center of the circle and taking their place in the circle.

CD Example

You will find a volume dynamics up and down section facilitated in "The Clavé."

Drum Circle Game: Dynamic Solo to Call and Response Break

Using an all-drum circle, play the same drum circle solo game as you did in Chapter Six, but add two new elements at the beginning. The whole group will play the in-the-moment groove very softly. As the soloist, you will also start your solo softly, and slowly get louder until by the end of your solo you are playing as loud as you want. The circle supports your solo by increasing the volume of the groove as you slowly increase the volume of your solo.

Let your circle know that the idea is for the group to play at a volume that is just under the soloist. If the group is playing the support groove for the soloist and you can not hear the solo, someone is playing too loud. When you have finished your solo, stop playing, look around at the circle to make sure that you have everybody's attention. Then do a call-and-response break with the circle to pass the solo to the person on your left. Have the circle respond to any pattern call you make with the same pattern. Every soloist can make up their own pattern, or in an advanced circle you can all decide on one particular pattern for the call and response break. After the circle does the call and response break, you can all go back to playing the groove very quietly and the person on your left will start their dynamic solo.

Layering

"Layering" is the process of adding more, or different, kinds of instruments, pitches, or timbral groups to the music.

An example of layering begins with you, as the facilitator, showcasing just the wood instruments in a drum circle groove, so that they are the only ones playing. Then you can sculpt all the bell players and have them layer onto the wood groove. While the wood and the bells are playing, you can sculpt the shakers and have them layer on top of the woods and bells, and while all the percussion are playing, then you can have the congas layer into that groove, and so on and so forth, until all the parts of the drum circle have been layered into a full groove.

Exercise: Layering In and Out

In a mixed-instrument circle, use the example above as an exercise. Make sure that you have a good mix of instruments for this particular exercise. Start by having only the people with wood instruments start the groove with their own rhythms. Then begin to sculpt and layer into the groove the different timbral groups and types of drums until everyone is playing. Then, begin to layer out those timbral groups and drums in reverse order, until no one is playing. Then it's someone else's turn to get in the middle of the circle and layer in and out, but this time do the layering in a different order. Experiment.

Exercise: Layering in Parts by Pitch

In this all-drum circle, before you start to play, identify three or four levels of drum pitch in your circle (low, medium, high, etc.). Let each drummer decide where their drum belongs among the pitch groups. Designate one person in each pitch group to be the groove leader. To start the groove, give the person who is groove leader for the low drums a simple pulse-oriented part, by playing it on your drum. That groove leader plays the rhythm and the others in the pitch group, after listening for a bit, play the same groove.

Listen to the low groove and create a responding or related rhythm that complements the low or bottom part. Then share a second part with the groove leader of the next higher pitch group. Have the other players in that pitch group reproduce the groove leader's part, layering their part into the groove. Continue adding pitch parts in layers until the whole circle is playing. You can then either keep the parts as they are, or tell them to add or take out a note at their discretion.

Enjoy layering in parts by pitch until the circle reaches a transition point. Then, bring the groove to a close with a rumble or a call and response sequence.

Take turns directing the layering of parts by pitch.

Exercise: Layering in Parts by Drum Type

In this all-drum circle, before you start to play, identify three or four different drum types (*djun-djuns, congas, ashikos, djembes,* or other small drums, etc.). Let each drummer decide where their drum belongs among the groups. Designate one person in each group to be the groove leader. To start the groove, give the person who is groove leader for the *djun-djuns* a simple pulse-oriented part. That groove leader plays the rhythm, and then the others in the pitch group, after listening for a bit, play the same groove.

Listen to the *djun-djun* groove and create a responding or related rhythm that complements the part. Then share a second part with the groove leader of the *conga* group. Have the other players in that group reproduce the groove leader's part, layering their part into the groove. Continue adding parts in layers until the whole circle is playing. You can then either keep the parts as they are or else let each player add or take out a note at their discretion.

Enjoy layering in parts by type of drum until the circle reaches a transition point. Then, bring the groove to a close with a rumble or a call and response sequence.

Take turns directing the layering of parts by drum type.

CD Example

There are two layering sequences in the second half of "Drum Call." I have individual players layer in one part at a time to start "Shiko." I also create a rhythm groove on top of the opening rumble in "Magic Chicken," by layering, one at a time, all the wood instruments, then the bells, then shakers, then *djun-djuns*, then *congas*, then *ashikos*, and lastly the *djembes*.

Exercise: Magic Chicken

In the exercise Layering in Parts By Drum Type, the facilitator provides parts for each timbral leader. Now we will do an exercise where each timbral leader creates their own part. Use an all-drum or mixed-instrument circle for this exercise.

Choose one timbral leader for each type of instrument represented in the group. If your mixed-instrument circle is small, use all of your percussion as one timbral group, or just use all drums. If you use all drums then choose one group leader player for each type of drum, or each of the three or four pitches represented in your circle. Have one of the timbral leaders start the groove. Each leader will create their own part. Then, have all the other players in your circle who have the same type of instrument join the groove, copying the part that is being created and played by their timbral leader.

Ask each timbral leader representing an instrument type to wait until the support players for the ongoing timbral groups have settled into the rhythm before layering their part into the ongoing groove. When all the parts are layered into the groove, everybody in the circle will be playing.

After you fully explore this particular Magic Chicken, close with a rumble and start another Magic Chicken by choosing another facilitator who will choose another set of leaders to represent and layer in instrument types.

Due to the layering format, every Magic Chicken is an entirely different composition. This piece requires a lot of trust by you, the facilitator, in the individual leaders you choose to represent their instrument groups. Be prepared for surprises.

Marking the Pulse

You can "mark the pulse" to direct the whole group to play quarter notes in time. Alternatively, you can mark the pulse for a group that is listening to a particular showcased element in the circle, making it easier for them to come back into the groove.

Marking the Pulse Body Language

To mark the pulse I use accent jumps. Prior to the jump or jumps, I hold up the appropriate number of fingers to let the group know how many of the pulses of a four pulse cycle I want the designated group to play. Then I make the appropriate number of jumps.

Marking the Pulse to Signal Re-entry into the Groove

The sequence described below is one that is best used with a rhythm circle that is cohesive and understands your body language.

- Sculpt a particular timbral group or section in the circle.
- Indicate that you want that timbral group or section to continue playing when you make the stop cut.
- Sculpt the rest of the group in preparation for a stop cut.
- Make the stop cut. This part of the drum circle stops and listens to the showcased timbral group or section as it continues to play.
- Mark the pulse for the intro for the stopped group, using accent jumps. Have the group mark the first pulse in a rhythmical cycle on their instruments while the showcased timbral group continues to play.
- Then have the group mark the first and second pulses in the next rhythmical cycle.
- Have the group mark the first, second, and third pulses in the third rhythmical cycle.
- Finally have the stopped group mark all four pulses before entering back into the musical groove with the showcased group.

There are many variations with which you can experiment to syncopate your group's support of the ongoing groove.

CD Example

 You will find me using the marking the pulse sequence in "Make Up Your Own To Surprise Groove" and "Shiko."

Showcasing

"Showcasing" happens when a drum circle gets sculpted and stopped during a full groove, exposing a single soloist or group playing their contribution to the larger song. You can use showcasing to help the group understand the many different parts and voices and smaller songs in its chorus, that make up the whole song. By showcasing timbral groups, pitches, or drum types, you educate your group about its orchestrational makeup, and help it hear itself better.

In showcasing, you identify a group, a person, or an instrument timbral group by sculpting. Indicate that you want them to continue playing when you make the stop cut. Then stop the rest of the circle using the stop cut, exposing the chosen group or person and thus showcasing them to the rest of the circle. Then you can bring the circle back into full groove by using a call to groove, a call and response, or by marking the pulse sequence.

The Showcasing Sequence

Identify to the circle the person, group, or timbral group being showcased by sculpting. Then give them the continue to play signal before signaling a stop cut for the rest of the circle. Give the stop cut, and the person, group, or timbral group continues to play while the rest of the circle listens.

As the facilitator, you have many ways to bring the whole circle back into full groove. You can vocally count the group in, or use body language to call the group to groove. You could use call and response to bring them into full playing, or mark the pulse in an intro sequence.

You can also showcase an advanced player soloing on top of a circle that is in full groove without stop cutting. You do this simply by having that person take a step or two into the center of the circle, solo, and step back into the circle when finished.

Drummer's showcase: Ayo Adeyemi, Babatunde Olatunji, Paulo Mattioli, Arthur Hull, and Chalo Eduardo

Showcasing the Ryder Truck

For each annual Berklee College of Music community rhythm circle, they pack a Ryder rental truck with folding chairs and instruments donated by the college and REMO, and deliver them to the park in downtown Boston where the circle is held. Dean Anderson is the chair of the percussion department at the college, and runs the World Percussion Festival. This event is part of that festival. At this particular circle, Dean was guarding the Ryder truck. It was parked near the circle, with extra chairs and instruments, in case they were needed.

The circle was in full groove and I had been individually showcasing the wonderfully talented players in the circle. I used the showcasing sequence described above, bringing the full circle back into groove at the end of each solo by marking the pulse sequence. Then I noticed that Dean was using the Ryder truck as his instrument, playing on it with two drum sticks. I was curious about what he was doing, but since the truck was on the outside of the circle and I was on the inside, I couldn't hear him very well. I showcased him by giving him the continue to play signal, and a stop cut to the rest of the circle.

Dean played the hubcaps, the side panels of the truck, and the truck frame itself. He used the bumper, back door, and the inside floor of the truck to bring his solo to a climactic ending.

Dean used every part available on the truck like a sound kit. Each part he hit had an entirely different sound. He played the hubcaps, the side panels of the truck, and the truck frame itself. During his solo, he worked his way to the back of the truck, which was facing the circle. There Dean used the bumper, back door, and the inside floor of the truck to bring his solo to a climactic ending as I marked the pulse with the rest of the circle to bring us back into the groove. At the end of Dean's Ryder truck solo we all gave him a rousing cheer.

CD Example

Showcasing different combinations of drums and percussion in your drum orchestra will give you a wide variety of soundscapes with which to work and play at your event. Remember as you listen to the CD that I am working with the same people, playing the same instruments throughout most of the event, but I was able to create different musical moods and sensibilities by sculpting and showcasing different combinations of instruments.

I showcase individual drums and timbral groups in the opening of "Drum Call." In "Make Up Your Own" I showcase different combinations of drums and percussion. In "The Clavé" I showcase small drums and percussion together. In "Shiko" I showcase *djun-djuns* with percussion, and later in the piece I showcase *djun-djuns* with *ashikos*. In "6/8," I showcase *djun-djuns* with bells.

Universal Grooves

Universal grooves are based on patterns found in many cultures throughout the world. When used in a community drum circle, these accessible patterns empower participants of all musical levels to explore and express their rhythmical sensibility, interpreting the music and improvising. Combined with a player's ability to listen to the whole circle, these universal groves can be a foundation for the circle to create beautiful, in-the-moment music together.

In this chapter I describe specific universal grooves. You can listen to the grooves on the Universal Grooves CD that you received with the book. These play-along rhythms offer a reference tool to use while you develop the facilitation tools and orchestration ideas presented in the book. An outline of the orchestration of each groove on the CD is included with each groove's description below.

A live community rhythm circle of over 30 drummers of all ages, sexes, and levels of musical and rhythmical experience gathered together, unrehearsed, in a recording studio to play as a community drum circle for one day, to create the Universal Grooves CD. The orchestrational compositions were created in the moment with my facilitation while the circle was in full groove participation.

This CD was created specifically for this book and is not intended to be a clean multi-tracked album for public consumption. The parts created by this group were "in-the-moment music" and I implemented facilitation ideas on the run and in the moment. Some of the breaks are not cleanly cut, meaning that someone has been surprised by the stop cut and played through it. The group's tempo sometimes falters, and the music is sometimes unruly, as any drum circle will be in the real world. You will find multiple layers of pitches and timbral groups. The group shared with me their musical spirit and their inspiration and I facilitated them into collaborative rhythmical and musical magic. These magical musical moments and messy breaks are exactly what you will find in any live, in-the-moment music, community drumming circle.

Each piece the group played that day was whittled from twenty or more minutes to a CD-appropriate size in the mixing studio. We kept most of the facilitated orchestrational cuts, dynamics, and transition points. Don Davidson, Cameron Tummel, and I added a few percussion part tracks in the studio to solidify some of the grooves, but the foundation and inspiration of the music was supplied by the community at the event. I thank the circle participants with all my heart as they have provided us with an exultant example of a live community drum circle playing universal grooves while being facilitated with the basic orchestration tools.

The Pulse

The pulse is made up of evenly spaced notes. This universal foundational rhythm can be found in any music that is played on this planet. The "spot in time" where you tap your foot when you listen to music is where you are hearing the pulse. This pulse is the beat that connects the music of the drum circle, with all its different parts, together in harmonious agreement. For the beginning-beginner player, the pulse is the simplest continuous pattern to play within a rhythm circle.

Even when the pulse is not physically present in the music, because it is not being played by any particular instrument, it is implied in the musical relationship being created. When the players in a rhythm circle are listening to each other, a magical thing happens between the different parts. The pulse is the glue to that magical musical relationship.

As the most basic and simple universal rhythm, the pulse is often used first in a rhythmical event to bring the rhythmical sensibilities of the group to synergistic agreement. Then you can use more sophisticated rhythms as foundations for jamming and improvisation. I notate the pulse as:

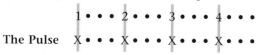

Bass drums and djun-djuns

Drum Call

As the first cut on the CD, "Drum Call" is a pulse-oriented warm-up groove that participants played while additional players arrived to form a fully-functioning drum circle. In "Drum Call" I showcase various types of drums and percussion and I establish basic body-language signals with the players. The progression of "Drum Call" is defined below. As you listen, you can imagine the body language that you would use to create these effects.

- The *djun-djuns* start.
- Layer in the percussion.
- Showcase the *congas*.
- Showcase the *djembes* and *ashikos*.
- Showcase the wood percussion toys.
- Showcase the bells.
- Take the tempo up.
- Showcase the *djun-djuns*.

Congas and asongas

- Layer the wood toys and shakers into the *djun-djun* groove.
- Then layer in the shakers.
- Then layer in the bells.
- Then layer in the *djembes*.
- Take the tempo up.
- Showcase the bells and wood toys.
- Layer in the *congas*.
- Layer in the *ashikos* and *djembes*.
- Layer in the *djun-djuns*.
- Rumble.
- I signal a dynamic rumble wave.
- I do a stop cut.

Make Up Your Own to Surprise Groove

"Make Up Your Own" is a pulse-oriented groove that begins with a simple call and response sequence. This orchestrational sequence empowered the group, as well as the individual players, to truly express themselves.

In "Make Up Your Own" I utilized call and response to set up a musical space with freedom for personal expression and improvisation, in the context of an in-the-moment rhythmical collaboration. I began to develop more complicated body-language communication, such as the marking-the-pulse-to-groove intro sequence. I also used the call-and-response sequence to take the group through a transition point to a second groove called the "Surprise Groove." The facilitation outline below defines how we created "Make Up Your Own" and then transitioned to the "Surprise Groove."

Djembes

- We begin with calls and responses among the participants.
- Then I do a vocal call to groove, "Make up your own!"
- Showcase the *congas*.
- Mark the pulse intro.
- Showcase the *djembes* and *ashikos*.
- Mark the pulse intro.
- Showcase the wood toys, bells, and shakers.
- Showcase the bells.
- Layer in the wood toys.
- Take the tempo up while the percussion is being showcased.
- Mark the pulse to intro.
- Take the tempo up.
- Showcase the *ashikos*.
- We do a call and response.
- Call to a new groove.
- Take the tempo up.
- Showcase a *djembe* player while in full groove.
- Make a call and response to end.

Ashikos

The Rocker Rhythm

What I call the "Rocker Rhythm" is a call and response melody line that can be found in many culturally-specific rhythms throughout the world. Sometimes the pitch moves from high to low, or low to high, but it will always be an evenly-spaced back and forth movement in the bodies of the players and in the sound of the fundamental rhythms on the drums.

I sometimes set up the rocker rhythm simply by having two players sit across from each other with differently pitched *djun-djuns*. I ask them to create a rhythm that has a teeter-totter dialogue between them.

This type of rocking rhythm sets up a foundation for safe rhythmical exploration. If a player gets rhythmically lost it is easy for them to find their way back to the rocker rhythm.

Here is an example of a two *djun-djun* call and response that will set up a rocker rhythm in a rhythm circle. I notate that example rhythm as:

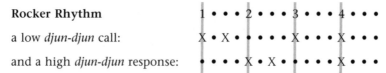

Rocker Rhythm	1 • • • 2 • • • 3 • • • 4 • • •
a low *djun-djun* call:	X • X • • • • • X • • • X • • •
and a high *djun-djun* response:	• • • X • X • • • • • X • • •

Layering Parts

In a drum circle, a universal groove can be created by adding different drum or percussion parts one at a time into the groove, generating a powerful musical experience. I call this layering parts. You can listen to three examples of different kinds of layering on the CD: "Shiko," "Magic Chicken" and "Boom Whacka Boom." They are each described in detail below.

Shiko

The next universal groove on the CD is "Shiko," a composition that begins using three simple Nigerian highlife parts, based on the different pitches of the drums. The simplicity of the parts empowers participants to improvise within the composition. This freedom supports their rhythmical and musical exploration. As the piece evolves it becomes a song unique to the particular time and place.

The first two foundation parts to "Shiko," the conga and the *djun-djun*, make it a Rocker rhythm. When you see someone playing the bottom conga part to "Shiko," you can actually see their body rock back and forth. They move their hands back and forth, in and out of the drum as they access the tones and the bass notes.

There are many ways to use "Shiko," or any other simple multi-part rhythm, inside a drum circle event. You can sculpt the group by drum pitch or drum type during a window of communication and then layer the parts into a groove. In this recorded version of Shiko I layered in the parts by drum type, first conga, then ashiko, then djun-djun. My notation for these three parts is shown below. Then I outline the progression of my facilitation of "Shiko."

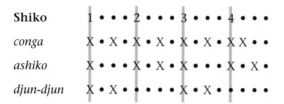

Shiko   1 • • • 2 • • • 3 • • • 4 • • •

conga   X • X • X • X • X • X • X X • •

ashiko   X • • • X • X • X • • • X • X •

djun-djun   X • X • • • • • X • X • • • • •

- We begin by layering in individual drummers on specific parts one at a time, first *djun-djun*, then *conga*, then *ashiko*.
- The rest of the group fades into the groove.
- Mark the pulse-to-groove intro with the whole group.
- Mark the pulse sequence with the whole group to tempo up.
- Showcase *djun-djuns* and percussion toys.
- Mark the pulse to groove intro.
- Showcase the *djun-djuns* and *ashikos*.
- Mark the pulse to groove intro.
- Mark the pulse with the full group to end.

Rolling to The One

The "Rolling to The One" rhythm is a universal groove. There is an opening pattern that starts before the first pulse of a rhythmical cycle and ends on that first pulse. The Rolling to The One pattern starts on the fourth pulse of the preceding rhythmic cycle and hits every sixteenth note between the fourth pulse of that cycle and the first pulse of the next cycle. The opening phrase of this rhythm rolls to the first pulse, suggesting the name of the rhythm, "Rolling to The One." This rhythm can be recognized as the *Merengué* rhythm from Puerto Rico, but it can also be found in many Polynesian log drum rhythms, as well as in the Congo, South Africa, and Nigeria.

The patterns, after the first five notes, vary widely in many culturally-specific rhythms, but the introductory melody of this universal rhythm is always the same. It is constantly rolling to the "beginning" of a continuous rhythmic musical cycle.

You can hear the "Rolling to The One" rhythm as the first conga drum part being layered on top of the opening group rumble in the CD piece Magic Chicken.

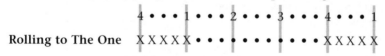

4 • • • 1 • • • 2 • • • 3 • • • 4 • • • 1

Rolling to The One   X X X X X • • • • • • • • • • • X X X X X

Magic Chicken

Parts are parts until you put the whole chicken together. In the "Magic Chicken" universal grooves piece, I facilitated the circle in an opening rumble, creating tonal waves. Then we built the drum song by layering into the groove, first the percussion instruments' timbral groups: wood, bells, and shakers; and then layering in the drums by timbral group: *djun-djuns*, *congas*, *ashikos* and *djembes*.

This piece sounds similar to what you get when you do the exercise Layering in Parts by Drum Type in the preceding chapter. The difference is that the simple drum and percussion parts are created by individual players in the Magic Chicken.

For the CD, the players have been pre-selected by me, each with a certain type of drum or instrument. They are layered into the groove one by one. Then, the other people in the circle followed the leader for their type of instrument, copying and supporting the part. The result was that all the conga drummers played one part while the *ashiko* drummers played their corresponding, but different part. As the other parts were layered in, a complete composition was created. An outline of the Magic Chicken you hear on the CD is given below.

A selected group of designated players, one person for each type of drum and timbral group, layer their own parts, on their instruments, into a groove and anyone with the same type of instrument plays that part as they join the groove.

- I initiate a soft rumble on a drum.
- Layer into the groove one at a time in this order: wood, bells, shakers, *djun-djun*, *conga*, *ashiko*, and *djembe*.
- Take the tempo up.
- Sculpt drums to dynamic rumble waves while showcasing *djun-djun* and percussion.
- I do a stop cut.

Boom Whacka Boom

"Boom Whacka Boom" uses six differently-pitched Boomwhackers® percussion tubes. Boomwhackers are a set of six plastic tubes cut to different lengths, created by Craig Ramsell. When they are struck they create a pentatonic C scale, where all the notes are in tune with all the other notes and can create beautiful harmonies. You can't play a wrong note. I created this piece with the circle by passing out simple syncopated rhythmical patterns that call and respond to each other. When the Boomwhackers are played together, the circle creates an intricate spider-web of music.

Village Music Circles owns two thousand Boomwhackers and uses them in almost every population that their facilitators serve. They are just as effective and fun for adults as for kids. The facilitation outline for "Boom Whacka Boom" is defined below.

- Layer in pitches of Boomwhackers to a full groove.
- Layer different percussion parts corresponding to the Boomwhacker rhythms on wood toys, bells and drums.
- Take the tempo up.
- Layer out percussion leaving only Boomwhackers.
- I do a stop cut.

Corporate Boom Whackage

This story happened at the Band Showcase Day for Silicon Graphics, a company near Palo Alto in the San Francisco Bay Area. The company is situated near a large open-air arena called the Shoreline Amphitheater. They rented out the amphitheater and had an all-day picnic for their employees. They had all their employee in-house bands play on the big stage. Halfway through the picnic day they were going to switch the program to do lip-synch presentations and office skits by employees of different departments in the company.

I had worked for many different departments at Silicon Graphics and the Band Day program planners figured that I would have some shills in the audience, so they brought me in to be the transition act between the bands and the employee presentations. They wanted me to facilitate the audience from the stage. I had done a few Silicon Graphics team-building programs where the company had purchased a drum for each of the program participants from my drum company or REMO drums. The program considered purchasing a small percussion toy for each person at the picnic band showcase but it proved to be too costly, so they bought five thousand Boomwhackers for the audience.

The house bands included musical groups of every musical description, including an all drum and percussion group that performed culturally-specific rhythms and songs. The group was led by Chuck Narad and called themselves Ancient Pulse. I knew Chuck and most of the drummers. They were happy to see me at their presentation and let me sit in on their last performance piece. I in turn asked them to help me in my Boomwhacker presentation.

When it was my turn to go on stage, they dumped thousands of Boomwhackers into the audience. Each person went home with more than one Boomwhacker. There was Boomwhacker pandemonium and chaos in the amphitheater for about five minutes while everybody tested their tube's sounds by bouncing them off each other's heads. I called the audience to attention with a group rumble. We practiced the group rumble a few times to get everybody's focus. Then, using the Silicon Graphics percussion group behind me as models and guides, we practiced individual note rumbles. Each note in the Boomwhacker pentatonic scale is color coded, so instead of calling out notes, I called out color rumbles, so the audience could hear the different notes available in the musical scale.

There was Boomwhacker pandemonium and chaos in the amphitheater for about five minutes while everybody tested their tube's sounds by bouncing them off each other's heads.

Once I established our chorus of notes, I taught simple dialogue parts between Boomwhackers by calling out sequences of colors. Each member of the Silicon Graphics percussion group stood behind me holding one of the six colored notes, and as I passed out a part for a particular color, the person behind me with that color demonstrated that part for the participants to model while I passed out other parts. We created three beautiful musical pieces this way in less than fifteen minutes. It was the only time that day that all the employees of Silicon Graphics entertained themselves. After that, all audience applause for the acts on stage were done in Boom Whackage.

The 3/2 Clavé

The 3/2 *clavé* is a universal rhythmical expression of call and response in music. It represents the push and pull, the rhythmical question and answer. *Clavé* is a Spanish word meaning keystone. A keystone is the foundational stone used in the construction of a building. It is a basic reference point in relation to the placement of the other building elements. In Afro-Cuban music, the *clavé* serves the same purpose. It is a basic rhythmical reference point in relation to the placement of the other notes played in the music.

In Cuba the 3/2 clavé is called the Son Clavé. There are other clavés, but this is the most universal of them all and can be found in music all over the world. I notate the three-two clavé as shown below.

Clavé: 1 • • • 2 • • • 3 • • • 4 • • •
X • • X • • X • • • X • X • • •

The Clavé

"The Clavé" groove sets up a creative space for rhythmical phraseology on the CD. The call and response of the pattern divides the rhythm cycle and creates a dialog among the community of players. I also use the clavé to set up a call and response in this piece for a group break without teaching it to the group beforehand. They just knew. A facilitator's outline of the clavé is defined here.

- The *djun-djuns* start.
- Layer in all drums.
- Layer in percussion with vocal call to groove "one, two, here we go."
- Take the tempo up.
- Take the tempo down.
- Groove dynamics: softer, louder, softer, etc.
- Take the tempo up.
- Showcase small drums and percussion.
- Use clavé as a call to groove for group intro.
- Use clavé as a call to dynamic rumble.
- We do a dynamic rumble.
- We do a clavé end.

The Gods of Clavé

I am in the Republic of China in a fairly modern mall. There is something strangely familiar about the music coming from the overhead speakers, so I stop and listen. The music is definitely culturally traditional but the soloing stringed instrument is playing around, through, and right on top of the 3/2 clavé...

I am in Jakarta, Java, drumming with a young Balinese man. I have my REMO *ashiko* and he has a traditional drum shaped like a small African *djembe*. We are exchanging rhythms. I have just taught him a simple Haitian *Bumba* rhythm, and he is showing me a drumming rhythm from his village that is almost like the heart part of the rhythm called Fanga from Liberia, Africa. All but two of the extra notes are played on the 3/2 clavé pattern...

I am walking through the black market in Moscow. I come across a group of street musicians who are singing and playing two mandolins, a violin, and a skinheaded tambourine. The tambourine player is the group's dancer. She dances while playing the tambourine to the music. Every once in a while, during her dance, she twirls around in front of the musicians and stops. On the next beat she and all the rest of the musicians play the 3/2 clavé break, wait for a four count and start the dance and music again. At the end of the dance and music piece the group plays the same *clavé* break, except that on the last *clavé* note the dancer thrusts her tambourine out to the gathered audience and freezes. We all clap and throw coins into the tambourine...

I am on the Caribbean coast of Belize the night before Easter. I am drumming on *carrib* drums with a group of men from a Garifuna village. The women are dancing around us, singing and clapping the 3/2 *clavé*...

I am in Kuala Lumpur, Malaysia, watching a kickboxing match between two young men representing their respective villages. Their supporters are on either side of the circle chanting for their warrior as they fight. One group's chant is in 3/2 *clavé*...

I dance the pattern with my poor tired sweaty body, and we all three stop on the last beat to the roar of the market crowd.

I am in a village market near Victoria Falls on the border of Zimbabwe and Zambia in southern Africa. The market is laid out in a circle. The huts on the outside of the circle are full of women selling their basket weavings and cloth goods and the men have laid out their wood and stone carvings and crafts for sale inside the circle. Amongst the crafts are cheap souvenir drums like the kind that can be found at any African airport tourist shop. To the people in the market, I look like a South Afrikaaner tourist with a vest.

I see a large ancient, carved, standing Ngoma drum in the back of one craft section. It is not like the flimsy airport tourist souvenir drums being sold in the marketplace. The drum calls to me, and I walk up to it and examine it. The craftsman says "It is not for sale. It belongs to the village. May I sell you a new one?"

I ask "May I play this one?"

He smiles at me and says, "Can you?"

I smile back at him and say, "Yes."

I begin to explore the drum, gently making a few tentative tones. Then I place my elbow in the center of the head of the drum, slowly stretching the head tight and making the pitch go up as I lean on my elbow with my weight and tap on the drum head with my other hand. I continue to play the drum as I release the weight of my elbow off the drum, causing the pitch of the drum to slowly go back to its original pitch. Then I play a glissade note by hitting the drum with my left hand while pushing a finger from my right hand across the vibrating head, causing the drum to moan like a cat in heat.

I look up from the drum. The market is quiet and all eyes are on me. I look back into those eyes and see the question, "Does he know what he's doing?"

My heart, eyes and hands say yes. I have made friends with the drum so I let my spirit fly into it. I play a standard hand over hand 3/2 clavé pattern. My hands move around the drum head pulling out its tones and slaps. A crowd is gathering, consisting mostly of the shopkeepers. The women come out of their huts, joining us. Someone grabs an airport drum that works and, standing next to me, plays an accompanying rhythm to my *clavé* pattern. A woman clears some of the people from in front of the drummers and dances. Another woman joins the first in the dance circle and challenges the drummers to play faster, which we do. The new dancer comes up and bumps our drums with her hips. This excites the crowd as they begin to clap in 3/2 *clavé* and chant together.

An excited woman runs up to me yelling in her native tongue while she pushes me off the drum. Without dropping a beat, she proceeds to play on the drum exactly the same pattern I have been playing. I stand there stunned, watching her excellent drumming, but she is still yelling at me. I finally figure out that she wants me to dance. I give her the dance moves I have, emphasizing the 3/2 *clavé* with my flailing body. She continues the rhythm for longer than my body would like in the African heat, and then plays what turns out to be the closing break. Both the other drummer and I miss the break, but she sees that I recognize what she intends and gives us a second chance by playing it again. The other drummer picks up the closing pattern and plays it with her. I dance the pattern with my poor tired sweaty body, and we all three stop on the last beat to the roar of the market crowd. The woman drummer immediately walks up to me with a serious face, grabs my wrist, pulls my arm to her, and with her other hand she rubs my forearm hard while saying with an English accent, "Where is your skin brother?" With a smile she turns away, heading for her hut. I watch her walk away, trying to figure out if that was a compliment or not, when the other drummer stands in front of me clutching the airport drum and says, with a stunned look on his face, "Who taught you our music?"

I say, with a smile in my heart, "The Gods of Clavé."

To-The-Pulse Rhythm

When the To-The-Pulse rhythm is played on a drum, using three basic tones, it creates a melody line that can be heard in the rhythms, songs, and guitar parts of contemporary West African music, as well as in many other cultures throughout the world. As a drumming style we collectively call it highlife bottom. This is frequently found as a bottom drum part when played in the context of a multi-part, culturally-specific drum ensemble. I played for three years in Kotoja, a thirteen-piece Nigerian highlife orchestra, where more than half of the drum rhythms were based on the To-The-Pulse rhythm.

The To-The-Pulse rhythm is related to the Rolling-to-The-One rhythm in the sense that there is an opening pattern that precedes the first note of each rhythm cycle. The first two notes are played just before the first pulse in a rhythm cycle, and the third note in the series is played on that first pulse. Thus the name of the rhythm: To-The-Pulse (or sometimes it is called To The One). The patterns, after the first three notes, vary widely in many culturally-specific rhythms, but the introductory melody of this universal rhythm is always the same. It constantly reinforces the beginning of a continuous musical cycle.

This rhythm encourages the drum-circle players to take risks in exploring their rhythmical improvisations, because if they fall off the beat, it is easy to find where to get back into the rhythm. The beginning beginner drummers call it "Where's The One?" or "To The One." Then they play it as they say it.

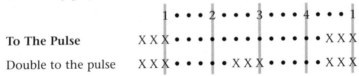

Highlife

The highlife piece on this CD is obviously a to-the-pulse rhythm. Individual players layer themselves into the rhythm at their leisure. The tones on the drums create a melody line that could be easily identified as a Nigerian Highlife bottom part. The middle Eastern drummers who play it on *dumbeck* drums would give it a different name, as would the Polynesians who play this pattern on hollowed-out logs with sticks.

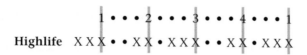

Highlife   X X X • • X X • X X X • • X X • X X X

- I start the groove on an low conga drum.
- Individual players layer themselves at their leisure.
- Take the tempo up.
- Rumble stop to a new groove.
- We do dynamic rumble waves for the closing.
- I do accent jumps to end.

6/8

The patterns that most people call 6/8 are based on 12 triplet eighth notes, or 12/8. They are commonly found in the music and rhythms of most African cultures, and are the foundations for polyrhythmic music heard throughout the world. Several 6/8 patterns are listed below.

6/8	1 • • 2 • • 3 • • 4 • •
Triplet pulse:	X • • X • • X • • X • •
The 6/8 short bell:	X • X • X X • X • X • X
The 6/8 Long bell:	X • X • X • X X • X • X
The 6/8 Clavé:	X • X • X • • X • X • •

6/8

This piece is based on a 6/8 rhythmical cycle: it is the only round triplet-form rhythm on this CD.

I start the rhythm by playing the 6/8 short bell, notated above, with a stick on a low drum. The rest of the group joins me in the moment whenever they are ready. The composition created by the participants is modeled after some of the universal patterns found throughout many African, Arab, and Asian musical traditions.

- I set the pace during the first few cycles using 6/8 stick drumming.
- Using a triplet break I call the other drummers into the groove.
- I use a triplet break to call out the drummers while showcasing the *djun-djuns* and bells.
- I use a triplet break to call the drummers back to full groove.
- I call an end of groove with the triplet break and the group responds.
- We do dynamic rumbles.
- I use accent jumps to end.

Vocalage

This CD piece is an example of how you can use voices in a rhythm-based event. As you can hear on the recording, it is a whole lot of fun! You will hear some of the people unconsciously singing vocal sounds in some of the universal patterns in this chapter.

The circle creates rhythmical vocal parts in-the-moment, and then, when I give them a signal, they translate their vocal rhythms to their drums. A surprise synergy materializes instantly.

- I start the vocal groove and the group joins me.
- When I call, "One, two, put it on the drum," the circle translates their vocal parts to their instruments.
- Showcase *djun-djun* and percussion.
- Layer in drums.
- Players translate their instruments back into vocals.
- Showcase women's voices.
- Back to full chorus.
- Showcase men's voices.
- Clavé call and response.
- Vocal rumble to end.

Heartbeat

This is the most universal pattern of all, found beating inside all of us. I have found this rhythm somewhere in the music of almost every culture that I have studied or visited. It is widely used as a call to community, or within a community context in drumming circles.

This simple two-note pattern leaves a lot of space for group interpretation and expression, The Heartbeat rhythm, played in the drum circle, connects the participants in that timeless place where the never-ending search for the one has brought us together as one.

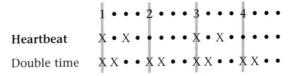

Heartbeat

At the end of our long recording day, our circle has been playing for more than six hours, and the group is in a deep rhythmical trance. I do little facilitation and play the heartbeat rhythm with the group for our closing piece on the CD. The *djun-djuns* lay down the foundation beat and we just play our hearts out.

- Heartbeat starts with the *djun-djuns*.
- Fades to community.
- Tempo up.
- The groove fades to *djun-djuns*.

Orchestrational Ideas

The orchestrational ideas presented in this chapter are ways of using the orchestrational tools described in Chapter 10, Tools and Techniques of Facilitators, to facilitate your circles. You can apply different tool combinations to facilitate a rhythm circle in full groove while on the run. Make sure that you have done the individual facilitator exercises in the earlier chapters and that you have integrated each tool into your facilitator's circuitry before you combine them into the exercises described in this chapter. Otherwise, you may find yourself in facilitator's crisis mode. In the exercises in the orchestrational tools chapter, I asked you to use one tool at a time. In the exercises in this chapter, you may be juggling three or more tools at a time. Happy juggling!

Orchestrational Exercises

 Each of these basic, fundamental orchestrational ideas is an exercise for your facilitation study group. Each one will open a door to limitless facilitation ideas and possibilities. Explore, experiment, and be creative, and then write to me and teach me your new ideas.

Sculpting

Sculpting is the act of identifying a specific part of your circle, as defined in detail in the Facilitator's Orchestrational Tools chapter.

Sculpting Group Sections for Listening

By sculpting groups and then allowing them to listen to the rest of the circle, you will improve your participants' ability to hear the many different elements that make up a rhythm-based orchestra. This also gives you the opportunity to empower them to create new grooves or change their parts within grooves already established. An example is described below.

Sculpt half of the group, part A, giving them their signal to continue. Sculpt the other half of the group, part B, and then give them a stop cut signal. By pulling on your ear and pointing at the group still playing, you can tell the non-playing group to listen to the other side of the circle. Now tell them to come up with something different than what they were playing before that will fit the groove they hear coming from the other side. Get them started with a call to groove.

After you give the B group a signal to continue, sculpt the A group. Give them a stop cut signal, and ask them to listen to the B group as the B group plays their new groove. Let the A group know that what is being played is a version, interpretation, or a response (or all three) to what they were playing. Have them come up with new parts that would fit with what the other side of the circle is playing. Give them a Call to Groove signal, so both sides are now playing. You now have an entirely new song.

Sculpting Two or More Simple Patterns from the Window of Communication

From the window of communication, tell the circle that the parts you will be passing out are only reference points for dialogue and creativity. Give them permission to interpret the parts to create something achievable at their current level of musical and rhythmical expertise. Encourage them to create successes for themselves. Then layer the parts in one by one.

You have many options of how and what to sculpt, as you pass out rhythmical parts to your circle. The simplest way is to sculpt the whole circle, physically dividing it like three pieces of a pie, and then passing out a part to each section that you sculpted.

Another option is to sculpt a circle by timbral group or by type of drum being played. A simpler version of this option is to sculpt all non-drumming percussionists in your circle, and give them one part. Then sculpt all hand drummers, and give them a second part. Finally you could sculpt all the *djun-djuns* and double-headed drums, giving them a third part to play

You can also divide the drum groups into three pitches: low, medium, and high. Pass out one part for each drum pitch, and let the percussionists in your group choose which part they want to support by playing it.

Experiment with your study group by working with an all-percussion circle, then with an all-drum circle, and lastly with a mixed-instrument circle.

Sculpting Two or More Simple Patterns On the Run

The circle is in full groove (on the run). You sculpt half the circle, and give them a continue to play signal. Sculpt the other half of the circle, and make a stop cut. Now half A of the circle is playing the groove and the B half is listening. You give the B half a simple pattern to play. Once they are playing the new pattern and you have given them the continue-to-play signal, turn around to the A half of the circle who are still playing the old groove and give them the stop cut. When they've stopped, let them listen to the new groove created by the B half of the group. You can give the listening half a new pattern that is in relationship to and supportive of the groove being played by the B half of the circle.

For a three-part variation of this exercise, sculpt the circle into three pie pieces and do a stop cut for the first third of the circle, while the other two thirds of the circle play the ongoing groove. Give a simple part to that first group, and when they are playing you can move to the second group, giving them a stop cut. After they listen to the rest of the circle, add another simple part, and when they are fully engaged, go to the last third of the circle, sculpt it, give a stop-cut signal, and have them listen to the first two parts. You can now either give them a third part to create an on-the-run groove, or else you can count them in with "one, two, play your own." Simply by creating two interrelated parts with the first two thirds of the circle, that last group will come up with their own parts that groove with what you have created.

Sculpting Two or More Dialogue Patterns from the Window of Communication

A dialogue pattern is a pattern played that leaves space after it for another pattern to respond.

From a window of communication, divide the circle into halves, or divide the circle into two pitches or timbral groups. Pass out two patterns that each leave space for completion of one before the next one responds. Then empower the players to add notes to their parts or otherwise interpret their parts, playing into and around and through each other's parts, creating a dialogue.

Sculpting Two or More Simple Dialogue Patterns On the Run

Sculpt and stop one half of your circle on the run. Pass out a part to them that lasts a cycle and then rests a cycle. Once that half of the circle can play their part of the dialogue, stop the other half. When you do this, half of your group will be listening to the dialogue being played every other rhythmical cycle. This leaves space in the rhythm for the non-playing half of the circle to respond. You can now give the non-playing part of your circle a responding part to create a dialogue. Once the full circle is playing, encourage individuals to listen and add or remove notes at will.

Sculpting Parts from Existing Parts On the Run

Let your circle groove. Listen to the parts being played. Pick one existing player's groove to showcase. Sculpt and stop the players surrounding the chosen player. Have the stopped players copy the part and join the showcased player. This can be done with one or more sections in your circle.

Sculpting Parts from Existing Parts On the Run By Type of Drum

Let your circle groove. Listen to the parts being played. Pick one existing player's groove to showcase. Sculpt and stop the other players with the same drum type. For example, let's say you choose a *djembe* player. Give that *djembe* player a continue-to-play signal, Then sculpt all the *djembe* players, by individually sculpting and signaling stop cuts. Now, with the circle in full groove, you have showcased that person playing a *djembe*. All the other *djembe* players have stopped and are now listening to your showcased *djembe* player. Have the other *djembe* players model the showcased player's part and join into the groove. You now have all of the djembe players playing the same part.

Next, pick a player of another type of drum, for example an *ashiko*, and go through the same process as you did with the djembe players.

Continue this process with each drum type in your circle and you will have four to six rhythm parts being played by distinct drum types. Most importantly, you have created a rhythm song with drum parts contributed by the individuals you have showcased in your circle.

To me, the ultimate in facilitation is when you take what your circle of players give you musically and rhythmically, and sculpt it into a beautiful musical piece that they did not know that they had in them.

Call and Response

 Call and response is defined in detail in Chapter 12, Facilitator's Orchestrational Tools. Here are some example situations and exercises.

Setting Up Call & Response from the Window

While setting up a call-and-response piece during a window of communication, empower the group to be creative as you explain the exercise. Let the drummers know that they need only respond to you in the next measure with the same spirit you gave them, without necessarily playing exactly the same sounds that you are about to make on your drum. This is especially true when you have multiple percussion instruments in your circle.

Keep in mind that there are a wide variety of drums and percussion instruments in the circle, and give your percussionists permission to respond by tapping out the pattern you played on your drum on their cow bells or shakers. In any community rhythm-based event you have many ages and levels of rhythmical expertise.

Call and Response from Participants to the Group and Back

While facilitating call and response you have the total attention of the circle. You can move around inside the circle between your calls and during their responses. You can pick participants to showcase by moving next to them as you make a call. Then, during the circle's response, you can tell them that the next call is theirs to play. At the same time point at them to indicate to the circle that the circle should give their attention to that person for the next call. The person calls, the circle responds, and you go on making calls until you identify the next person you want to showcase.

It is empowering for a person to play a simple pattern as a call into the circle when the circle sends that pattern back to them in response. It is as if they had called their full name into the circle and the circle called it back to them with the full force of its attention and intention.

Initiate a call-and-response sequence. While the group is responding to your last call, go to a participant and indicate to them that it's their turn to make a call to which the group will respond. When the group has responded to your last call, it is that participant's turn. You might want to choose people with whom you now have rapport: participants who have good listening and playing abilities. You want to feel confident that they will make a solid call on time in relationship to the ongoing beat established by the group.

Be careful if you decide to showcase your advanced players. Hopefully they will understand that call and response is for communicating with and empowering the circle, rather than using the call as a place to show off their chops. When you choose an advanced player, understand that you are handing your circle over to them for one full call-and-response cycle. If they use the call to play their hottest and most intricate licks, they may be playing beyond your circle's ability to respond. This can disempower rather than empower the circle. If that happens, your circle may trip over itself trying to reproduce a rhythm beyond its grasp. If they lose control of the call-and-response groove and have a train wreck, you can take back control of the circle by playing a simple and reproducible pulse-oriented pattern on the next call. This gives your circle an opportunity to return to the groove, and allows you to continue calling and responding to a close or a transition while on the run.

If the person you choose to do a call panics, freezes, starts their pattern out of time with the rhythm being played, or loses time with their call-and-response pattern, you can regain control by going to the orchestrational spot and making calls and getting responses from the group until the groove sounds strong again. You can then decide whether to choose other participants to make calls, do a transition into another groove, or stop.

At these transition points your choices are numerous. You have many choices and the trick is not to think, but to use your radar and three peripheral listening tools to let the group tell you where to go in the next transition.

Call and Response On the Run...

Call and response on the run is an excellent focus enhancer and can be used to facilitate a transition point to another pattern, a faster tempo, or a full stop.

Call and Response On the Run to A Full Stop

While the circle is in full groove, when you reach a transition point where you want the groove to stop, go to the orchestrational spot in the circle, get the group's attention, and give them the signal for call and response. If you are playing a drum, as you begin making calls, back up to join the circle so that everyone can see your hands. If the group is attentive, most of the group will respond on your first call. As you give the second call, you will get even more responses. By the third call most of your group will respond to you, as only a few people might play through calls until the peer pressure from the group forces them to join in the responses. Do calls and responses with the group until you feel it is time to stop. When you do your last call, they respond, and you indicate by your body language that you are not going to give another call. There is a powerful silence. Depending on the state of consciousness of the group and the placement of that piece in the event, you may decide to call a rumble to give them a celebratory release from their last piece, or you may speak during the communication window that you have just created.

 You can listen to call-and-response sequences that end the full groove in "The Clavé" and in "Make Up Your Own to Surprise Groove" on the CD.

Call and Response On-the-Run Transition to New Groove

You can do an on-the-run transition from the call and response to a groove simply by starting a groove as one of your calls and repeating it on the response. Repeat the call every rhythmical cycle until the circle is grooving with you. Away you all go into the next piece.

When the circle is in full groove and you have reached a transition point, deciding that you want to change the rhythmical direction of the group, you can activate a call-and-response sequence. With the full focused attention of the group, you can continue a particular pattern that is groove-oriented as your call. Continue playing the same call and they continue to respond. Then, play the same call while they are responding, no longer calling and leaving an open measure for the response. Some members of the circle will continue to play the groove as soon as they hear you playing it again. With each measure, as you continue to play the groove on top of their response, more of the participants will join in, and you will be playing a new rhythm.

 On the CD, I use call and response on the run to make the transition to a new groove. This generates the surprise groove in "Make Up Your Own to Surprise Groove."

Call and Response On the Run with Half the Circle

With the circle in full groove, sculpt half the circle and signal them to continue. Then, sculpt the other half of the circle and make a stop-cut. Now you have half of the circle grooving, and the other half listening. Do call and response with the stopped group while the other half grooves.

At the end of the call and response sequence you are at a transition point with that half of the circle. To bring them back into the groove, you can count them off and call them back, using one of the versions described in "Vocal Call to Groove." The sculpted half will join the groove of the other half of the circle.

Call and Response On The Run While Maintaining A Groove

When you do call and response on the run while maintaining a groove, indicate to your group that you want them to continue playing their groove after each response. Then give a call. They will respond and then continue playing the groove. Make your call to the group every 4th or 6th rhythmical cycle, letting the circle rest a few measures while playing their groove before you make the next call.

Rumbles

 Rumbles happen when everyone goes into musical chaos and makes a group noise. You get to facilitate their rumbles!

Group Rumble as a Focus Call

When there is a break in the action at a drum circle event, there is a natural tendency toward sound chaos. People begin talking to each other, adjusting their chairs, and tapping on their drums while tuning or playing a quick personal drum rhythm to themselves.

When you are ready to bring the circle back to focused attention you can call for a rumble, and then make a full-group stop cut. You then have the attention of the group, and can speak to them in the window of silence that follows the rumble to prepare them for the next piece.

You can use the group rumble as a facilitator's focus call, rather than yelling over the cacophony of noise to get attention.

Group Rumble as a Closing

You can use a group rumble as a closing for a particular rhythm piece. At the closing point for a group rhythm, give the rumble body-language signal until the group is fully rumbling, and then bring it to a closing note with a stop cut. This completes the piece and you will find yourself in a window of communication.

Building a Rumble by Layers

Building a rumble by layers creates a tonal and volume dynamic that modulates to an exciting climax. I usually do this from a window of communication, sometimes using a rumble to start a rhythm by doing a start count after all the instruments are layered in at the top of the rumble climax, with a call of "1, 2, let's all play."

To layer in a long sustained rumble, starting with low drums and ending with high-pitched timbral groups, start with *djun-djuns* rumbling, then add, one by one, the *congas*, *ashikos*, *djembes*, woods, bells, and shakers. Alternatively, you can reverse the process, building a rumble by layering in the instruments from the high pitches to the low pitches.

Creating Timbral Parts from the Rumble

You can orchestrate from the communication window, or while the group is in the groove. Call for a group rumble. During the rumble, sculpt by holding up an instrument that represents that timbral group. After sculpting that particular timbral group, play the part that you want them to play and they will stop rumbling to model and play the part. For example, when you hold up a wood block and give the people playing wood instruments a particular pattern to play, they will begin to play that pattern on the wood block. You could hold up bells, shakers, and wood blocks all at the same time, and direct the whole percussion ensemble to play the same part while the drummers are still rumbling. You can then identify another timbral group by holding up another instrument for sculpting. As you continue to identify instruments and pass out parts, fewer instruments will be rumbling. Any leftover instruments can be encouraged to pick whatever part they want to play and join in. This process creates a smooth transition from a group rumble to a multi-layered rhythm-ensemble based on timbral groups.

Rumble Stops to New Groove

Use a series of rumbles at the end of a rhythmical piece to start a new groove from the ongoing one. At the appropriate time, when the group is in full groove and heading for a transition, start a closing rumble and bring it to a closing note with a stop cut. Before the group stars to celebrate, start another rumble to stop cut. Keep repeating the rumbles, each one a little shorter until the rumbles encompass an evenly-spaced note, and your stop cuts have turned into accent notes. Because the facilitator hops up and down to facilitate these rumbles and stop cuts, I sometimes call this a "Rumble To Bunny Hops." The group, with your direction, is now doing a short rumble on each pulse.

As the rumble pulse gets established, some participants may begin to play rhythms on top of and through the group rumble pulse. Other players get the idea and add their rhythms until there are more people playing to and through the pulse than there are people playing the rumble pulse. A new groove starts out of the earlier rhythm's closing rumble and the group finds itself making music to a different pulse in a new way.

 On the CD, I use the rumble-stops-to-new-groove sequence at the end of the "Highlife" bottom groove to start a new groove from the ongoing one.

Group Rumble to a New Rhythm

When your circle is in full groove and the dynamics of a particular musical piece have reached a transition point, you can use the rumble to facilitate this transition.

Call a rumble. While the group is rumbling, sculpt out half the group. Give that group the body signal to continue to rumble. Sculpt the other half of the circle and bring them to a stop. Encourage the first half of the group to continue to rumble. Then give a basic rhythmic pattern to the second half of the circle that has stopped. That group will create a groove with the basic pattern. Give them a signal to continue, and then turn around and stop the rumbling group. Have this stopped group listen to the other side of the circle groove. Then you can choose one of the following options: give them the same basic rhythmic pattern or give them a rhythmical part that has a supportive relationship to the ongoing groove. Alternatively, you can have them each create their own rhythm that is in relationship to the ongoing groove. With any of these choices, your circle can make the transition to a totally new groove.

Rumble to a New Groove with *Djun-Djun* Sculpting

A simple rumble transition, while on the run, from one groove to the next is *djun-djun* sculpting. While the group is playing a groove, you, as the facilitator, give the body signal for a rumble. With the group in full rumble, you identify the double-headed *djun-djuns*, sculpting those instruments to a stop, and then indicating the pattern that you would like the *djun-djuns* to play while the rest of the group is rumbling. The chosen pattern could be any of the basic universal drum circle patterns such as the Heartbeat or Clavé or even a simple pulse. Once the *djun-djuns* are playing the new groove, you can count the group in from the rumble to play whatever rhythm they want that accompanies the *djun-djun* pattern. Boom! You're in the next groove.

Call and Response with a Rumble

Call for a rumble. Sculpt half the group with a continue-to-rumble signal. Sculpt the other half with a stop cut. Give a call and response sequence. Then you can sculpt that group to rumble again, so that the whole group is rumbling again. Your choices are numerous: you can sculpt the other half of the circle to call and response, take the whole group into another groove, do call and response with the whole group into another piece, or facilitate them to a full stop. You can also take your rumbling circle into a dynamic rumble wave.

Rumble Waves

 Three variations of rumble waves are described below: the dynamic rumble wave, the tonal rumble wave, and the football wave.

The Dynamic Rumble Wave

The dynamic rumble wave happens when the group gets louder or softer in response to your body language. Holding your hands high in the air, palms up, represents a loud volume. As the hands, palms down, come down past your shoulders to your waist, you are signaling for a lower volume. Crouching down, with your hands down below your knees toward the floor signals for an even softer, lower volume.

By moving your hands up and down in a rhythmical fashion, you can create sound waves, with high-volume rumbles at the peaks of the waves and soft volume rumbles at the bottom of the waves.

 On the CD, I facilitate different dynamic rumble waves at the end of "Drum Call," "The Clavé," and " High Life."

The Tonal Rumble Wave

A tonal rumble wave happens when you lead your group to play in and around the tonal area of their drums. This creates different sounds on the drum as rumbling hands move from the edge of the drums to the center of the drums and back. You lead the tonal rumble wave from the edge of the circle, so that folks can see your hands on your drum. You want the group to do exactly what you are doing, so that as you all play your drums you create a total group sound.

Do a rumble, playing with just your fingertips on the edge of the drum head, creating the highest and quietest sounds. Then as you add more of your fingers onto the drum you begin to play in the tonal area of the drum, creating a more rounded and deeper tone. Finally, as your rumbling hands move into the center of your drum, using your palms as well as your hands, the rumbling sound of the drum becomes a deep bass sound.

As you move your hands in and out of your drum, as described above, you create a tonal wave with the whole group. You can control the rhythmical pattern on every wave, or you can lead the group into a rhythmical wave pattern in a way that empowers them to create their own wave pattern. As another variation of a tonal rumble wave, you can go from slaps, to tones, to bass notes and back again.

Depending on the speed and dynamics of the waves, you can facilitate a tonal rumble wave to create a new groove. On the CD I use a rumble wave to start "Magic Chicken."

The Football Rumble Wave

During a football game, the crowd watching the game sometimes plays the wave game during lulls. One group begins by standing up and moving their hands up in the air and then sitting down. This initiates a wave of people standing up and sitting down, traveling around the stadium, going from left to right. As the person sitting next to you begins to stand up, you also stand up, and then the person next to you gets up and slowly arches their back from a bent-over position. Then you all straighten your backs and raise your bodies and hands into the air. Next, you lower your hands down, and then your arms and back, bending over and finally returning to a sitting position. This creates a wave of people standing, making a wave, and then sitting, that runs across the stadium seating area like a wave on a pond radiating out from where the pebble dropped into the water.

The football rumble wave is usually done with a standard rumble, fluctuating the volume. If I have a responsive group that is in tune with itself, I can also use the tonal wave while facilitating the football rumble wave.

The football rumble wave starts from a quiet rumble, and the drummers go from quiet to loud. You start the rumble at any point in the circle by pointing and giving the volume up signal. The people in the immediate area where you point will start to rumble loudly. As you move your pointing finger around the circle, the people you are moving your finger toward begin to rumble loudly as the people that you're moving your finger away from rumble more softly. You can facilitate the sound rumble by waving your right "loud" fingers upward and your left "quiet" fingers downward.

After you start a football rumble wave, it can be self-facilitated by the group, and have a life of its own, just like a wave in the football stadium. To stop the rumble wave you can bring the whole circle to a rumble to close, or just let the rumble fade to a stop.

Facilitating Rumble Waves Over the Groove

While your circle is in full groove, sculpt a type of drum or percussion, facilitate a rumble wave sequence, and then count them back into the group groove.

Marking the Pulse

 A definition and body-language description of marking the pulse are in Chapter 12, Facilitator's Orchestrational Tools. Now I present some exercises for marking the pulse as you facilitate.

Marking the Pulse while Showcasing

While your group is in full groove, sculpt one half the group, indicating for them to continue the groove. Sculpt the other half of the group, and make a stop cut. Indicate to the stopped group that you want them to play one pulse note. Raise one finger up in the air as a physical indication for one note. Mark the note at the beginning of the rhythmical cycle by jumping up in the air. When you jump up in the air their hands go up. When you come down, their hands come down. Boom! The stopped half of the group marks that first note, while the other half of the circle is in full groove.

Next you indicate that you want your stopped half of the circle to accent two notes. As you indicate that to the group, your body indicates where those two notes are in relationship to the groove. Jump up and hit the ground twice and their hands jump up with you and hit their drums as you hit the ground.

Next, indicate that you want three pulses with three fingers, and show them with your body where you want them to place those accent notes in relationship to the ongoing groove. As you orchestrate with three jumps, they play three notes.

Finally, indicate that you want them to play all four pulses in the cycle, and then to continue to play by joining the groove that the other half of the circle is playing. Mark four pulses and play. Some of the members of the group will get your signal while on the run. Others may need more time or vocal energy than you have for explaining to them while on the run. The people that read your body language correctly will understand you. When you indicate where to start the sequence, they will play and accent the pulses on their instruments in the proper sequence and then at the beginning of the next cycle, they will join the groove. The ones who accent the four pulses and then stop and wait for another signal from you will, upon hearing the group playing the groove after marking the pulse, join in as well.

By marking the pulse with one half of the group while the other half of the group grooves, half of the group learns the accent sequence. Give a continue-to-play signal to the sculpted group that just finished marking the pulse sequence. Sculpt the other half of the group, make a stop cut, and go through the sequence described above for marking the pulse with your new group.

By marking the pulse with half the group while showcasing the other half on the run, you educate and practice the marking-the-pulse sequence for showcasing, and for your use later in the program.

Marking the Pulse while Showcasing Timbral Groups

Showcasing timbral groups and drum types in a circle early in the event educates the circle about the different sounds and orchestrational possibilities that are available. After showcasing your timbral group and instrument range, you can bring your circle back to full groove with a simple call to groove. Later in the event, when the group is somewhat synergized, you can use the marking-the-pulse sequence with the whole group while showcasing a particular timbral group or instrument.

As an example, while the group is full groove, consider showcasing the *djun-djuns*. Go to each *djun-djun* player, give them the indication to continue to play, then give the rest of the group an attention call in preparation for a stop cut. Stop cut everyone but the *djun-djun* players. While the *djun-djuns* play, do the marking-the-pulse sequence with the other members of the group, having them return to the group's ongoing groove, after the marking-the-pulse sequence.

You can also showcase the *congas*, *ashikos*, *djembes*, or all the percussion players in the same way.

 On the CD, you will find me marking the pulse to a groove intro while showcasing different instruments in "Make Up Your Own to Surprise Groove."

Marking the Pulse while Showcasing a Soloist

Once the circle learns how to mark time by accenting the pulse or pulses, your group understands a new orchestrational body language and you can showcase individuals, by indicating to a particular individual to continue to play when you make the stop cut. Choose a person that you feel confident enough in to continue playing and to solo by themselves while the rest of the group marks time. Then sculpt the rest of the circle to make a stop cut.

To do this, simply walk up to the person who you are going to showcase, and make the signal very clearly to everyone that this is the only person who will continue to play when you make the cut. Stand directly in front of the chosen person and make a sculpt that goes from the left side of that person all the way around the circle to the right side of the person, indicating everyone else in the circle, in preparation for the stop cut. Then go to the orchestrational spot and make the stop cut. This leaves only one person in the circle playing.

Next, give the indication to the rest of the circle for accenting the pulse. Some facilitators will give the indication for two pulses and have the group play two pulses every rhythmical cycle as they listen to the soloist. At the appropriate time in the solo, bring the group back into the groove by initiating the marking-the-pulse sequence by running the full sequence of marking first one pulse, then two pulses, then three pulses, then four pulses and then having them play the groove.

Layering a Multi-Part Rhythm On the Run

Save this orchestrational piece until your program has progressed long enough for you to identify the different levels of players in your circle. Before you do this piece with your circle be sure that you know who your intermediate and advanced players are. Hopefully they will be dispersed throughout the circle.

As an example, start with these indications for a three part rhythm. As you practice the model you can add more parts.

Start the circle with everyone playing the same simple pattern, with lots of space between the notes. Once the rhythm settles into its groove, deliberately sculpt your intermediate and advanced players. Sculpt players individually with a stop cut. Show them, one at a time, a second part that you want them to play on top of the groove that you have established.

This second part could be a totally new part, or it could be an extension of the first part, adding more notes and syncopation onto the original part, or changing the tones of the first part by replacing tones with slaps or bass notes. By sculpting out and giving a single intermediate or advanced person a new part, you have also shown the other members of the group the new part. As you progress around the circle sculpting out and adding more intermediate and advanced players to the new part, two things happen.

First, each time you show the new part, the next person who you sculpt will be more ready to play it, until all you have to do is point at the next person you want to sculpt and they will immediately play it with the rest of the intermediate and advanced players. They have seen you show the part multiple times and have been waiting for you to sculpt them. By the time you sculpt one-fourth of your players, you will only need to point at others to get them to play the new part.

Secondly, by adding one person at a time to the new part, you are slowly increasing the volume of the second part so that you are dynamically layering in an on-the-run transition in the groove. The second part is born out of the first part as you add more players.

Now your circle song is made up of two parts: the original basic part played by the beginner players in the circle, and the syncopated part played by the intermediate and advanced people in that circle. With the first two parts playing, identify and individually sculpt out advanced players who are playing the second part with the intermediate players. Give them a third even more syncopated part to play. You now have three parts in the circle, each being played by the people most capable of holding it together.

Showcasing Your Advanced Players During the Groove

 A good time to showcase people who have the ability to play lead on top of a full groove is near the end of your event. These advanced players might be drum teachers or elders in your community circle, or all of the above in one person.

You showcase advanced players because you know that they have the technical ability to play on top of the groove being created by an ongoing drum circle without being overwhelmed. You can showcase these players without stopping the rest of the circle, marking the pulse with the group, or doing any fancy sculpting.

While the circle is in full groove, walk up to the person that you would like to showcase and invite them to take a few steps into the circle and share their spirit with their community through their drum. When they have made their statement or when you feel it is time to move on, you walk up to them, politely thank them, and invite them back into the circle. You may showcase as many people as you want, considering both how well and how long the circle is capable of maintaining the groove while someone plays lead. Consider who you want to acknowledge and showcase in the community for their skill, service, perseverance, commitment, work, and eldership in the community.

 A good example of showcasing a djembe player while in full groove can be heard on the CD at the end of "Make Up Your Own to Surprise Groove."

Manipulation Versus Service

Avoid driving your circle like a sports car unless it is one! Now that you have all these fancy orchestrational ideas under your belt, be careful about trying too many of them with your circle all at once, or you will burn out your circle. Overfacilitating a group may give them the feeling of being manipulated rather than being facilitated. The more you empower your circle to facilitate itself, and the stronger the rapport developed between you and your circle, the more you can instigate the more intricate orchestrational ideas addressed in this chapter.

There are two keys to successfully facilitating your group to their highest potential without overpowering or overfacilitating them. The first key is to read the group at all times so you are aware of what they are capable of doing. That way you will be more likely to give them just a little more than they think they can handle to create their small successes. This will usually be a little less than you think they can handle. The second key is your proper use of the group's transition points. It is unnecessary for you to apply highly intricate orchestrational ideas at every transition point. Sometimes a small adjustment or re-focus gives them what they need.

You can occasionally initiate orchestrational ideas outside of the points of transition. However, initiating too many transitions outside of the natural transition points will create the feeling in the group that they are being manipulated by you. Let them enjoy where you take them musically, before you take them somewhere else. Even a roller coaster has plateaus and breathing spaces in its wild ride.

When used within the context of service, these facilitation and orchestrational ideas are powerful in their ability to transform a totally disorganized and disconnected body of strangers into a totally unified body of participants, thus creating a powerful musical experience. When used properly these are tools for helping the group establish rapport with itself.

When the tools are used as tricks, they become tools for manipulation and eventually disconnect you from your group and destroy any rapport that you might have created. Even though you might utilize these tools with grace and beauty, if you utilize them as tricks to impress and manipulate then sooner or later your group will know. If you force a preconceived outcome without listening to the group's needs as well as your own, then whether you know it or not, you are manipulating. If you focus on service to community, then you can use the tools to empower and transform the community.

It may be necessary to guide an individual to better serve the group, if it can be done in a positive, constructive manner for the betterment of the group as a whole. An example of one way to use these tools is described in The Billed Cap Story that follows.

The Billed Cap Story

This story unfolds at the close of a Hawaii Facilitator's Playshop event, when we had a celebration party in Honolulu and invited the Hawaii drum and dance community to join us. Many of the islands' drum and dance troupes performed, as well some world beat bands. During the breaks we would go outside and I would facilitate a quick twenty-minute drum circle piece.

I'm facilitating a drum circle piece at that event, when an excited young person brings four friends and a bunch of standup congas into the ongoing circle. He is excited and looking forward to participating in the program. Wearing a baseball cap and looking at his own drum, he is constantly losing touch with the rhythm of our circle, getting mostly the sound of his own drum in his face and not hearing the rest of the group. He keeps missing the breaks. I go over to him two or three times to bring his attention out to the group, but his head continually goes back down to his drum, and he is playing with the bill of his cap down, so he can't see the rest of the group.

A little positive guidance comes into play here. I walk up beside the guy, who has two standup drums and ask him if I can play one of his drums, and he lets me. We play for awhile, and I make comments to him, while we're all drumming, telling him that he's playing strong and clear (which he is). I tell him that he's contributing to the group, and that I like what he's playing. Then, in a playful manner, I exchange hats with him, so that he is wearing my hat and I am wearing his. I tell him that my African-style cap is just like his baseball cap, except that it doesn't have the bill on it. I tell him to notice that now, with the bill of his hat gone, he is more a part of the group, and can hear and see everybody else while he is playing. When it is time for me to go facilitate some more, I exchange hats with him, but I playfully put his hat back on his head backwards with the bill in the back. For the remainder of the circle he keeps his hat that way and stays totally in focus with the rest of the group.

Closing

Following your bliss will open many doors for you, and at the same time offer you many challenges. If you follow your bliss, you cannot go wrong. You can make mistakes and learn from them. You can have failures and be strengthened by them, but your bliss will always lead you down the path that fulfills your innermost needs.

The more you follow and serve your bliss, the more it will serve you. The more it serves you, the more it will lead you to challenges. When the challenges come, do not be afraid to say yes. Do not be afraid to try something new. Take a chance on an idea that may or may not work. Just do it, and find out what part of it works and what part of it doesn't. Be strengthened by your experiences, and use the knowledge you gained from your last challenge for the next one.

Just say yes, and do it.

This book is about how to take what you know and give it to others. The better you get at the giving, the more powerful will be the gift. I have seen the gift of rhythm change many lives in many ways, and always for the positive.

Rhythm is a way to release stress and emotion, express yourself musically, get in touch with your own life rhythms, make relations with each other, connect with and express your spirit, create a deeper relationship with the earth and nature, and create and strengthen community while celebrating life, the greatest gift of all.

I have put my life's work and knowledge into this book. Please use the information and experiences in this book to help make that rhythmical spirit that lives inside us all more accessible to the community at large. As an orchestra creates musical and rhythmical harmony by cooperatively playing together, a community can create harmony by living, working and celebrating together in all forms of rhythmical entrainment. Every rhythm-based program you facilitate in any population will take us one more small step toward developing the value-based rhythmaculture we all so desperately need to work, play, and live together in peace and harmony. If you are following your bliss by using rhythm to create and serve community, then we are on the same path together. I offer you all my blessings and support on the rest of your journey.

The Child In All of Us

I have been the rhythmatist for a number of Neuro Linguistic Programming (NLP) programs in Sydney, Australia, and have been the catalyst in the creation of quite a few percussion puppies in that community. At one particular program, fifteen of the participants had cajoled me into dedicating the one week of lunch breaks into a series of hand-drum classes. The challenge I gave myself was to consolidate my two-month university beginners' village music class into seven, one-hour sessions in a way that sincerious students could take the material home and develop it as if we had shared twenty hours in a percussion class, instead of just seven.

One of the students set up a video camera on a tripod and recorded the sessions. He was from Adelaide, on the southern coast of Australia, and was involved with a drum study group. According to some people from Sydney, Adelaide was Australia's equivalent to Russia's Siberia. He had guaranteed me that if I tagged a side trip to Adelaide on to my next trip down under, his study group would learn everything that was on the tapes, in preparation for my visit. I agreed saying "No worries, mate!"

Every once in a while as I'm departing a plane, walking down an off-ramp, I hear the unmistakable sounds of a percussion ensemble floating up the tunnel. It is always a surprise to me, because the words drum circle and airport don't seem to fit in the same sentence. I know my particular role in this little ritual. That is, if these people are going to take the time and trouble to bring their drums to the airport and through security to greet me with a rhythm, the least I can do when I get into the terminal where they are drumming is to dance to their music.

Six months after my last visit to Australia, I arrive in Adelaide. As I depart the plane, I hear an old familiar rhythm called Fanga floating up the off-ramp toward me. Fanga is a dance and rhythm from Liberia, Africa, that is traditionally used to greet a dignitary as they enter the village. It is one of the rhythms that Babatunde Olatunji brought to the U.S. to share with us. I teach it, with Baba's permission, in my beginning-beginner drum classes as one of the many manifestations of the universal clavé in action.

Upon hearing the rhythm, I realize that my NLP student has kept his promise. His study group has done their homework and is greeting me with a rhythm from his video class. I feel that I need to honor them, as they are honoring me, by doing the proper Fanga dance moves to their rhythm when I reach the terminal.

I am running the dance moves that I can remember through my mind as I walk down the ramp. I adjust the strap of my computer case over my shoulder in preparation for the dance, when a little five-year-old blond-haired girl with pigtails flying behind her skips lightly past me down the ramp. It is obvious that she is heading for the source of the music. Her heart, spirit, and body are responding to the call of the drums and the voices singing the Fanga song.

All of a sudden there is a sharp bark from behind me. It is in a language that I do not understand, but it is in a tone of voice that is universally understood by all children. The tone said, "Stop. Act your age, and get back here right this minute." It startles me and stops the little girl in the middle of a skip. She stands there facing the direction of the music, with shoulders slumped, pig tails drooping and head down, waiting for whoever is behind me to catch up to her. The child in me wants to turn around and stick my tongue out at such a person who would suppress an innocent spirit like that.

I find myself in a predicament. Do I continue as planned and greet the drummers with the greeting dance, or do I validate the little girl and take her skip dance down to the drummers and singers that called her spirit? I pass the girl, get her attention with a smile and a thank you, as I copy her skip dance and head down the ramp toward the music.

In the airport terminal the drum circle participants, who have only met Arthur Hull as a sincerious drum teacher on a video tape, play Fanga for a forty-five-year-old man in a funny hat and vest, skipping around them as lightly as he can, like a five-year-old in high spirits.

Life Is A Dance.

Done.

Resources

Drum Circle Spirit Players of Universal Groove CD

This CD was recorded by Daniel Thomas, Jeff Sterling, and Mark Weldon at Sonic Images Studio, San Jose, California. Daniel Thomas did the digital editing and mixing at Solo Sound Productions in Bonny Doon, California. Daniel Thomas, Keith Hollister, and Tim Favro mastered the CD at Moon Rock Audio in Santa Cruz, California.

The people listed below came together from afar and united themselves into a percussion orchestra through the spirit of the drum. I thank them for letting me capture their spirited community drum circle in action on my CD. They represent many cultures, religions, age groups, and lifestyles who use the drum as a tool for unity and expression.

I thank them all from the bottom of my drummer's heart, and to the top of my Arthurian spirit.

Mark Schneider	Tom Kraus	J. Jeffrey Cuda
Chuck Narad	Devorah Ginden	Forrest Foster
Francine Joy	Walter Levison	Richard Guadian
Thiemm Sornasse	Terry Craven	Zorina
Michael Dalmadge	Janis Aziza Varo	Alison Severson
Tim Bolling	Laura Worth	Max Montgomery
Robert Bornn	Linda Scarborough	Tim Haight
Karen Bedard	Robert Peizer	Daniel Worthman
Chuck Stein	David Wilcox	Steve Gan
Shawnee Undell	David Amooi	Sam Herzberg
Rich Fongheiser	Fred Witt	
Don Davidson	Cameron Tummel	
Jeff Severson-Papa Djun-Djun		

Resource List

An up-to-date listing that includes the resources list provided here as well as an extensive set of links to related Internet sites is available at http://www.drumcircle.com.

Books That Influenced Arthur

Adzinyah, Abraham Kobena, Dumisani Maraire, and Judith Cook Tucker. *Let Your Voice Be Heard! Songs from Ghana and Zimbabwe* (Book/Tape set). World Music Press, 1986.

Baldwin, Christina. Calling the Circle, *The First and Future Culture*. Swan Raven & Co., 1994.

Banek, Reinbold, and Jon Scoville. *Sound Designs, A Handbook of Musical Instrument Building*. Ten Speed Press, 1980.

Borden, Barbara. *Dare to Drum*. Cloud 9 Productions, 1995.

Diallo, Yaya, and Mitchell Hall. *The Healing Drum—African Wisdom Teachings*. 1989.

Flatishler, Reinhard. *Ta Ki Ti Na, The Forgotten Power of Rhythm*. LifeRhythm,1992.

Hart, Mickey, and Frederic Lieberman. *Planet Drum, A Celebration of Percussion and Rhythm*. Harper Publishing,1991.

Hart, Mickey, and Jay Stevens. *Drumming at the Edge of Magic, A Journey Into the Spirit of Percussion*. Harper Publishing, 1990.

Hayden, John. *Jamtown Percussion Improvisation, A Teacher's Guide for Pre-K Through 12th Grade*. John Hayden, 1997. (206) 632-9136.

Hayden, John. *The Road to Jamtown, Play a Beat You Can Repeat, A Percussion Activities Guide* (comes as part of a kit with instruments and rhythm cards). John Hayden, 1995. (206) 632-9136.

Kristel, Dru. *Breath Was the First Drummer, A Treatise on Drums, Drumming and Drummers*. QX Publications,1995.

Olatunji, Babatunde. *Drums of Passion Songbook*. Olatunji Music, 1993.

Redmond, Layne. *When the Drummers Were Women, A Spiritual History of Rhythm*. Three Rivers Press, 1997.

Thompson, Robert Farris. *Flash of the Spirit, African & Afro-American Art and Philosophy*. Vintage Books, 1983.

Wilson, Sule Greg. *The Drummer's Path, Moving the Spirit with Ritual and Traditional Drumming*. Destiny Books, 1992.

Magazines

Drum! Magazine
www.drumlink.com
(888) 378-6624

RhythmMusic Magazine,
email rhythm@interport.net
1 (800) 464-2767

Other Stuff

Boomwhackers® Percussion Tubes are available through Whacky Music, Inc., toll-free: (888) 942-2536

American Music Therapy Association
(301) 589-3300
email: Info@musictherapy.org.

Beginning-Beginner–Friendly Resources

Greiner, Jim. *Community Drumming for Health and Happiness*. Latin Percussion, 1994.

Olatunji, Babatunde. *African Drumming (Djembe/Ashiko)*. Interworld Music, 1995.

Bermudez, Jorge. *Conga Drumming— A Beginner's Video Guide*. Dancing Hands Music, 1995.

Dworsky, Alan, and Betsy Sansby. *Conga Drumming, A Beginner's Guide to Playing With Time*. Dancing Hands Music, 1994.

Hull, Arthur. *Guide To Endrummingment*. (Book/Video) Interworld Music, 1995.

Johns, Geoff. *Drum! How to Play the Rhythms of Africa and Latin America*. Sounds True Recordings, 1997.

Kalani. *African Beats (Djembe)*. (Video). Interworld Music, 1995.

Matthews, Bill. *The New Conga Joy, Traditional African and Afro-Caribbean Rhythms for One Drum, Two Drums, and Full Ensemble*. Bill Matthews, 1995.

Mattioli, Paulo. *Hands on Drumming— Universal Keys to Hand Drumming! (Djembe)*. 4 volumes (Video). African Percussion, 1996.

Sole, Doug. *The Soul of Hand Drumming, A Comprehensive Book for Beginner to Advanced Solo and Circle Hand Drummers*. Soul Drums, 1993.

Internet Resources

On my website I maintain an up-to-date extensive listing that includes the resources list provided here, plus organizations and other web sites that pertain to drumming and drum circle facilitation. My website address is: http://www.drumcircle.com

If you have Internet access, I suggest you first peruse the amazing amount of information available to you on the Djembe-L mailing list FAQ site (Frequently Asked Questions) http://www.drums.org/djembefaq/index.htm.

The Djembe-L mailing list is a large group of hand drummers and percussionists worldwide who dialogue in open format on one mailing list site. To reduce redundant dialogue, they provide a FAQ list containing the most frequently asked questions of new people who join the list.

Credits

Illustrations: Peter Cerny
Cover Design: Lightbourne Images
Cover Photography: Paul Schraub
Interior Book Design and Layout: Cliff Warner
Rhythm Temple poem reproduced from *Guide to Endrummingment*, INTERWORLD MUSIC, 1994.

Photos
Foreword: page 7, Paula Bickham / Dedication: page 8, Michael Buchanan / Introduction: page 12, Paul Bousquet / Chapter 1: page 21, Rob Berkowitz; page 24, Jan Avinger-Jacques; page 25, Benét Luchion; page 29, Carol Carpenter; page 30, Village Music Circles / Chapter 2: page 32, Dean Monroe; page 34, Al Hartmann; page 37, Dean Monroe; page 38, Dean Monroe; page 42, Geoff Johns / Chapter 3: page 48, 49 Arthur Hull; page 52, Dean Monroe; page 54, Dean Monroe / Chapter 5: page 73, Dick Markus; page 78, Joe Songer; page 79, Jan Avinger-Jacques; page 80, Village Music Circles / Chapter 7: page 94, Marian Oliker / Chapter 8: page 97, Arthur Hull; page 99, Anna Daraban; page 101, Seth Cashman; page 104 Arthur Hull; page 106 Dan Coyro; page 109 Don Davidson; page 111, Arthur Hull; page 113, David Alexander; page 119, M.A. Bjarkman; page 121, Arthur Hull; page 123, Village Music Circles; page 124, Dean Monroe / Chapter 9: page 126, Joe Skaggs Chapter 10. page 131 Dean Monroe; page 132, Arthur Hull; page 134, Dean Monroe; page 137, Dean Monroe; page 138, Jim Greiner; page 141, Bob Bloom; page 144, John Avinger-Jacques / Chapter 11: page 148, Dean Monroe; page 150, Seth Cashman / Chapter 12: page 156, HappyShel; page 157, Christine K. Stevens; page 158, Dean Monroe; page 159, Paul Schraub; page 159, Reggae McGowen; page 160, HappyShel; page 161, Arthur Hull; page 162, A. I. Fischer; page 163, Christine K. Stevens; page 166, Jan Avinger-Jacques; page 171, HappyShel / Chapter 13: page 174, Arthur Hull; page 175, Arthur Hull / Chapter 14: page 200, Bill Van Bloom

Index

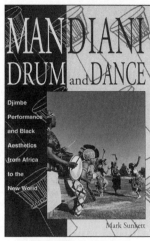

Drum Gahu
David Locke.
Book with Compact Disc,
ISBN 0-941677-90-7,
$29.95.
*"Recommended for all
music scholars and all
music students."*
— Ethnomusicology

Drum Damba
David Locke.
Book, ISBN
0-941677-10-9, $17.95.
CD WCM 9508, $15.95.
*"A book of unique value for
its retention of traditional
African teaching methods."*
— Dr. Rodric Knight,
Oberlin College

**Mandiani Drum
and Dance**
Mark Sunkett.
Book, ISBN
0-941677-76-1, $19.95.
CD WCM 9826 $15.95
Video $29.95.
*"Required reading...a major
work in this field."*
— Percussive Notes

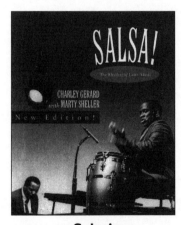

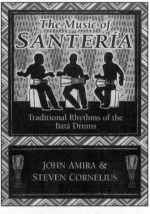

Salsa!
The Rhythm of Latin Music
Charley Gerard
with Marty Sheller.
Book with Compact Disc,
ISBN 0-941677-35-4, $24.95.
*"Takes the mystery out of
Afro-Latin music without
destroying its beauty or power."*
— Fernando Gonzalez, arts
editor, The Boston Globe

The Music of Santería
**Traditional Rhythms
of the Batá Drums**
John Amira
and Steven Cornelius.
Book with Compact Disc,
ISBN 0-941677-70-2 $24.95.
*"A useful intoduction
to batá drumming."*
— The Beat

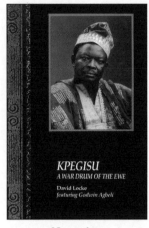

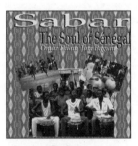